WOODY BARNES—A FARMER'S LIFE IN JULIAN

SCOTT T. BARNES

NEW MYTHS PUBLISHING

Also Available in This Series

Alice Genevieve Barnes—Gold Mines and Apple Pie by Scott T. Barnes

CONTENTS

MAPS

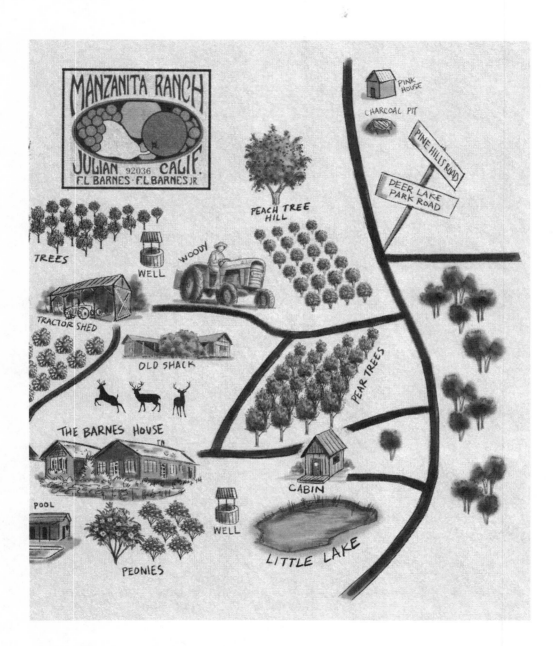

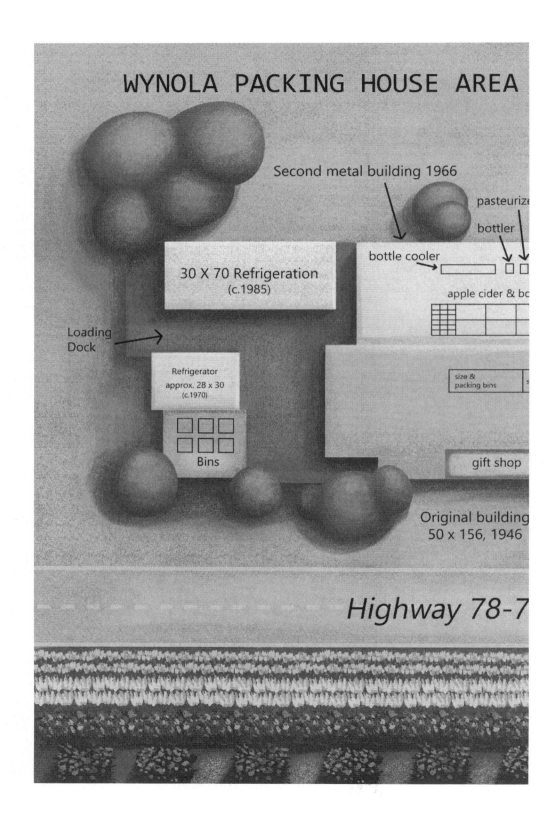

WYNOLA PACKING HOUSE AREA

Second metal building 1966

pasteurize

bottler

bottle cooler

30 X 70 Refrigeration
(c.1985)

apple cider & bc

Loading
Dock

Refrigerator
approx. 28 x 30
(c.1970)

size &
packing bins

Bins

gift shop

Original building
50 x 156, 1946

Highway 78-7

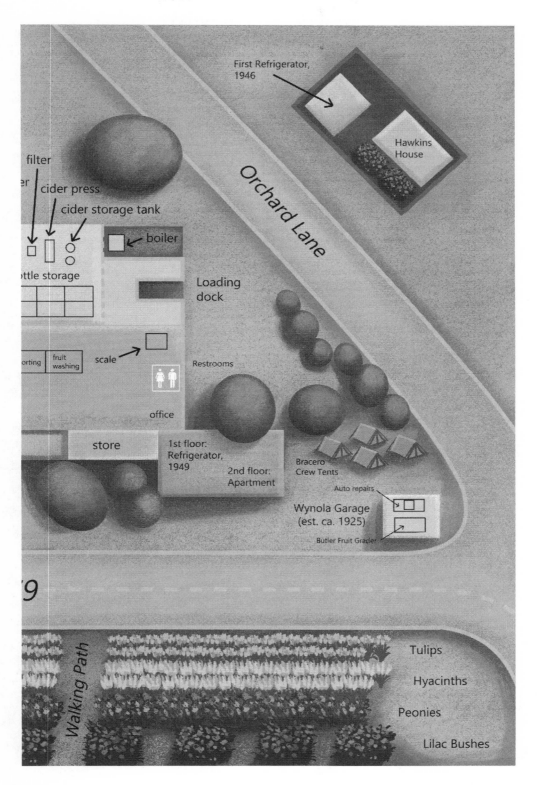

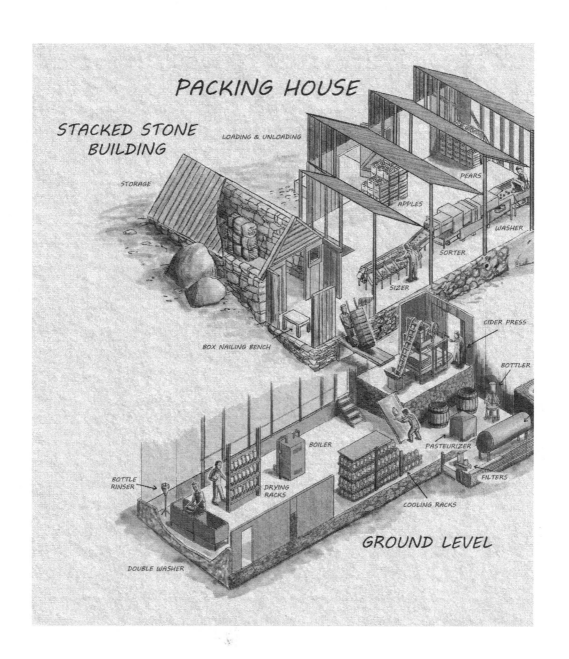

PACKING HOUSE

STACKED STONE
BUILDING

LOADING & UNLOADING

STORAGE

PEARS

APPLES

WASHER

SORTER

SIZER

CIDER PRESS

BOX NAILING BENCH

BOTTLER

BOILER

PASTEURIZER

BOTTLE
RINSER

DRYING
RACKS

COOLING RACKS

FILTERS

GROUND LEVEL

DOUBLE WASHER

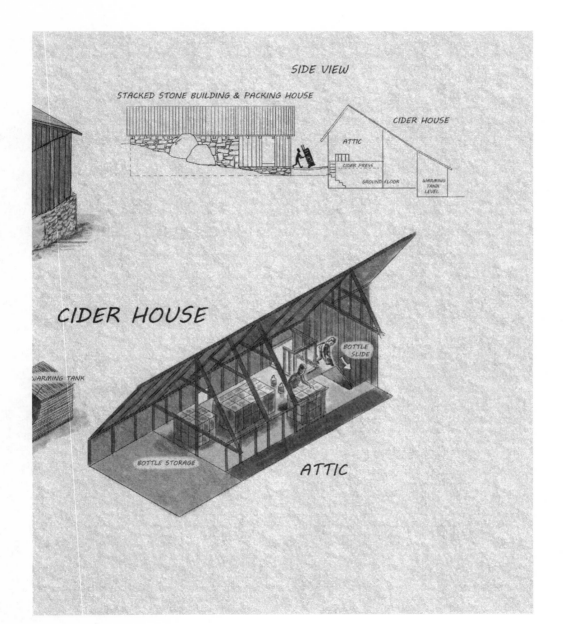

SIDE VIEW

STACKED STONE BUILDING & PACKING HOUSE

CIDER HOUSE

ATTIC

CIDER PRESS

GROUND FLOOR

WARMING TANK LEVEL

CIDER HOUSE

WARMING TANK

BOTTLE SLIDE

BOTTLE STORAGE

ATTIC

INTRODUCTION

In many ways this project began in 1991 when I started inter-viewing my grandmother for the oral history *Alice Barnes—Gold Mines and Apple Pie*. Alice was born in 1906 at the Helvetia Mine just outside of Julian, though her oral history begins earlier than her birth year as Alice, in the tradition of story-tellers, related pre-Julian family lore almost as if she had been there.

As her son Woody continued farming the same land as his parents, and managing the Manzanita Ranch store and packing house his father built, this is very much a continuation of the story. Woody's narrative begins in World War II, the heyday of the local fruit business (which in Julian was pears rather than apples) when price and demand was at its highest, and the high cost of transportation inhibited competition. It takes us through the difficult years that followed, when improvements in trucking and refrigeration began to kill the small family farm, through Julian's great transition to tourism and modern times.

Still Woody and Manzanita Ranch soldier on, the man in his eighties, growing apples and cut flowers, lilacs, lily of the valley, and peonies, albeit on a smaller scale. Woody always said, "If you love what you do, you never work a day in your life."

He continues not working to this day.

The first recorded interviews of Woody date from 1995 on a handheld cassette recorder. The latest are Voice Memos on an iPhone from 2019. As much as possible I left sections of the interviews intact, though with the interviews taking place over such a long period the same stories were told multiple times. If a tidbit of information or turn of phrase was irresistible I would splice it into the narrative on the theory that giving a complete picture is of primary importance.

Much beloved by the community, Woody Barnes has grown up with the town. Volunteers and volunteer organizations grease the wheels in any small town, and Woody volunteered for many of them. These include the Julian Volunteer Fire Department; San Diego County Cattleman's Association; the San Diego County Farm Bureau; the Julian Planning Commission; Julian's Architectural Review Board; the Council of California Growers; California Rangeland Trust; California Board of Forestry; California Agricultural Leadership Foundation, and probably a few I have forgotten. For most he served as president at least once.

Despite all his volunteering, Woody was a family man. (Allow me to call him 'Dad.') Dad never failed to be home for dinner at precisely six o'clock. Even if he returned to work for another two or three hours afterward. Each year the family would take a vacation whose goal was to see as much of the country as possible. Reviewing photos the other day, I found photos from Brice Canyon, Zion, the Grand Canyon, Washington D.C., Yellowstone, Mount Lassen, and the redwoods of Northern California: all from one trip. Any day where less than 400 miles was covered was a failure. And yet on these trips, with a generous and gregarious personality, Dad always found time to stop and chat with local farmers, often pulling up the car and stopping them as they worked in the field, often making business partners, lifelong friends, or both in the process. (And embarrassing his teenage sons to no end.)

Despite the fact that the Ford station wagon's air conditioning invariably broke the first day out, and the bickering started soon after (and any time we couldn't stop for lunch or dinner at 12 or 6 P.M. sharp), I have very fond memories of those trips.

In the days when Dad ran the Manzanita Ranch store in Wynola, he went to work in the early morning, lit the wood Franklin stove, and prepared a pot of coffee. Which he didn't drink. The coffee was for the locals would would drop by to have breakfast. Bob Dugan did this for as many as thirty years, Bill Cain for slightly less, and any local in the know would stop by from time to time, including friends such as Dana Reed and Erik Pollock from my generation.

I remember with nostalgia the angst Dad had about whether or not Manzanita Ranch should close one day a year —Christmas day. All through the fall season he would start work around 5 AM, come home for dinner at 6, and return to work for another two hours or so after dinner. Seven days a week. Barney (my brother) and I never felt neglected. Dad was always there. If possible, we would shoot some hoops at work. (Dad set up a basketball hoop in the middle of the Wynola packing house.) And of course, we worked together. And still do. I just spent an hour reviewing the subterranean irrigation system. Enough pipes crisscross Manzanita Ranch to drive a civil engineer loony. I still smile to myself whenever one of my friends complains about their 'long hours'... and they only work five days a week.

It has been a joy to relive and discover new memories with my Dad. I hope you enjoy his story as much as I loved putting it together.

Summer, 2020.

Scott T. Barnes

1

CIDER HOUSE VISIT

Manzanita Ranch is quite possibly the longest continually-operating orchard and farm in San Diego County. Started before 1900, leased by the Barnes family ca 1906 and purchased in 1916, the farm remains in commercial operation today.[1] The farm totals 160-acre acres to the west of Pine Hills Road and Deer Lake Park Road. Most of the farm is rough canyon country; only a handful of acres have ever been cultivated.

Picking his way through debris, boxes, and abandoned machinery, Woody narrates the whys and hows of fruit packing and cider making as it transpired in the heart of the Pine Hills operation from 1939 through 1956.

Two primary interviews were used for this information, one done in 2009 and one in 2016. The story can be appreciated much more fully if you along on the three-d diagram in the Maps section.

Woody: One reason I thought we'd go down to the Cider House today is that it's an era that is completely gone and I'm probably the only person alive who remembers most of it.

Even (my sister) Jo probably doesn't remember a lot of this down here. You see, we left here in '46;[2] Jo would have only been eight. We left the packing part of it—the cider making remained. There are really three buildings that were all used together in the fruit business here: the Stacked Stone Building; the Packing House; the Cider House.

I will explain to you the incredible history as best I know it when we get down there.

Stacked Stone Building

Okay, this is the oldest building on the place that's extant. There were a couple of others, probably older, that have since collapsed. This was a stacked stone building—there was no masonry in it at all. The original roof was two-foot clear redwood shingles that were quite thick. We finally had to replace them with metal because they had reached the end of their life.

This is pre-1900, we don't know exactly when. When Edward Young Barnes[3] started leasing the place in 1906, the freestanding [stacked stone] part was already here then. It was used for two purposes: it was used to store hay for draft horses, which in those days was not baled, the hay was just hauled over from the meadow on the other side from where the pond is now and put in here; and it was also used for apple storage. They brought the hay in this side and took it out the other side, so they took advantage of gravity—also with fruit. Originally most of the fruit was not sorted, packed or anything fancy.

The reason the concrete was pushed into some of the cracks was to reduce the amount of mice that can get in.

(Walking further.) This was the end of the original stone building. And you can see that this end was, again, all free stacked with no masonry. Most of the people up here prior to 1900, except if they were around a mine, didn't have masonry material. The sand, in general, had to be hauled from Banner Canyon, and that was a long haul in a horse-drawn wagon.

This would be quite old. Originally there were dirt floors. The concrete was added much later.

Now the next part, this little porch area here on the end of the Stacked Stone Building, was added on and I don't know exactly when. I think this was also pre-1900 but it may have been when Bope first got here. This was the original place where they would sort their apples. It had a window on this side and a door here. You can see that the rocks are mostly Julian schist or schist-related rocks. So the rocks in this area were probably hauled over from near the town of Julian some-where, because there's very little schist here, although there is some in Pine Hills and they might have hauled it from there. Some of this schist looks like it might have been near a stream or something, but you can't tell that for sure.

I try to leave it because I think it's kind of interesting. This is one of the oldest buildings in Julian—and clearly one of the oldest agricultural buildings. We don't know exactly how old except we know it was old when they leased it in 1906 and it has lasted that long. (Pointing to the adjacent section.) I think this part of the building was the next oldest. You can see it's a different kind of stone. This schist is not really found much here, so I suspect this may have been brought over from the Julian Grade area. The older section is all stone that you can find here pretty easily.

There was a lot of schist over at Timm's[4].

Scott: Which one was Timm's?

Woody: That's the orchard north of Van Duesen Road and east of Pine Hills Road.

In this stacked stone building there's shook, wooden pieces, left over from that era for making boxes. A lot of the lugs we had to nail because the pears ripened so fast you couldn't find enough used lugs. There was a fellow by the name of Hammer 'n Nails Johnson who was one of the fastest. He could nail about two hundred boxes a day by hand. Every nail was one hit that went in, using a box hatchet.

They had a thing called a nail stripper that you put the nails up here and they vibrated down. And as they vibrated down they would point this way. They came down two thin wires that held them. He could just pull them off, pow, pow, pow.

Packing House

Note: the Packing House adjoins the Stacked Stone Building. (See diagram in the Maps section.)

(Pointing to a different section of wall/floor.) This was where the Packing House originally stopped. And then this newer section, a lot of this was the dynamite stuff from Pine Hills Road. See how that has the fresh cuts? Those rocks were blasted, either out of the [hand-dug] wells or out of Pine Hills Road.

Scott: I did notice a different color and texture, more gray, sparkle-y.

Woody: It's the same rock except that this has been blasted, freshly opened. Here's some more of that schist-type stuff. They poured the slabs a little at time over the wood floor as it rotted out. They started back here and worked back that way except for this piece, which was still wood when I was a kid.

We went up and visited Dad's cousin Eddie, who is 95, the other day. He lives in Paradise, California—which I always felt was ironical for a guy his age. [laughs] Anyhow, all of the T.L. Barnes family I think worked at one time or another for Dad.[5] But Eddie was the one who worked the most. Over here, if we can still see it, you can see when they put about the last piece of flooring in. I remember them working on it. You can see how there were boards put in at different times. Eddie did this section in here.

Scott: (Reading a name and date drawn in the wet concrete floor by finger before it hardened—a common practice around Manzanita Ranch.) Oh yeah. 'E. Barnes, July 29, 1939.'

Woody: Now, that could have been Bope because Bope was an E. Barnes too.

Scott: E.Y., wasn't that what Bope liked to use when he signed concrete?

Woody: E.Y., yeah.

I don't know for sure, but I think E. Barnes was Eddie's initials. After working here, Eddie went into the military during World War II and he was an aviator. He completed 31 missions over Germany. He has a picture where he came back and the plane was so badly shot up that it didn't quite get to the airfield. He had been a nose gunner all the other missions and he was a side gunner on that one so he didn't get hurt when it crash landed in England. The nose gunner got hurt bad.

E.Y. (Bope) and T.L. (Theodore Lockwood) Barnes were brothers. Eddie was one of T.L. Barnes' four children. David was the first one, he was a very liberal educator. Ted was the next one, he worked down in the salt flats down in South Bay (harvesting salt from sea water) and was very good guy. Virginia was the next one, and she lived up here in Julian. That's Kiki's mom. She was a school teacher in the L.A. area before moving back to Julian. And then Eddie was the one that lived up there in Paradise. He and Ted, I think, ran the gas station that Bobby Hathaway owns in town (next to the drugstore). I used to think it was the one that Fred Slaughter owns, the Julian Cider Mill, but it was one of those two.

(Pointing to an old wooden box.) This is an "LA lug." That was what pears were ordinarily shipped in. They packed 'em high. They always had these cleats on them so you could pack 'em higher than the sides.

One of the reasons our [Manzanita Ranch] label is big is because it would cover the other guy's label when we were using a used box.[6]

Then when they got to apple season they went to apple boxes. It's taller than a pear box. There were two kinds of apple boxes. A "California long box" which they only used really around Watsonville, and the "northwest box" which everybody else used. We mostly used "northwest" boxes.

Scott: How many apples could you fit in one of these?

Woody: A bushel.[7]

One of the reasons that they used this area was this giant oak tree which shaded the building.

Scott: The live oaks were all pretty much here?

·   ·   ·

Woody: Yeah, yeah. That big one that we cut down, which is over here, we measured the other day. It is pretty near a five foot diameter oak tree. It shaded that whole area pretty well. The two things you wanted was to have light, and that's why you had the building with the funny slopes and the openings in the roof, and shade to keep things a little cooler. Because usually in late August, September and early October it's pretty warm, or apt to be.

Scott: Did Grampy design the buildings like that?

Woody: Yeah, and he built all of those. The only one he might not have built would be that little porch out the front, I don't know about that, and this Stacked Stone Building here. The amazing thing is that they managed to pack, oh, 30,000 lugs of pears in a two, two-and-a-half week period, using this little tiny building.

This was the area they backed the trucks in, both to unload the fruit and then to load the packed fruit. These things across the top edge of the foundation are rails from a little railroad. Before the rails were brought to the cider house, there was a cattle guard made from railroad iron right where the lower peach orchard road comes in. When they took that out, they put those rails down here (so the trucks wouldn't damage the concrete if they backed into it).

Scott: You're talking about Pine Hills Road.

Woody: On Pine Hills Road. They used to drive the cattle from down Boulder Creek along the road and over to Julian. I don't know when they had the cattle guard built, but by the time we came they weren't driving as many cattle and I used to go out—I was the keep-em outer. (Woody kept the cattle from entering the orchard from Pine Hills Road.)

This little flat area here, there was about a six or eight foot place where you walk into the place, and there were some boards out here, a flat platform with wood. That was where they brought the boxes down.

This part of the wall was done in the 20s. As they kept getting a larger scale operation they kept adding. The fruit packing was still done by hand. They then got an apple washing machine. There was no electricity down here at that time.

When I was here[8] they were just finishing putting the cement floor in, replacing the wood floor here. Originally— and I just barely remember this—there was a hollow place under here. They had an old Ford motor that sat here and flat belts that went up that ran the washer and the grader. I was just a little kid when they got rid of the Ford motor.[9]

So at first they had these belts and they had to do all their packing in daylight. By the time I was six or seven or eight they had electricity and then they could also load at night and still see what they were putting on the trucks without using flashlights and so on. But that time of year the light stays fairly long. The picking crew started at seven AM and went until four thirty. The packing crew started at eight and went until five. That was their hours.

But anyhow, that's what was happening here.

What little storage they had for fruit was in the old Stacked Stone Building.

Now, when the fruit came in [from the fields], over in this area was a washer and a grader. There was a low place in the concrete where the washer sat and where they ran the water out after washing the fruit. Like I say, it was 90 percent pears.

The reason they washed everything so thoroughly—they had a double washer—was because they used to spray the apples with lead arsenate to keep the worms down. You had to wash with acid to get the lead arsenate off, and then you washed with water to get the acid off. So there was a double washer all the time. I don't know if we have any photos of the original equipment.[10]

At that time we had three little bitty wells: one over here about 150 feet from where we are standing; one up at the old tractor shed area; and one down in the front canyon (by Pine Hills). Those two were thirty feet deep. This near one was nineteen feet deep. They produced, maybe, 200-300 gallons a day apiece. And they did all the washing for all the fruit and all the cider making on that little bit of water...and also our household use. They were very efficient with the water.

The pears would run up. They'd wash them, and there was a sorting table, which would have been right about there. I can tell you that it pinched fingers, because Jo got her fingers pinched in it. Then there was a sizing thing here. The sizing was kind of interesting. They had two shafts that ran along about six inches apart. There were balls on the shafts that were about the size of tennis balls, and there were little elastic belts that went around it. As you went down, it got narrower so it would kick the big fruit off first into a bucket to pack. And then it would kick the medium ones off. You could make about six sizes. It was a very poor sizer, because if the stem stood up a little the fruit got kicked off right off the bat.

The ones we had in Wynola were weight sizers. They were far more efficient. But the one here was a physical sizer.

You can see the various iterations of building gradually getting bigger as the business and operation increased. This was the final wall and they actually used concrete in here and had it formed. The rest of it was all freestanding except where they filled in where the motor had been.

Remember how there were shed roofs that sloped up, like a series of triangles that went up like this and then straight down, and then up like this and then down, open on the north side?

Scott: Right.

Woody: That was to protect the operation from the sun but also get north light, which was pretty good. They were shed [tin] roofs. They went up (at around a 45 degree angle), and then there'd be rafters coming down (open to the air), and then there'd be a slope up and down, and a few posts to hold it up. Repeat. We have pictures of those before it fell down.

This was where they brought the fruit in and hauled it out at night. The next section was approximately here. The next one came to here. The third one came here. And the fourth one went over to the Stacked Stone Building and just was a half a section. The first three sections were roughly the same width. Your ceiling height here was roughly seven feet or so. There was a three-foot door here. There were roller doors here. You can see some of the boards down there from the leftover doors.

It worked pretty well. They even, one time, whitewashed the inside of it to give a little more light.

About 1940 they got electricity roughly this far. The [public utility] electricity stopped right by where the swimming pool was later built; we ran our own line down to here. I think the old transformer is still in here that we used to reduce the voltage.

You get some idea of when this stuff was finished, the last pieces of it—you can see the names when they did this little piece right in here [etched in the concrete]. I'm not sure they did the wall but they did the slab. (Reading) H.N. Williams (Herman Williams), Eddie Barnes, July 1939. And over here there's a floor piece that says Eddie Barnes, 1939.

. . .

(Chris Tindall and Dana Reed participated some of the interviews.)

Chris: I kind of understand how it all works, how was it laid out. Fruit came in from this direction.

Woody: And went through here.

Chris: They washed it here. Then there was a table for sorting.

Woody: Table for sorting right about here. Sizing there.

Chris: Then it was staged here in wooden boxes.

Woody: Yeah, and the staging was usually pretty fast. They packed on both sides. As you can see, this gave them enough room. Then they could go around with the fruit and put it right back in the first section. They loaded it on trucks at night in the same place.

It almost all went to San Diego. Some went to Long Beach. They were running as many as three thousand boxes a day out of this place. Pears were the big rush thing.

Everything was used, including the boxes we shipped out in. Eventually it got to be where you couldn't buy as many used boxes as you needed so they would nail them by hand. I don't know if I can find the remnants of the nailing benches...

These were fairly low beams in here—they're probably about 6'6" this way. So you couldn't stack too awfully high.

Okay, here's one of the nailing benches—the benches that they made the boxes on when they were nailing them by hand. There was a metal plate like this on each side. There was what they called a nail stripper that would kind of line the nails up. You'd throw the nails in here and the vibration would line 'em up so they'd come out point down. And the guys would take 'em like this and they'd start at the back—one hit, they'd put 'em in. There was a guy we used to call Hammer 'n Nails—he was probably 65—and he could just nail those boxes up so fast you couldn't believe it. They usually did that out at that end [of the Stacked Stone Building] or else outside—they used to have a wooden platform out here.

During my lifetime the Stacked Stone Building was no longer used for hay because they'd gotten rid of the horses. They weren't doing horse power; they were using tractors.[11]

Most of the fruit was hauled by the Porters. You know Jim Porter, the fellow that has one arm? His parents. When they moved up here, they didn't have any trucks at all and they were trying to get started. The Folks made a deal with them to (help them) borrow the money to buy some trucks. The Folks[12] had to tell whoever the Porters were borrowing the money from that the Porters would get all of our business so that they had enough creditworthiness at that time to borrow the money to buy the trucks. It worked out very well for both of us.

The Porters had three trucks, two Chevy green trucks and one orange truck. They all had about twelve-foot beds. They were old, used trucks. They would just barely pull out of our home place with a load of fruit.

One of the reasons they built this here, and the reason this building has such a funny shape, is that this was such a giant oak tree. It shaded most of the first two sections. (The building wrapped around a live oak tree. The tree was cut down in 2003 because it threatened to fall and crush the building.)

Chris: Did they count the rings?

Woody: I don't know if we ever counted them. That's the stump lying over there. It broke their crane trying to move it. Not our crane, but the tree people that were chipping all the stuff around here. (The government hired loggers to clean up after the Cedar Fire in 2003. Woody allowed the loggers to stage from the ranch, parking their equipment and dropping the dead trees there if they would chip the wood and scatter it as mulch. He also hired them to do some odd jobs such as cutting down this massive tree).

One of the things that you learn about trees is that the diameter of the tree is not necessarily related to the age, because they grow at different rates.

Scott: (Measuring the stump.) If we're conservative, the diameter of the trunk is five foot six inches at the narrowest place.

Woody: Okay, let's do the maximum.

Scott: Six foot one.

Woody: Depending on the shape. And the nice thing is the darn stump sprouted and is growing again.

(Walking to the South end of the Packing House: looking at a small live oak tree growing from the foundation.)

We quit taking care of this building because we were so busy down in Wynola. And that oak tree grew up in there and cracked the foundation—an acorn somehow got in there.

We had pear trees all the way along here when I was a kid (along the south side of the building, between the building and the road). The pears were planted before the building came this far out.

Trying to do 3,000 boxes a day in a place like this was just chaotic. That was only during pear season. Dad always said that they made money on the pears and they lost it back on the apples. And that was pretty much true at that time. Now it's the other way around. Pears aren't hardly worth picking.

Chris: Really? Because tastes changed? Or because you've got pears from Brazil or—?

Woody: Well, a whole lot of things changed. Partly the economics of transportation changed dramatically. When they started this they had essentially a pickup on a Model T bed, you know. They were just beyond the horse and buggy stage, barely. In fact, at first they weren't. When they first started they were trying to haul stuff to San Diego on [horse-drawn] wagons. (Roughly 60 miles on dirt roads.)

To answer your question a little more, pears are short lived and supermarkets came in and they wanted to have the same thing year round. So you had to have super refrigeration and multiple sources and big operations. They didn't want to deal with anyone who had a little tiny operation.

Chris: So do you mostly have apple trees here or are they still pear trees?

· · ·

Woody: Well, all those on the south side of the building are pears. On the north are all apples. There are more apples than pears now. But actually, as far as production is concerned, it's very difficult to justify growing anything in Julian economically.

Chris: Because of the lack of water?

Woody: Well, it's a broad variety of things. One of them is marketing. One of them is water. One of them is production. A lot of it is the rules that the government has are much easier for a large, flat area to obey than it is for a mountain area. Just a whole bunch of things. But primarily your costs are more than your production.

Cider House

Now this was the place: there was a ramp across here from one building to another, three two-by-twelves (forming a makeshift bridge about 4' above the ground and 10' 8" long). When they were making apple cider and when they were packing apples they used the same line. The cull apples came over here and were wheeled across. That was pretty exciting when it was slippery and wet.

Scott: I would guess.

Woody: There was no railing. And, of course, they picked the boards up every once in a while and did other things. Towards the end, after we moved the packing house away (to Manzanita Ranch store in Wynola), they put a support under the middle of the ramp. But originally when you went across the boards kind of sagged.

Scott: Oh yeah. That's a lot of weight.

Woody: There was a tub that sat right there, much like we had in Wynola. (A tub of water to put the cider apples in). And an elevator (to lift the apples from the tub of water into the press). The cider press sat right in here. They would grind the apples up and the juice went down below.

　　Originally they threw the apple pulp out here on the dirt. Later they built this cement trough. Then they had to scoop it up onto a truck, haul it out for the cows to eat. This was a door where you flipped the pulp out. I don't know if it still works anymore.

Scott: That is a door. After all these years I didn't even know that. I can see it now.

Woody: It was hard work. The juice went over the edge here. I don't know if you remember the old type of press, essentially like (the Palmer Press) Freddy Slaughter uses at the Julian Cider Mill.

Scott: Yes.

Woody: That type of rack and frame press is what they had here. You'll see there are no rafters. That's because the press was so tall that there wasn't room for the supports on the crossbeams. We probably should have replaced them after we took the press out. We moved out of that packing house building in '46. We kept making cider in the cider house until '56. And somewhere I have some fairly decent pictures of cider being made here.

This section (of the foundation) was made out of rock largely from well digging. You can see the fresh cuts. They made cider in that little square there. By the time I came along they had gone into a larger scale operation and they had added this room on and you can see the change in the rock and the line where it was added on. This was the press room when I was born, but originally it was the press and bottling room.

In later years they got scientific and put an edge on the concrete. Cider is very hard on floors. It ate the floor off and they put another floor in. I think it's the third floor in there.

The cider press was an old Palmer-type press which had a platen; I think it was a 32 inch platen.[13] You'd make a stack of cloths and lathes and the press would come up and the juice would run out. Well, this was fine until you decided, 'How are you going to keep the stuff?' So most of the people at that time were loading the cider with preservatives. But we were pasteurizing it. There was an old boiler in here.

You can see here (further north) this was a different era of building, obviously, different material. As you go along you will find all kinds of different layers of buildings.

Anyhow, we can go downstairs. This little porch, where the beam goes across there, the juice would run down here via gravity and they would bottle it. There was a square oven that they could heat with the steam from that boiler. You'd heat the cider up to, I've forgotten now, 170 degrees, 175, for so many minutes. There was a thermometer on top. The thermometer is in behind my desk in that treasure chest of things that nobody needs. And that was basically unfiltered pasteurized.

It was pretty primitive.

You have to have seen a lot of these things to appreciate them, but there were two wooden tanks that sat downstairs—about 500 gallon tanks. Some of the boards from the tanks are used as shelving up in the old shed, and there are still some unused boards down here.

They would let the cider settle overnight in the tanks, and then they would bottle it. When they first started they put it in barrels. Here are a couple of the barrel types that they used (around 45-55 gallon barrels). The barrels were not terribly satisfactory because the cider would almost instantly start to ferment, so they very shortly went to glass bottles.

The next thing they did was they built this section here, where the boards start and go this way. This is almost all Julian lumber. You can tell by the high quality of the knots—not the quality of the lumber.

After pasteurization they would lay the hot cider bottles on their sides on wooden racks which went along here. And you'll see those swing-out doors—they'd swing 'em out so the bottles on the cooling racks could cool faster. Then they would label it.

All of this was done by hand, of course.

I can remember—

Watch your step, there's a killer here.

I can remember Mother standing right in here labeling cider by the truckload. And it would be put in here 'till it was ready to load. They loaded it out this door. So this section was built before I was born but after those two (southern-most) sections.

After that they put the lean-to down there and moved the filter room there. By then they had reasonable electricity. I remember them building that room.

The cider tends to get cloudy if you just bottle it. Everybody wanted clear cider at that time. And so you would put what you call Pectinol in—an enzyme that would break down some of the gelatinous material in the cider. They had a stainless steel tank that would warm it a little, because the Pectinol enzyme filtered better if it was warm. (We learned to get around that when we got to Wynola. But even there we found sometimes we'd heat it to keep it from clouding afterward.) Then there was a filter at this end of that lean-to room.

The same process we used in Wynola, exactly.

Scott: I didn't realize we used Pectinol.

Woody: Yeah. There were several other enzyme companies but the original was Pectinol,[14] a Rohm and Haas product, as I remember.

Then the cider would be pumped up and bottled—that was the only pump we had. Everything else was gravity.

Over the years they made a lot of cider in here. They used to make as much as 50,000 gallons here in a season, they claim—nobody has any real records. But there weren't that many apples in Julian so even when I was a kid they had to buy cider apples. They bought them from all around Julian, and they bought them from Oak Glen. We used to make most of the cider, except for Los Ríos Rancho, for Oak Glen. Los Ríos was made by the Utt Juice Company, who we later did a lot of dealing with.[15]

Now you have to remember they had basically no electricity, just enough for minimal things. The boiler had no pump or blowers, it was just open fire. That little platform up there (outside, under the oak trees off by itself, near the stacked stone building) was for the fuel tank. The first boiler didn't have a pump to pump the oil in. It went over by gravity and just trickled into the boiler and there was a fire.

Scott: Oh really?

. . .

Woody: Yeah. So it didn't vaporize it or anything. It was a vertical tube boiler. That was the reason the fuel tank was up there outside, so the gravity would let the oil run over to here when they were pasteurizing. They pasteurized practically all of the cider because there was not much refrigeration anywhere in the world. Most boilers today have vaporizers, "burners" they call them, that vaporizes the diesel and gets much more efficiency. But the original boiler here was just a bunch of tubes with water in them and a fire underneath it.

After I was about six or so they put in a good boiler downstairs. It was made by Steammaster Automatic Boiler Co. in Los Angeles.

(Walking outside.) This part here was put on in '46.

Scott: That's the part above the little apartment.

Woody: Yeah. The downstairs you and Barney turned into a kind of an apartment. Originally, see that rock on its edge up there (by an oak tree and where the diesel tank sat)? For years the outhouse sat there by that rock pile, before they built these restrooms on the end of the building. That was pretty convenient, as you can see.

Grammy used to tell a story about that outhouse. During World War II when they had vaceros working here, most of them had never had even an outhouse. But Mother (i.e. Grammy) was going out there and one of the men went running by her and said, "Me first señora, me first," and beat her to it. She said she pretty near pooped in her pants she was so astonished when he went charging by. [laughs]

Grampy was so frustrated when they built the restrooms. The septic tank was supposed to be built low enough so that the restrooms could be down in that other building, level with the floor inside. Well, they put the septic tank high enough that we had to build the restrooms up on stilts (higher than the rest of the building: you need to climb stairs to reach it)—which has been a problem ever since.

The leach lines go out that way right along that pear line, in case you ever need to find them.

Anyhow, it worked out. It's still being used.

Now the upstairs here was where they stored the cases of empty bottles when they'd come in. We'd get a truckload of bottles and put 'em up here. When they were bottling they went down that metal slide (to slide them downstairs).

Scott: Oh really? It seems like they would crash.

Woody: Well, they had a way to catch them at the bottom. They came in cardboard cases just exactly like these, except most of them, until the later years, did not have printing on them. Jo and I used to spend a lot of time in the off season digging tunnels in the [boxes of] bottles. And we used—the wood that they use to make boxes out of is called "shook,"—and we used that shook because it was a little bit longer than the cider carton to make a roof over our tunnels. You could just lay the cartons on the edges (without reinforcement) but that got pretty narrow. And as we got bigger, why, they'd fall down on us.

Anyhow. This piece of building came down to here. There were no windows. It just had that metal screen, and this was solid metal (tin siding) down to here. There was a platform where they would unload the bottles. The trucks would back into here and they would unload 'em. And again, the trucks kept getting bigger, and it made this place more and more difficult. We used to have a heck of a time getting a semi in here. We had to pull it way out there into the orchard and back it in here. It just wasn't practical anymore. Everything was done by hand.

This section was the last thing built here. You can see the change in the construction right about there. You have to remember that during World War II you couldn't buy any new building material. All the boards were used. All the galvanized iron was used. You can see all the extra holes in it and stuff. It's done pretty well considering it was well worn.

That was when the restrooms came in. I found the permit, one time, on the back side of this thing, and I was too stupid to put it in my files. But there was a septic permit and an electrical permit in 1946 for this addition here.

I forgot to mention that this was the original siding, this kind of cardboard-y stuff. They insulated it with sawdust. So this is just termite heaven. The kids (Barney and Scott, Woody's sons) put the shower in—there was no shower here.

We have to go inside this restroom to get to the lower level because the lower door blew off in a windstorm and we had to board it up. Ron Morgan is going to replace it someday.

Scott: And the reason for the wooden handrail rail on the stairs leading to the apartment is because I forgot to put in the metal one when they poured the steps.

Woody: Well, we were all here. You can't get all the credit.

Scott: That was my job.

Woody: [laughs]
We'll go down below and I can kind of give you a verbal

thing of how stuff was made. The empty cider boxes, bottles in paper boxes, would come in here. See how they were nice and square boxes?

Scott: Right.

Woody: Those are some of the latest ones. They were done in '56.

Our distributor was Pacific Coast Packing Company, the Edic family.[16] One semi load would just about fill this room. Originally the empty bottles came in small trucks like everything else. And the semis wouldn't make the (90 degree) corner by the house. They always had to pull them around with tractors. Trucks didn't have much power in those days.

The way they brought the trucks in here was that they'd come around this way (a loop road around the oak trees and the building) and they'd park up there. All of the fruit tramps would park under the oak trees as they could cause we were trying to keep the dust far away. They'd bring the trucks down one at a time and back 'em in here. And then they'd haul 'em out that way when they'd get 'em loaded. They had the oak branches trimmed up a little higher and the road actually went about where the electric poles are lying, not quite where it is now. We kept making cider here from '46 to '56, before we built the back room to Manzanita Ranch in Wynola.

I remember one time after we built the packing house Tom Coleman and I were supposed to hold the cider on the truck bed as it went up over this hill. And it tipped over on us. [laughs] It wasn't tied.

Scott: You didn't get hurt, apparently.

· · ·

Woody: No. We squealed and yelled and ran.

Where the posts are in the other room (downstairs in the cider house building, under the apartment) was where we used to do the bottle washing. During World War II you could not buy new bottles, so we used mostly Coke syrup bottles. At that time Coca Cola syrup, and I think all the other soda pops, came in one gallon bottles. The bottles had a little metal strip on the top and you'd take that off and wash 'em. Somebody was always washing bottles—during the off season too. And then we had the problem that it came with a case that said Coke on it. So we were always hunting for new boxes to put the cider bottles in.

Do you remember the tubs that we used to heat the bottles in down there in Wynola before we filled them?

Scott: Were they square?

Woody: Yup. Square tubs. Well, three tubs used to sit along there. One of them you soaked the bottles in. One had soap. And one had water to rinse 'em. Along here we had boards nailed—you can still see the nail holes where the boards went this way. And they had pegs. You put the bottles upside down on the wooden pegs to drain 'em.

This was the only place we had hot water, at first.

I forgot to tell you, after that original boiler went out then there was another boiler upstairs for a little while, and then the good boiler sat about here. We had steam pipes going both ways. So there was hot water everywhere at that time. It was relatively satisfactory.

If you look at the rock walls and the things, ah, would not meet today's standards.

·   ·   ·

Scott: Oh yeah. [laughs]

Woody: But they worked fine and we never had any problems with it. There was very little water wasted. What they did use they ran it out on the ground by gravity. Which we used to do in Wynola until somebody turned us in. (After which they built leach lines.)

Do you remember what year you did this (apartment into the building)? You must have been about a freshman and Barney must have been about a senior.

Scott: Well, Barney was out of high school when I was a freshman, so I must have been in eighth grade. Nineteen eighty two.

Woody: (Speaking to Dana Reed and Chris Tindall.) We decided we needed to have a house for our employees, so Barney and Scott converted this thing into two bedrooms, one of which now serves as my postcard room, and one over here.[17]

Scott: We worked hard. Barney knew what he was doing, and I worked pretty hard too.

Woody: Yeah. They did a good job, I thought. We used it for a house for seasonal employees for about three or four years. I can tell you what year the last year was, maybe. (Reading a Mexican calendar over the stove.) Marzo... Febrero... 1988. That was the last year we used it for a house.

·   ·   ·

Scott: That would be about right. I graduated high school in '86.

Dana: It's nice and cool down here.

Woody: Yup. I think for a couple of high school and grammar school kids they did a pretty nice job of remodeling it. They put the windows in—there were no windows in it. They also put in the shower. A friend of ours, Fred Rickon, did the wiring. He was a licensed electrician. We had him replace all the wiring in the building with conduit. The old wiring was BX[18] and it was getting pretty dilapidated. We didn't know if there might be a short or anything. So the wiring should be pretty darn good. You know, it's not abundant, but it's pretty good. But again, we had to use all used fixtures and everything.

Dana: There's a Franklin stove over there.

Woody: Yeah, that was one they put in in 1946. That was for the heating for the Boys [employees]. There was no heat in here when it was used for cider.

Scott: So you say you moved the operation down to Wynola in '46?

Woody: Yup. We only moved the fruit packing. The cider packing went down in '56, ten years later. One of the reasons they moved to Wynola was that they had to haul all the fruit up to Pine Hills from Wynola. At least half of it was grown in Wynola, probably a little more than half. Up to here. Down into this hole (downhill to the building). Take care of it. Then haul it back up and down into Wynola.

We were still selling wholesale. But within a few years after we moved down there to Wynola we went from selling in boxes in retail or wholesale in San Diego to selling retail in Wynola.

Helmus Andrews was the broker that handled our fruit in San Diego, Andrews Brokerage. Years later Tom Segawa bought the Andrews Brokerage and we bought fruit back from him to make cider, for many years. But even in those days, there were not enough apples in Julian to make the cider we made.

Tom Segawa was an interesting guy. He was one of the people that was interred during the war. He had Japanese ancestry, so they immediately slapped him into prison—which was foolish. But he came back and did very well. Almost all the other Japanese that we knew were really good citizens in spite of the poor treatment they got.

One of the camps that they put them in was in Yuma and another one was up in the Owens River Valley area. It you go by there they have a monument to them.

You just have to hand it to those people, they were treated very, very shabbily for no real reason. Just paranoia. They took their property, they stuffed them in a camp, and didn't treat them very nice. And they came out and almost all of them became very good, prominent citizens.

Scott: Very true.

Woody: We distributed cider through Pacific Coast Packing Company, the Edic family, as far north as Long Beach, and as far east as Phoenix. To do that we had to buy a lot of cider apples. A lot them used to come by rail to Escondido.[19] There would just be a rail car loaded full. Most if it came from Hood River where they had very good Pippin apples, yellow, Newtown Pippins, as we called them. They only gave you something like three days to unload the car without charging you extra. So we would all run down there and push 'em out so we wouldn't have to pay that demurrage charge. You can imagine trying to haul a full railroad car full of apples up here to Pine Hills from Escondido. And you can also imagine that they were dumped in the rail car loose—they were culls to begin with—and dumped out here in Pine Hills, and they still were pretty darn good apples. Pippins were a wonderful apple.

Scott: Yeah. You wouldn't do that with a Red Delicious. [laughs]

Woody: No. Well, not at the speed they went, and how many they used.

I don't remember how many rail cars they got there, but I can remember going down to Escondido several times. Of course I could only go when I wasn't in school. They usually made cider from the local apples first, used them all up, and then would start hauling them in. Years later, we started getting them delivered up here in trucks.

Today, nobody would think of taking apples in a truck, dumping them into a rail car, then bringing the rail car over here, unloading it, hauling the apples up here in a truck. The handling cost a great deal.

They worked extraordinarily hard to make anything work in a place like this.

. . .

Scott: I can't imagine the number of hours. I mean, I know how many, but I can't imagine doing it myself for as many years as they did.

Woody: Dad was six foot four. He used to weigh about 220 pound when the season started, and at the end of the season he'd weigh about 190.

Scott: Really? Working so hard.

Woody: Working. They'd get up at 4 or 5 in the morning, wake us up at 6 or so and get us off to school. Dad would work all day down here and into the night—load all the trucks at night. Sometimes they'd finish at two at night, loading trucks.

Electricity came fairly quickly; I just barely remember it not being here. When Jo was born (1938) they got electricity at the house and I think they put our own poles all the way down here right away because all the old gas engines at the wells came out about the same time, except the one at the shed. That one lasted a while longer; there wasn't electricity over to that one. But it had almost no water.

So, anyhow, it was interesting. And none of that stuff will ever happen again.

Wearing a protective mask, Bope washes equipment in the snow, 1929.

Bope and his grandson Woody, one year old, at the Packing House in 1935.

Bope with Woody and Jo, Nov. 1941. Row upon row of cider bottles are cooling on racks behind them.

*The crew fills apple cider bottles at the Cider House in the early
1950s. Pedro Mireles is furthest from the camera.*

*Franklin in protective rubber gear with a load of apple pulp
outside the door to the cider press room, early 1950s.*

Scott (left) and Barney pose after converting part of the cider house into an apartment for employees in 1981. A calendar left on the wall shows it was used by employees through 1988.

After the cider operation moved to Wynola the cider house was converted to storage. Rubber boots are essential gear when moving irrigation pipes in wet grass.

*The packing house in 2005. It collapsed soon after in a
snowstorm.*

*In 2012 Woody gave the first of two tours of the packing and
cider houses which became this section of the book. Dana Reed
recorded Woody's narration; Scott Barnes took photographs and
notes; and Chris Tindall took measurements and made a CAD
drawing which helped inform the artist's rendering by Larissa
Marantz.*

*Woody, Dana Reed and Chris Tindall (rear) descend into the
bottling room of the Cider House for the 2012 tour.*

---

1. For a thorough description of the acquisition of the ranch see Alice Barnes
   – Gold Mines and Apple Pie, pp123-124.
2. They stopped packing apples at the "cider house" in Pine Hills in 1946
   when Woody was 11 years old. They continued making apple cider there
   another 10 years.

3. Edward Young Barnes (1873-1948), also known as "Bope," was Woody's grandfather.
4. 'Timms' was an orchard totaling approximately 80 acres.
5. Theodore Lockwood Barnes was Edward Young "Bope" Barnes' brother, Woody's great uncle. He married Myrta Hoover and they had four children, David, Ted, Virginia (later Skagen) and Edward (Eddie). They are Woody's second cousins. For complete details, Alice Barnes – Gold Mines and Apple Pie, p191.
6. A lug box is 17" x 13" x 7¼", around 25 pounds of fruit.
7. A bushel is 8 gallons or around 38-40 pounds, which is around 125 apples.
8. I.e. When Woody was old enough to remember, around 1940.
9. Electricity came to the town of Julian in 1931 but did not come to more remote areas until later still.
10. The sorter was made by Food Machinery Corporation (FMC) of Los Gatos and Riverside, California.
    Lead arsenate (PbHAsO4) is an insecticide used primarily for codling moths on apples. The codling moth caterpillars bore into young fruit and prohibit growth, causing severe damage to production. Lead arsenate was banned in the U.S. in 1988.
11. The stacked stone building was often referred to as the "poison room" because in later years it had been used for pesticide storage.
12. "The Folks" means Alice and Franklin Barnes, Woody's parents.
13. The plate which presses against the mash in order to squeeze out the juice.
14. "Pectinol" is the brand name for an enzyme produced by the Rohm and Haas company. The enzyme is commonly called pectinase. Pectin is a jelly-like substance that helps cement plants together. Pectinase is an enzyme used to break down pectin and clear the cloudy aspect from the juice. Pectinase is also commonly used in wine production.
15. Los Ríos Rancho was apple orchard on roughly 300 acres (not all of it cultivated) in Oak Glen planted by Howard L. Rivers beginning in 1906. The ranch remained in the Rivers family through 1995 when it was sold to The Wildlands Conservancy.
16. William "Bill" Edic produced the "Imperial" brand of jam at the Pacific Coast Packing Company from 1929 to 1959. He lived to be over 102.
17. For many years Woody ran a postcard business, selling postcards for Julian, Carlsbad, and the desert regions.
18. BX is a bundle of plastic-coated wires protected by metal sheathing.
19. The San Diego Central line was 22 miles long and opened in 1888 with depots in Oceanside, Vista, San Marcos, and Escondido. Primary freight through the 1950s includes grapes, avocados, and citrus.

2

WOODY EARLY YEARS

This section deals with Woody's early years on the ranch, friends from Julian, and a very exciting tractor adventure.

Scott: So, Dad, why don't you tell me where you were born and so forth.

Woody: Well, I was born at Mercy Hospital in San Diego but I've lived all my life in Julian, on Manzanita Ranch in Pine Hills most of the time with a few timeouts for college and 14 years in Wynola at the little house across the street from Spencer Valley School.

Scott: What year were you born?

Woody: February 24th 1935, and attended the Julian Elementary school for eight years and the Julian High School for four years, Pomona College for four years and the University of Michigan for a year and a half and got a Master's there.

Scott: Wow. Those were the days when you could actually finish in four years. [laughs]

Woody: Well, in those days we had an incentive program because it was the universal military draft[1] and when you were 18 you had to register for the draft and if you didn't go to college you were drafted and if you did go to college you would get a deferment with some provisions. In your first year you had to be in the top 25% of your class or you would not get a deferment grade-wise. And in the second year, because they had already taken a group out, there was a lower percentage—I think it was around 50% because they had drafted all of the people who had lower grades than that. And so on. Grampy Barnes had an enemy on the local draft board, which was interesting in that each time I had to appeal. And the enemy was also on the appeals board. So each time I would be turned down for my deferment. It would go the appeals board and the appeals board would come back two to one and I would get to go to college.

Scott: [laughs] Who was this enemy?

Woody: Well, the gentleman's name was Lou Lipton and he ran Lipton Savoy Café downtown. He was in cahoots with Arnholt Smith's group who was attempting to buy the racetrack at the time. He wasn't a truly longtime enemy, but they wanted to get control of the racetrack and were trying to get

Grampy (Woody's dad), who was on the fair board that controlled the racetrack, to vote for his particular group at the time. In addition to little games he played with me he offered Grammy Barnes anything she wanted if she could get Grampy to vote for them to run the racetrack.

Scott: Anything she wanted meaning...?

Woody: Well, I assume it was in clothing or something, fur coats and things. Arnholt Smith and his brother J.A. Smith ran the U.S. National Bank at the time. They were well known financiers and I don't know exactly how Lou Lipton was hooked in with them but he was.[2]

Scott: So then you had one sister.

Woody: Yep. Jo. Still have one sister.

Scott: She's younger than you.

Woody: Three and a half years younger.

Scott: Did you wish you had brothers?

Woody: I was happy to have her. That's kind of an interesting story because when I was little we had a wood stove and a wood fireplace and that was the sole heat for the house. Electricity came to the Ranch when I was about three and a half...the same year Jo (Mary Alice) came along.

When Mother was in the hospital having Mary Alice— they used to keep them there for ten or twelve days, which is something they don't do anymore—why, Grampy Barnes got a washing machine, an electric stove, a hot water heater, and an electric refrigerator. Previously we'd had an ice box and it would last the whole week if you were lucky.

Scott: Wow.

Woody: I don't remember the hot water heater particularly but I remember the other three because they were really a big deal. Hartwick Barnes' wife Wilmeth, and (their daughter) Rosemary, sat with me when Grandma Barnes was in the hospital, as I remember it.

When Jo and Grandma Barnes (Woody's mother) came back from the hospital I remember being kind of astonished at how little she was. [laughs] I thought I was going to have a playmate immediately!

That's about what I remember of her arrival.

Scott: You couldn't take her down to the lake and toddle around.

Woody: No. We couldn't do much of anything there for a while. It was a surprise.

A few years later we ran our own electric line to the packing house - cider house area. And later still on down to the lake to run the pump for irrigation.

. . .

Scott: We replaced some of those poles when I was in high school after they had rotted out. We tied the new poles to a backhoe with a chain, lifted them up, and then eased them into the holes by hand. I was the person who maneuvered the bottoms into the hole. Down by the corrals one of these giant poles slipped free from the chain and came crashing down. You yelled for me to run! I was lucky it fell the other way because I hesitated a bit too long.

That was dangerous and scary, but the worst part was climbing up the extension ladder and pulling the copper wires tight. I was never fond of heights.

Getting back to when Jo was born, 1938, at that time you didn't have the Wynola store.

Woody: No. This ranch in Pine Hills was the center of the Manzanita Ranch operation from the time they began leasing it in 1904 or 5, we don't know for sure when, and when they bought it in 1916, until about 1946 when they built the store down there. They actually bought the property where the store is in 42 and we did sell stuff retail and do a little bit of packing there in the garage.[3] It was a multi-purpose room auto garage and retail fruit business. They also bought the big ranch at the north end of the Wynola Valley (at the end of Orchard Lane) somewhere around 1928 and were gradually paying for it up until around 1940.

Grampy Barnes moved here to Pine Hills permanently in 1922 and built the rock house with stones gathered on the ranch. I think he finished it shortly after they were married on December 25th of 1924. He and Alice lived in the old shack for a short time before they finished the house.

Scott: Was the old shack still there when you were growing up?

. . .

Woody: Oh yeah. It was used occasionally. It was a one-by-twelve board and bat structure with some sort of a fibrous board cover on portions of the inside. Some of those pictures that we have from Hartwick show it back in the 20s when it was in better shape than when we remember it. It had no electricity, no running water. They had a single faucet outside that they could get water from when I was little, but that was a later edition. And they had an outhouse, of course.

My Granddad (Bope) lived in it for quite a while. I think he came up here in '28 and they eventually remodeled what was going to be Grampy's office in the back of the garage into his room. (A single-car garage with rock walls located near the house.) Bope lived there and they put in the restroom around 1942 or 3. Bope passed away in 1948.

The last thing we did was put that room on where you used to sleep. (Scott lived there part-time when working from 2003 to 2006). That was done, I believe, the first year Pete (Pedro Mireles) worked for us, which was 1948. There's a mark on the wall (on the cement outside) that says 1956, so that might very well be when the bedroom was built.

The main original house just had the two bedrooms. In about 1940 to 42, somewhere in there, they added where Jo's room and Jo's office is—the two bedrooms and the second bathroom. I can remember them doing that but I don't remember the exact year.[4]

Scott: At that time there was a pretty big fruit operation here.

Woody: The scale of operations of everybody in those days was much different than it is now. They didn't have the super-large chain stores and so on. We produced a lot of pears, far more pears than we ever produced apples. In fact, we produced more pears in Julian than will ever be done in apples. The pear business was the engine that made the business possible for many years. They had, previously, tried a lot of other crops. The area in front of Jo's house was a cherry orchard for a while. It was a walnut orchard for a while. Previous to that I think they had raised wheat there. We see in some of those pictures of Hark's (Hartwick Barnes) some other crop between the young trees. By the time I came along there were just about four walnut trees and four cherry trees. They raised plums, fresh market plums, not dried ones, for quite a while in that area. So that area had had a lot of variety.

The area in front of this house had been mostly apples. When they started leasing the place everybody said the trees were beyond their productive years. We finally took out all the original trees... I think there's one tree left just over the hill behind the shed. They probably were planted in the 1880s but we don't know for sure. They were planted on a very wide spacing and they were designed for non-irrigation. Because nobody had any water. Non-irrigated fruit was practical in those days. They did what they called 'clean cultivation.' They tried to not let the weeds get any moisture. And they disced and everything to keep the weeds down.

Scott: Which is not really encouraged nowadays because of erosion.

Woody: Well, it would not be practical. They also put contour ditches throughout the orchard so that when the rains came in the winter the water would run around. In some of those pictures of Hark's we can show you a lake they used to have halfway down to the old cider house where they would run the water off in the spring. Then it would soak into the ground in the sandpit out there. Somewhat like what we do with the pump from this lake, only in a different area. They did it in several areas.

Scott: What was your favorite thing about growing up here?

Woody: I don't think I have a single favorite thing. We had a great deal of fun. We were, of course, limited in the number of people we knew, but the folks had a wonderful group of friends. So some of our friends that we hung around with were business associates and friends from San Diego because Grandpa Barnes (Bope) had grown up in San Diego. San Diego was a small town. For example, our attorney had two daughters and one of them was roughly our age. (Luther and Dorothy Ward, and their daughters Barbara and Linda.)

Life was simpler in those days. Attorneys didn't make quite as much money as they do now. He used to come up on his vacation, stay at the house, and plant tulip bulbs. And they would come up whenever we had a snowstorm.

Barbara was the oldest one and Linda was roughly our age. They lived in Point Loma most of the time, but they had a beach house out at Windansea Beach (La Jolla), where it's now Windansea Beach. We used to go down there on the Fourth of July. It was a marginal house, kind of a screened bungalow thing. It did have running water and flush toilets but that was about it. We still use a legal firm sometimes called Ward and Thorn. That was the descendants of Ward. Dick Thorn is the active person now.

Scott: I've spoken to him.

. . .

Woody: At one time it was called Ward, Thorn and Jessop, and that was part of the Jessop family, the jewelry family. Jerry became a judge, and now he's retired. The Jessop family sold all their stores. The clock that they had was a wonderful thing. Somebody defaced it the other day.

Scott: Oh, really?

Woody: They've already gotten the funds to redo it. People are so silly.

Our fruit broker in San Diego—who was a wonderful guy by the name of Helmus Andrews, his wife's name was Billy—had a daughter named Pat and she was a very nice girl. She was roughly the same age as we were. We used to hang around with them.

The cider broker's name was Bill Edic—we made cider all this time. His company was called the Pacific Coast Packing Company, and he had three sons, two of whom were of a very similar age. They were twins, about two years younger or one year younger. They rented houses from us for quite a while and spent their summer months up here.

So those were some of the non-local people.

And then some of the local people: Bobby Jane Green, who at that time was Bobby Jane Hathaway, lived right across Pine Hills Road. The Reddings moved up when I was about a year old. They lived in Julian at first, and then moved out to Cuyamaca Road. The drugstore was run by the Tozers and they had three kids, but two of them were in our similar age group, Mitzi and Tom. We're still good friends with the three Redding kids after all these years. And then the Porters had a feed and supply and trucking business and they hauled much of our fruit for many, many years. Originally there was a fellow by the name of Parker and he was a very unreliable trucker. But Milo Porter and Lelah were wonderful people and they ran the Julian Feed and Supply. They had three kids, one of whom was a babysitter for us and the other two were good friends and still are good friends all these years later: Jim Porter and Mervyn Porter. Mervyn now lives in Montana. We went up just this last year to their "last" annual party. Again. Jim lives in Deer Lake Park.

Scott: So many people that you grew up with stayed here and are still here. Why do you think that is?

Woody: That's a harder question to answer. Julian is a pretty nice area to live in—and a very difficult area to make a living in. I think that's always been true.

A lot of the people who did stay had some reason to stay. For example, Jim Porter ran the trucking business, then he worked for the County until he retired. Mervyn went away to college and then was a Vo-Ag (Vocational Agriculture) teacher in Petaluma (Sonoma County, California), for many years. Then he came back and ran the cement transit-mix business. Norm Feigel was in our class and his family had a portion of the Santa Ysabel Ranch and he stayed. Bud Segni was in my class and he went away and went into construction and when he retired he moved back here. Aleta Hayton stayed here almost all her life. Her name is Starnes now. Bobby (Hathaway—Green) lives right across the road. Her husband traveled around quite a bit but when he retired they moved back here. He worked for Grangettos (Farm and Garden Supply) for a while and I think he was a part-owner. Pat Lewis Mushet was in our class. And my grandfather moved up here permanently after he sold his share in Doyle-Barnes. Doyle-Barnes Company split up and sold out in 1928.

Many of the people voluntarily lived here; they didn't have

to stay. I think they did it because Julian's a pretty nice area. It has a lot of nice people and a lot of talented people who may not look talented but they are.

Scott: [laughs]

Now I remember Grammy was always cooking apple pies and cookies. And other things too, but especially that's what I remember. Was that true when you were growing up?

Woody: When I was growing up was before there were freezers. So almost everybody canned a great deal of produce during the growing season to eat during the off season. Mother and Betty Angel would pack fruit, stop at noon, run up here, put something on the stove, and can it. Run back down, pack fruit 'til five, and then come up and can all night.

Scott: Really?

Woody: All during the fruit season. Betty Angel Okey was her married name. A really neat person. They did that for a number of years. At the end of the fruit season the basement would be full of various kinds of canned things (meaning glass mason jars).

My grandfather Barnes (Bope) would always have a big garden. So there would be beans and berries and all kinds of things to can besides just apples and peaches and pears and things that we raised commercially. There was always something going on. Plus we always had chickens for eggs and meat and much of the time, at least when I was a little kid, we had milk cows. Grammy Barnes would make butter, cottage cheese. The milk cows and pigs we kept down at the Hawkins place which is where the packing house is in Wynola, during the time that I can remember.

And we had pigs down there (in Wynola), so we also had pork. When we butchered them we would take the meat and —we didn't have freezers up here even then, although we did have refrigerators—we would take the meat to a place called Cuyamaca Meats, which was at the west end of Main Street in El Cajon. They had a slaughter house and a place to freeze meat. You could rent a locker there, which we'd do because otherwise you had too much meat to handle. We used to butcher the pigs in the spring when they'd been gaining a lot so the meat was somewhat tolerable, hang it for a couple of weeks so they would tenderize somewhat. And it would be somewhat edible.

Scott: [laughs] So you are saying the meat is better now?

Woody: Well, the best cuts of grass fed meats when they're gaining is quite good. But if you tried the average cuts, they are better now (with grain-fed animals). Plus the fact that when you butcher your own you have oxtail. You have lots of liver—you'd be surprised how big the liver is in a cow. I happen to like liver. We used to eat the tongue. A lot of people don't like tongue; I love tongue. We used to eat the heart; a lot of people don't eat heart. So when you butcher your own, there are a lot of things that you get that are not choice cuts.

Most of it should have been ground up, probably, the chuck roasts and so on. Or they needed to be cooked for a very long time and made into stews because they were rather firm. They had good flavor but they were low in fat. Fat in the meat is called marbling and that's what makes it both flavorful and tender.

. . .

Scott: It's funny, I think that I know history fairly well compared to most people, but you don't think about little things like there were no freezers back then.

Woody: Nope. The first refrigerators we bought would have about half a cubic foot to one cubic foot area that would freeze things. It was a very, very tiny space.

Scott: It probably was not all that reliable.

Woody: Well the electricity would go off for four or five hours (daily), but if you didn't open the refrigerator it would hold the temperature pretty well compared to being outside. Which was what they'd had before.

World War II Era

Woody: There are a whole series of things that happened during World War II which are kind of interesting, not things that you would think of now. The first thing I can remember about World War II was coming one day, just bubbling over, and my parents and grandparents...

We had an old Monitor Radio. It was about, oh, height of a desk. Very terrible radio. You could barely hear anything on it. Full of static. And we'd take a wire and hook it to the window screens to improve the antennae sometimes.

I came charging in and my parents and grandparents said SHHHHH!

It was Roosevelt giving his "Day of Infamy" speech. Now they had very little use for Roosevelt, like zero, but this was the beginning of World War II when Pearl Harbor had been bombed. So that was kind of the starting of things there.

World War II was a very interesting period in that we didn't feel the problems like they did in other places, but we had rationing on many things that you wouldn't expect. For example, shoes were rationed. Sugar was rationed. Gasoline was rationed. Tires were rationed. Butter was rationed. These were all things that you had to get a little coupon for to purchase. Because we had the milk cows, which were high butter-fat cows, Jerseys and Guernseys, we had lots of cream, which mother made into butter. So we had far more butter than we could possibly use. We would trade it to people who weren't using their sugar so we could can more things.

Gasoline had a quota that was very limiting. That's one reason we didn't visit our family in Berkeley very much, about twice when we were kids during the war years. Maybe only once. Because you couldn't get gas coupons for travel, but you could for farming. So we could get gas and diesel for the tractors, and diesel for the trucks that we used for hauling fruit, because there was a priority system set up. The gas used to be delivered by a fellow by the name of Leo Crickmore. He brought Signal Gas up. Leo Crickmore was a really nice fellow and, if we were temporarily needed more gas than our ration tickets, he would make sure that somehow we had enough gas to keep the tractors and trucks running.

Scott: Which family members lived in Berkeley?

Woody: Mother's sister Helen and Loren Wilson Hunt. That's Emily Cowan's dad and mom. I think Emily has gone back to Hunt now.

Scott: I think so. Okay.

. . .

Woody: Emily had an older sister that was my age exactly, Ann Hunt. She died of diabetes. Ann's husband was a dentist, and he was going through dental school when they got married. They lived in a basement in San Francisco. I remember visiting them and looking up and watching people's feet go by through the little glass. They had three adopted kids, and one committed suicide or was murdered, never knew the truth of it, in San Francisco. After Ann died... well, when she was still hospitalized with her diabetes up in Redding, she moved up to Redding, [her adopted kids] were stealing all her stuff and selling it. I suspect they were on dope, although I don't know that. That was a tragic thing.

Emily had two kids, John and Jennifer Cowan, and they both have been very successful.

Scott: Yeah. John I know fairly well.

Woody: Going back, one of the early things I remember, I believe it was in 1938, Grampy Barnes bought a new D2 tractor, and a new disc, and a new diesel tank. The diesel tank is still in the tractor shed. They built that tractor shed about that time. The diesel tank is the one that's up on the concrete.

Scott: It still works.

Woody: It's empty but it would work if we put diesel in it.

That tractor was a really big deal because it was brand new. Prior to that we'd had disaster tractors. The reason Grampy bought it, we had a thing called a Cletrac,[5] which was a small track tractor. The Cletrac had a seat on a spring and one day Grampy was driving it and the spring broke and almost dropped him into the disc. He managed to hang on. You know, when you're hanging off backwards trying to stay up, he just hung on to these levers and steering things. Grampy managed to get it stopped. He never even got it fixed.

He went down to San Diego and borrowed—I assume he borrowed the money—but anyhow, bought a D2[6] from Gunnard Gunn, Gunn Tractors. He didn't want to take a chance on dropping in again into the disc! When it dropped the only thing that kept him from falling in was he fell into the steering devices. And he managed to get the tractor stopped without getting hurt.

Another time, Ralph Slaughter, who was another great contractor but who had one weakness—he was very fond of alcoholic beverages—was working for us prior to starting his contracting business, and I was riding with Ralph and I fell down between the disc and the tractor and Ralph managed to stop without running over me.

Scott: Wow.

Woody: I'm sure a lot of people regretted it ever since. [laughs] Anyhow, that was the end of my riding with Ralph.

Another time, on those three trucks that the Porters had that I was telling you about... The folks had an apartment at Fourth and Upas for quite a few years,[7] and for some reason I was down there and Charlie Gates was hauling me home in one of those three Porter trucks. On those sharp turns just above Ramona—before you cross the creek—the door fell open on this old truck. I pretty near fell out. Charlie grabbed me and pulled me back in. I can remember that just as clear as anything. [laughs]

Charlie's sister Mary Gates worked for us a lot.

Tractor Swimming

Scott: You had a recent tractor escapade. Why don't you tell about that while it's still fresh in your memory?

Woody: Well, Heriberto and I were planting tules on the face of the big dam in the canyon down here and I was hauling the tules from the little dam down and I was dumping them over the edge.[8] They were to be a natural barrier against erosion. And it was a long walk for Heriberto to carry them to the water's edge. So I got a little close and shook the bucket of the tractor. The tractor went forward a little bit, enough to lift the rear wheels up so I had very little traction, and starting sliding down the side of the dam. What I had forgotten, and I shouldn't have forgotten but I did, was that brakes are only on the two back wheels on a wheel tractor.

That was two or three mistakes that I made. One of them was that it wasn't in four wheel drive. Another one was that I had the loader a little high with a big load. And I got close to the edge. But anyhow, that being behind us, it started skidding down there and I thought, 'Well it will go right straight down and I'll get out when I get down there.' I can remember that thought. And then it hit a telephone pole (lying sideways in the water to reduce wave erosion on the earthen dam) and flipped on the right side. Then it hit a rock and flipped on the left side and Heriberto thinks it turned over twice.

Scott: Rolled completely over twice?

Woody: He thinks so. I remember flipping to one side and flipping to the other side. Then I remember grabbing a breath of air as it was going underwater. And then I was underwater thinking, 'How in the heck do I get out of here?' astonished that I didn't have any broken bones and wasn't pinned. I started to get out but I had the seatbelt on. I was trying to undo the seatbelt and I was fumbling around on the right side, and it wasn't over there. I was beginning to run out of air. Then I remembered that the tractor was made in India, and I thought maybe the latch was on the left side. I rumbled around on the left side and was able to undo it and get up, get out and get a breath of air—which was very nice.

Scott: [laughs]

Woody: The tractor was one hundred percent underwater. The shallowest place was one wheel that was about three feet under. I pushed myself up on that and then started swimming towards shore. It's pretty hard to swim with boots full of water and clothes full of water and probably being pretty shook up from being tossed about. But I made it. And Heriberto was pointing me a tule because that was the only thing he had.

Scott: I was wondering if he jumped in the water to save you.

Woody: [laughs] No, he hadn't yet. You know, this all happens pretty fast. He thought I was underwater two minutes; I figured it was a good minute. But it was a long time to be underwater.

Scott: To be holding your breath! I don't know if I could hold it for that long.

· · ·

Woody: I didn't have many choices. I was thinking, 'I really don't want to croak under here. I'm probably going to drown but I don't want to.' I remember trying to figure out, 'How to get outta here?!'

Scott: Well then, if you swim directly to the surface you bang into the roof of the tractor.

Woody: No, the tractor was on its side. (The tractor had a sun shade roof but did not have an enclosed cab.) I could tell which way was up because there were bubbles. I didn't know what position the tractor was in 'til I got out, but the bubbles kinda told me where up was.

Scott: That's scary. Good thing I paid the life insurance on time.

Woody: And then Heriberto called Roman Gutierrez, and Roman came over while I went to the Old Timers Picnic. On the way out from the lake, Heriberto was bringing me up to the house to change some clothes, two of my college friends happened in: Del Weins and his wife Carol. So I had to stop and find them some maps. And then I went to the Old Timers Picnic.

Scott: Were you all wet when your friends...?

Woody: Yeah. I was all wet. I had to change clothes.

. . .

Scott: They are going to be talking about that forever.

Woody: I probably will too. [laughs] I told him about it and Del said, "You're the coolest person I've ever seen." Hey, he was right, I was cool. I was cold and wet. But he was thinking I was calm after that was all over.

By the time I got back from the Old Timers Picnic, Roman and Heriberto had dragged the tractor up with Roman's backhoe until it poked out of the water, but was not clear of the lake. Then we got Robert Redding to come over and between the two backhoes they were able to pull it to the top of the dam.

Scott: Now I don't feel so bad about getting that same tractor stuck in the muddy edge of the lake a year or two ago.

Woody: Oh yeah. The funny thing is the day before when we were starting to do this planting, or two days before, we went over and looked at that same area (the same arm of the lake where Scott got stuck). We were going to dig some tules there. It looked a little bit muddy. I said, "No, we're not going there." Heriberto said, "Oh yeah, you can do it." And I said, "Nope." I remembered what happened to you there.

Scott: It looked dry. It was dry. But an inch underneath the dry there was slippery mud.

Woody: That's exactly the way it looked. But having been there once, why, I knew better.

·   ·   ·

Scott: But the dam, it wasn't muddy, it was just...

Woody: No, it wasn't muddy. When we came out you could see the skid marks where the brakes were on, but it had so little weight on the back tires when it went over that edge. Once you get your engine over the lip it starts to lift everything; the weight was all on the front wheels. Once you start going downhill at that speed there is nothing you can do.

Scott: You are going have to take less risks. You always take more risks than I ever did.

Woody: I don't like to take risks.

Scott: I don't know if I agree with that.

Woody: That's why I quit sweeping the roof this morning.[9] [laughs] Well, anyhow.

Scott: You always do too much ladder work and too much roof work and you always drive the tractor faster than me. I know because I have never broken one of the bolts that holds the discs and mowers on the tractors. I've bent a couple, but you seem to break one every other time you take a disc or anything![10] [laughs]

A Historic Desk

Scott: It's August 21, 2018 and I just took a picture of a desk. It's in storage at Jo's garage in Pine Hills. Can you tell me about the desk?

Woody: Yeah, the desk was built by my great-grandfather, Edmund Carson Thorpe. I don't know exactly when it was built, but it was the desk that I used all the time I was in high school, and it's somewhat historic because of that.

Scott: Did he build it specifically for you?

Woody: No. No, he was dead long before I was born. I don't know how it got up here from Fourth and Upas but it did, and I don't know exactly how it got into my room, but it did. That'd be 100 plus years old.

   I can't remember when he died right off hand, but it's now 100 years old, I would say, and maybe more.[11] He was a carpenter and built a number of the houses in La Jolla when they were really not mansions like they are now, but houses when they were first opening up La Jolla. When they were still living in Pacific Beach where they raised lemons with the other great-grandparents and Granddad Barnes. They sold out that area around 1907, give or take a year or two, and moved over towards Fourth and Upas in San Diego. One of the houses he built in La Jolla is a house that was much, much later owned by Shirley and Roe Tuttle, Jo's first in-laws.

Scott: I did not know that.

.   .   .

Woody: Well, I'm just full of bologna.

Edmund Carson Thorpe had an interesting history. He married the author and poet Rose Hartwick Thorpe. Before Edmund was born his father accompanied Kit Carson on one of his early trips. That's why he was Edmund Carson Thorpe, he was named after Kit Carson.

When he was about five years old, Edmund's dad Lucian went on another trip with Kit Carson. Lucian was a great admirer of Kit Carson because he felt Kit Carson treated the Indian people very well and was an enlightened explorer. Well, the son, who was only five or so, missed his dad so much that he ran away from home. After a year or two when his father came back from exploring with Kit Carson the son was gone and so Lucian started out looking for him and fortuitously they found him selling newspapers at a railroad station, and that's how they eventually got back together. It was just an accident that his dad found him and that they recognized and found each other.

Edmund Carson Thorpe one day, when they still lived in Pacific Beach, went to La Jolla to get groceries. When he came out he started to crank his car and dropped dead. That's when Rose Hartwick Thorpe became a widow, from then on.[12]

The Barnes' Model T navigating December snow on the road from the shed to the packing house. Franklin hauled cement for his house from San Diego and sand from the bottom of Banner Grade in this Model T when building his home.

Franklin L. Barnes (left) and his brother Hartwick Barnes touring the ranch in Pine Hills on December 22, 1918 in a Model T. The Barnes family began leasing Manzanita Ranch farm (they always called it a "ranch") in 1906 and purchased it in 1916.

Franklin L. Barnes working on the foundation of his home. He gathered all the rocks on the ranch in Pine Hills, hauled the cement from San Diego and the sand from Banner Canyon in the Model T pictured earlier. He had one carpenter help him for two weeks, and the rest of it Franklin did himself. The photo says it was taken in 1920 but it may have been as late as 1922.

The rock house, Woody's childhood home, as completed in 1924.
A later addition to the left on this photo added two bedrooms and
a bathroom.

Grading the driveway with Bope on the grader and Franklin
driving the Cletrac tractor, 1929, before the near-fatal accident
convinced Franklin to sell it. (The seat, welded to a spring, broke
off and nearly dropped Franklin into the disc trailing behind the
tractor.)

Alice Barnes holding Woody at 5 weeks old. Everyone in Julian named "Frank" or "Franklin" was nicknamed "Pete" including Frank "Pete" Lane, Franklin "Pete" Barnes, etc. Being as Woody's dad was called Pete, Woody became "rePete." For a brief time they tried out "Locky," but the nickname "Woody" began in elementary school and stuck.

Woody at three digging in the iris bed.

Franklin L. Barnes holding Jo (Mary Alice) around 1939.

Woody at five at home.

Woody at six. Note the tulips growing between the apple trees.

Woody in front of pear blossoms in Junior High.

1. Passed by President Franklin D Roosevelt on September 16, 1940, the universal draft was called the Selective Training and Service Act. Initially requiring registration of men from the age of 21 in 1942 the age was dropped to 18. In addition, selection was moved from a 'lottery' system to administration by local draft boards.
2. Lou Lipton was a bank executive at U.S. National Bank—a bank chaired and controlled by C. Arnholt Smith. (Arnholt Smith called Lou Lipton "kind of a public relations man" and standard bearer in the local Democratic Party.)

    C. Arnholt Smith was a business tycoon who controlled both U.S. National Bank (with nearly $1 billion in deposits), and Westgate-California, which owned U.S. Steel, Yellow Cab Company franchises in many California cities, and much of the San Diego tuna industry—the third-largest industry in San Diego in the 1950s, behind the U.S. Navy and aerospace. He also owned the San Diego Padres from their inception through 1974. In 1979, C. Arnholt Smith was convicted of grand theft and tax evasion.
3. The "Wynola Garage" next to Manzanita Ranch Store. The Garage predated the store and was probably built in the 1920s.
4. Franklin Barnes built the house himself. The primary building materials were stones gathered on the ranch. The house is still being used by Jim and Jo (Barnes) Geary and their cat Up.
5. Cletrac Tractor—Manufactured by the Cleveland Tractor Company.
6. A track-type tractor first manufactured in 1938, the Caterpillar D2 was the smallest diesel tractor manufactured by Caterpillar. The model was discontinued in 1957.
7. Fourth and Upas—Two blocks west from the northwest corner of Balboa Park in San Diego.
8. Tule plants, also known as California Bulrush, Schoenoplectus californicus, were an important plant for Native Americans in wetter areas of California. Used as a food source (the fresh shoots could be eaten or dried and ground into flour), a source of black dye, and as a construction material. Tule plants are effective as steam bank (or in this case, dam) stabilization.
9. This interview was done on September 23, 2009. Woody was 74 at the time.
10. Discs are held to the tractor with a "bolt" or hitch pin through the tongue of the equipment and the drawbar "eye" of the tractor. If the disc gets hung up on a rock or some other impediment, the hitch pin will break before the tractor or disc suffers serious damage.
11. Edmund Carson Thorpe was born July 6, 1849 in Berea, Cuyahoga county, Ohio to Corinna (Pixley) and Lucian Rowland Thorpe. He died in 1916. The desk was used by Bope, and when Bope died it was moved to Woody's bedroom.
12. According to James Miller Guinn's *A History of California* (1907), Lucian made a trip across the country with Kit Carson the year his son was born, 1849. Guinn does not record the second trip though it may very well have happened. When the Civil War broke out, Lucian enlisted in Company G, Sixty-seventh Ohio Volunteer Infantry "where he was a drum major." He

passed away on October 15, 1864 at the Hilton Head, South Carolina General Hospital. Cause of death is listed as "congestive intermittent fever."

3

ELEMENTARY SCHOOL AND HIGH SCHOOL

Scott: How many people were in elementary school and high school at that time?

Woody: [In elementary school] we had three rooms and there were three grades in one room, three in another room, and two in the third room. Sometimes Bobby Jane (Hathaway) and myself and two others were put in with the class ahead of us to make the rooms balance out a little better. So we were in the year-older group than we would ordinarily have been. I think the other one was Peggy Brown, and I don't remember who the fourth one was. We were presumably a little less immature or something. [laughs]

Here's a list of some of the teachers we had. This is partly my memory and Martha Gwen's memory. Martha Gwen Redding (Thum) was a year ahead of me, but because it was a three room school, we were in the same room I think all the time we were in grammar school.

Ms. Tait was our first grade teacher.

Mrs. Moore was our second grade teacher. She was fatter than a pig. The main thing we remember about her was she sat on a table to give us a lecture and the table collapsed... and we all cheered. Of course that made her furious.

And then they had Mrs. Burford who chased Tom Tozer around the room while yelling at him. We all yelled, "Run, Tom. Run!"

Scott: She wanted to hit him with a ruler or something?

Woody: Yes. She was crazy.

Then Mrs. Medford was really... She left after Christmas.

Then Claudine Swycaffer. The Swycaffer family has been in Julian forever. Grammy Barnes used to ride with Tot Cumming around down to Ballena where the Swycaffers mostly lived. The other Swycaffer was a principal for awhile. I can't remember her first name.

In the sixth grade we had a Mr. Fox and he was Janice and Patricia Fox's uncle. His brother Denver Fox ran the County School Camp for a while.

Fox was an interesting loser. We diagrammed eight sentences in the morning and then we played till noon and then in the afternoon we diagrammed eight sentences and played until the school was out. That was it for the year.

We had Claire Duermit in the seventh and eighth grade. She was an excellent teacher. When we graduated she gave the girls something to keep clean with and she gave me and all the boys nail clippers. I still have the nail clippers. Her son, who was much older than we were at that time, just quit living in Julian Pines and went into an assisted living home. Her granddaughter Shirley lives in Julian Pines and runs a horseback riding business. Shirley's husband used to run a bike shop in town. So all these years later we still have a connection with our grammar school teacher.

Minnie Woodard was the principal much of that time.

Her husband, Manuel, when we were little kids, drove a stage that went daily from Julian to San Diego and then ran errands for people (who couldn't go down themselves). Can you imagine a stage running errands for people?

Scott: Is this a horse-drawn...?

Woody: No, this was motorized. Manuel he did that for several years. Then he became a bus driver for the school which took both grammar school and high school kids around. The school bus went to Pine Hills, Farmers Corner, and over to Cuyamaca.

The Woodards lived in the house that is now the Book House (Woody and Jane own 2230 Main Street, Julian which is leased to The Old Julian Book House). Minnie's dad, whose name was McGowan, built the house there and the next house, which is now the Julian Grill. Those two houses right side by side.

Edith McGowan was the postmistress for many years. That was in Foresters Hall right directly across the street. She was a bit of a tartar, but she got the job done.

The phone central was there, I can't remember the name. It was a plug-in central. Gwenny Clark was there many years and the Clark kids all went to school in Julian.

But anyhow, you could call up central, dial it, and they would say, "Number please." And if you said, "16," they would plug it into 16. Our phone number was three, four F, two. Three four was the hole you plugged it into, F was a farmer line: that meant *you* had to maintain the farmer line. And two was two rings.

Scott: Because there were other people on the same line.

· · ·

Woody: Not on our line because we had our own. But most of them had one ring, two rings and different codes. On all the other lines, almost all of them, you could listen in when somebody else was talking.[1]

Another teacher was Mrs. Feeler. She came up to Julian school when they closed the Inaja school. There used to be a one room Indian school down there.

High School

There were about a hundred and thirty in the high school. The high school included what is now Warner's High School and Borrego High School and all of the kids from those two areas' elementary schools came to Julian for the high school.

Scott: That's why it was bigger than the elementary school. Because now it's smaller in number of students.

Woody: Yes, that's right. It's four years (as opposed to eight for elementary school). But at that time there was also an elementary school at Witch Creek—which is now the library[2], or was the library for many years and is now the Historical Society building in Julian. There was also a school in Inaja, which was closed about the time I was in the fourth or fifth grade. That teacher came up to Julian. Her name was Mrs. Feeler. And so did the students, obviously. There were about three students down there.

At one time, I believe there were something like fifteen one-room schools in the Julian Union High School District as it existed at that time. There was one in Inaja, and there was one here (in Pine Hills) near the little white bridge called

Orinoco, there was one in Spencer Valley which still exists, of course. There was one in Witch Creek. There was a school at the Santa Ysabel Indian Reservation. There was one at the Mesa Grande Reservation. Off and on there was one in Banner, which is interesting because it was moved to the other side of San Felipe and dragged back and forth several times. And there were several out at Warners and one down in Borrego—that I know of offhand. Oh yeah, there was Oberlin School at what is now Farmers Corner—the one that Grandma (Mary Agnes) Jacobs taught at when she first came up here. She lived with the Marlettes out there. That was before she was married to Jacobs.

Scott: Ah, so it was a different last name. Mary Agnes McConville.

Woody: She married Martin Jacobs in 1897 and she didn't teach after that. They had six kids. His family used to call him sterile because the rest of them all had 10 or 12.

Somewhere in here I have a list of the high school teachers. I got them just the other day. Here they are.

Was Mister Rikansrud still there when you were there?

Scott: No.

Woody: Well Alvin (Rick) Rikansrud, Rudy Rikansrud's dad, was a teacher there and he taught civics, coached basketball, baseball and track. They're still in the community. Mrs. (Winona) Rikansrud worked with Jo in the State Parks I think.

. . .

Scott: Okay.

Woody: Pretty sure. And then there was Jane Muir who was a single lady for many years and then became Ms. Shumway. A math teacher. She was deaf, but she was very good. But of course because she was deaf, the devilish kids, and I don't know who those would have been (guilty expression on his face), would go "Mm" (make a humming sound). Then she'd go turn her hearing aids up and she couldn't hear anything.

Scott: So they had hearing aids in those days?

Woody: Yeah, she did have a hearing aid. I don't know what it was.

And then there was Mrs. Patton, Aurelia Patton. She was a single lady, had two daughters, and they were good kids. One of them was really bright, Eugenia was less bright, but her sister was very bright. Mrs. Patton was a very good Spanish and English teacher in our high school.

One year we had a lady by the name of Zimmerman and she married somebody named Barnes. Not related. She was an excellent English teacher, just taught one year.

Talk about coincidences, Barney (Woody's son) was showing somebody around over in Arizona and in the back seat was an ancient lady who was named Barnes. They got talking and this was our high school teacher.

Scott: Wow.

.   .   .

Woody: I called her and talked to her a little bit and didn't follow up on it as much as I should have.

Scott: Amazing.

Woody: Then there was Ray Robertson who graduated from Redlands. He taught chemistry and was a coach. He was a very good coach and a very poor chemistry teacher.

Al Doth was a teacher. He married Dotty Tozer and was the brother-in-law of Tom Tozer. He was recalled in midyear to the military and he spent the rest of his career in the military.

And then there was a Miss Clay. Miss Clay was interesting because we found out that she had worked her way through San Diego State by being a bubble dancer.

Betty Boger was gone by the time I got there. She taught there several years. Her husband ran a grocery store in Ramona when she married him.

And then there was Bob Finch. Now Finch was a really interesting character. Very good music teacher and just a live wire, I mean just full of bologna. And he worked also at the Starlight Opera House in the summer and he got comedy roles with Charlie. Wasn't Charlie Chaplin, but it was Charlie someone at the Starlight Opera House.[3]

The interesting thing is, at the same time we had a second music teacher in Julian whose name was Selland. Finch had been in the service. Mister Selland was teaching in his place. When Finch came back they had to give him a job. And so we had two music teachers for one year... which was hard on their budget.

Scott: Sure.

· · ·

Woody: Mary Louise Goodman did Home Ec. and English and she moved out to the Imperial Valley. We kept track of her and Mrs. Tozer, whose husband ran the drugstore. Tom is still a friend of mine. He worked in U.C. San Francisco all his career. Mrs. Tozer played piano and she wasn't a full time.

And then there was a fellow by the name of Lowell Plinke who came up and taught English and journalism one year.

And then there was Maurice Rennick who was for shop and agriculture, and he very good.

Okay, that's the teachers.

Elementary school grades three-four and five. Woody is in the back row, second to right. The teacher was Harriet Swycaffer.

This is Woody's second car, a 1949 Chevrolet Deluxe. His first car, a 1937 Ford, was involved in a fatal accident. Woody said, "Two of the fellas that worked for us were living in the old garage in Wynola, and it was the beginning of that big snow storm in '49. They were driving up to Julian and they got stuck right about where the scrimshaw place is, and John Collins drove into them while they were trying to put chains on. Broke both their legs, all four legs, and then one of them died. Fermin Fuentecilla who was a Spaniard that was working for us, and Agapito Aguilar who was a native of Mexico who was working for us. Agapito lost both his legs, and Fermin died from the legs being cut off. They were all good people.

Senior breakfast held at the rock house, June 8, 1953. Back row from left: Bob Finch (music teacher and advisor), Bob Winterton, Johnny Grammar, Tommy Tozer, Betty Mae Brinley (with glasses), Woody Barnes, Mildred Taylor, Bud Signi. Front row from left: Betty Clap, Aleta Hayton (with purse), Bobbie Jane Hatheway, Dorris DuMouchel (with necklace), Anne Kent (striped dress), Mildred Mee (with purse), Dorothy Osuna, Diane Domenigoni, Nancy Barringer, Peggy Brown, Pat Hearn, Cleason Lachusa, Winston Carter (stripes), Norman Feigel ("J" jacket).

Woody and Jo at graduation in the high school auditorium.
Woody remembers being valedictorian while Jo (who was most
certainly valedictorian in her year) remembers Woody being
salutatorian. This author is staying out of it.

1. Alice Barnes worked at the phone central. See *Alice Barnes—Gold Mines and Apple Pie* for more details.
2. The one-room Santa Ysabel School was built in the 1880s in Witch Creek on land donated by the Sawday family, and continued serving first through eighth graders until 1954 when it finally closed. The building was saved from demolition by the Julian Historical Society, an all-volunteer organization, and moved 10 miles to 2133 Fourth Street, Julian to serve as the local library. Currently the building serves as the home of the Julian Historical Society.
3. Charlie Cannon. (September 11, 1911 – August 14, 2003). Besides being a singer and theater performer, Cannon co-founded the San Diego Civic Light Opera Company in 1945. This later became the Starlight Opera.

4

WOODY AND JO INTERVIEW

This section combines two separate interviews done with Woody and his sister Mary Alice 'Jo' together spliced with a few snippets from other interviews. It contains biographical information on Jo as well as early Julian history.

Scott: When were you born, Jo?

Jo: 1938.

Scott: So you were three years younger than Woody?

Jo: Three and a *half*.

Scott: That's important for babies and, um...middle age people.

. . .

Woody: I can tell you a little about when she was born. I don't remember everything, but Wilmeth, Hartwick's wife, came up and took care of us while mother was in the hospital. And they used to keep 'em there ten days or so. So while they were in the hospital, Grampy Barnes took out the wood stove and put in an electric stove in the kitchen; took out the icebox in the back porch and put in an electric refrigerator; and we got electricity full time.

Before that we had what's called a Kohler Plant, which was a generator out in the garage. They used to turn it on in the evening for a couple hours. We had a deal were if you pulled a switch it theoretically would start itself. It had an electric starter that somehow sensed when you put a draw on the current. If that didn't work, you had to go out and—I don't know what they did—crank it, or whatever.

I was pretty young, so they may have had electricity a little before that but I don't think so. When Jo came home from the hospital in a car I went out thinking I was going to have somebody to play with. [laughs] It was just this little tiny thing. I was astonished.

The pool was built in '44. The hole was built in '44. The bathhouse was built in '45 and the rock walls and sidewalks. Most of the kids in Julian at that time learned to swim at our pool. There was no filter. It was bright green by the end of summer. The only other pool in the area (Camp Marston might have had one) was Hathaway's, a funny little triangle thing. It was really slimy.

Scott: I swam in Hathaway's. It had a 10-foot high platform that we'd jump off.

Woody: When we were kids they had a metal slide that went down. You had to be very careful that you didn't hit your fanny. But they didn't want people around very much. They were slightly different people.

Scott: You said there was a hole in the wall near the fireplace in your house?

Woody: There was a hole in the wall so that you could pass firewood through for the fireplace. There was a wood box there.

Scott: How did they close it off?

Woody: There was some kind of doors that closed on it.

Scott: It seems like it would let in a lot of cold air.

Woody: There were only two warm places in the house, the kitchen and living room. Grampy had put water pipes through the stove and into what I call "my room" back there. In that closet was our water heater. If the stove was hot and water was going through, we had hot water.

Scott: He hooked that up himself?

Woody: Oh yeah. Grampy was an amazing builder. You figure he pretty much built that house by himself. He built most of the pool bathhouse in one day. (Two changing rooms of around 10' on a side plus a bathroom and wide porch.) People said, "How could you have ever built that in one day?" He answered, "Because that was all the time I had." But the back side of it Bill Cain put the rocks in while Grampy was at lunch. You can see the crooked place in the rocks on the far corner.[1]

Grampy built most of this stuff down at the cider house. He built the packing house (Manzanita Ranch Store in Wynola). He built the house where you grew up in Spencer Valley.

Scott: I didn't know he did that.

Woody: Oh yeah. I think that time he bought the (cement) blocks. For the packing house they made all the blocks out there in the parking lot. You couldn't buy them, it was war time, or right after the war. I think he finished it in '46.

Mother was pretty good at managing stuff too, but she was not the construction type. Grampy would always manage to get his vacation time (from the Farm Security Administration) to coincide with harvest. He was primarily in the pear business. That's what the people have forgotten. Julian raised far more pears than they ever did apples.

Scott: There's an interesting photo of the school in 1910 in Heritage Hill, which is a museum in Old El Toro. All the girls are dressed very nice in their Sunday best, and not one of the boys had shoes. They all look like Huckleberry Fin. Was that kind of the way it was? The girls dressed up—?

· · ·

Jo: We have pictures of the students in the old elementary school at Julian and the girls are all pretty well dressed. But I don't recall if the boys are barefoot.

Woody: You'd find that the temperature in Julian would preclude that.

Scott: A little cold. It was really striking because, not only are they barefoot, but their clothes are rags.

Woody: That's pretty much true today.

Jo: (Gestures to Woody.) Exhibit A!

Scott: So all the work was done at what we call the "packing house" today. Which recently collapsed.

Woody: There was no electricity down there when I first remember it.

Scott: Oh really?

Woody: On the low side you'll see a place where there is a cement wall that looks pretty good and the rest is all straggly rocks. Well, that was a hollow. Under there there was a motor, and flat belts that went up and drove all the machinery for the washer and the grader. We had no refrigeration but they could keep apples for a few days in that part where we call the 'poison room' (stacked stone building).

That is a really old building, clearly built before 1900. How many years before we don't know, but I'm guessing it was one of the first buildings around the mountains.

Jo: I have a scar on this finger, right here, from keeping my hand on the sorting belt too long and it went underneath...

Woody: Pulled it under the roller.

Scott: That must have hurt.

Jo: Well, I don't remember if it hurt or not but I know where the Band-Aids were kept. That little wooden cupboard on the way in. [laughs]

Woody: That's the building (eastern building) that you started to take down...that we've never finished taking down.

Scott: The termites will finish the job before we finish the job, probably.

Jo: The east wind.

．　．　．

Woody: Today the Julian Historical Society is picking up the two gas pumps that were in front of the packing house and taking them up to Julian to the Historical Society.[2]

Scott: That's probably a good thing.

Woody: We felt that they would not get broken, they would not get stolen, and if they do, it's not our fault.

Jo: And also if you have 'em on your property now someone's gonna think you have a tank somewhere and want you to prove that you dug it up and it didn't leak and all of that.

Scott: I remember Grammy and Grampy working all the time. I assume they worked even more when you were kids. Didn't they have Indian gals that helped look after you?

Jo: Occasionally they had someone that was staying at the house, primarily for me. Woody was old enough to go back and forth to the cider house. They never did a lot of work. They just were there so that—

Scott: You didn't get hurt.

Jo: Right. Later on they did some preparation of dinner, get the potatoes ready to put in the oven. But Mother (Alice Barnes) did most all of the work. The help never did a heck of a lot.

. . .

Scott: Was she also sorting apples and...

Jo: Oh, absolutely. She was there all the time.

Woody: They started the sorting at eight. They started the picking at seven in the morning. Pickers quit at 4:30; packers quit at 5. But mother and a lady who was a longtime family friend—one of the Angel family, Betty Okey—used to run up to the house at noon and can some fruit. Then they would run back to continue sorting. Then they would come back in the evening and can fruit.

Scott: It was half an hour lunches? They must have had an hour.

Woody: Thirty minutes for the pickers but an hour for the packing crew. We used to hire a lot of what they called "fruit tramps." They were people who went from one packing house to another as the season progressed. They were paid by the box. The sorters were all local people. But the packers, a lot of them, were these fruit tramps. And most of 'em, you really had to watch their packing numbers because they would either pack 'em poorly or 'miscount' the boxes. But Oscar Oberg was one that came year after year. His wife Tenny, after we quit doing this, went down and took care of Tot Cumming[3] for a number of years.

Jo: What happened to Oscar?

·   ·   ·

Woody: I don't know. I think they split up, but I'm not sure what happened to Oscar.

There was an old German fellow, August Lepley, who used to come down only to prune. He didn't like to do anything but prune and graft. He was a very good grafter and he grafted a lot of the trees over on the "Timm" place—which no longer has any trees at all. We had a bunch of Bellflowers (variety of apples) and he grafted 'em into Winesaps. He also pruned all of the Drury place, which is at the corner of Frisius Drive and Deer Lake Park Road.

You were asking about people who kind of watched over us. There was a year or two when Virginia Skagen watched over us. We were a little older then.

Jo: Boy could she tell stories.

Woody: If she had written 'em down she would have been a great, successful author. She could sit there and make up stories and put us in 'em as part of the story, and they were just fantastic.

Jo: Adventure stories. Places and things were always incorporated that you knew and they were just fabulous.

Woody: One of the T.L. Barneses family had a son Jerry who was roughly between our age and he was often in the stories too. He died in Hawaii, probably ten years ago now.[4]

Jo: This was probably before Kiki was born—or even thought of. Virginia was still a Barnes, wasn't she?

.   .   .

Woody: No, I'm pretty sure she was a Skagen. It may have
been during World War II; Ed may have been in the service. I
think that was when T.L. Barneses may have still been living
in the house in Wynola Orchard.

In 1916, the flood, the T.L. Barneses were in the gravel
business with Henry Fenton, and their whole rock crusher
went out to sea when the Otay Dam[5] broke. It really devas-
tated him. Fenton came back and made all kinds of money
but Uncle Theodore never did. A few years later he got an eye
knocked out. A chip of rock when he was working on a rock
crusher hit him in the eye. They didn't wear safety glasses in
those days.

During the Depression they came up and lived at the place
at the end of the [Wynola] valley. Hubbells' is part of that
place. Raymond and his son Dana Reed's place was part of
that land when we bought it. Benjamin Reed was Dana's
grandfather. There was a piece that came out, an L shape that
took in the Reed and Hubbell places, a couple of hundred
acres in there.

Anyhow, when a barn fell down Uncle Theodore (T.L.
Barnes, Bope's brother) and Aunt Myrta built a house out of
the lumber. The kids were hard pressed to find work, and so
they lived there. Ted and Eddie, two of T.L.'s kids, ran a Shell
station where Fred Slaughter's place is now.

The Doyle-Barnes Company

Woody: Jarvis Doyle (partner in the Doyle-Barnes Company)
had I think three daughters. One of them married Elmer
Blossom. And that daughter, whose name I think was Reba
(Doyle) Blossom, used to come up to the store pretty often.
That was another one of those ancient connections that lasted
for years. She came up even after we were in Wynola.

The Doyle-Barnes Company I know practically nothing about except that Jarvis Doyle was a brother-in-law of Colonel Ed Fletcher. And that my grandfather E.Y. Barnes, whom we all called Bope, and Doyle, were in a produce and other kinds of things business, a wholesale business, for about 20-plus years and never had a written agreement and never had an argument. They terminated it in 1928 and I don't know exactly why they did but it was perfect timing.

I was always curious about where their business was. I still don't know. But I learned a little more about Jarvis Doyle.[6]

Doyle was a partner of Colonel Ed Fletcher in a produce business. I always wondered if Bope bought out Colonel Ed's interest in that business when Jarvis and he got together.[7]

Jo: We have a picture of a produce wagon—presumably produce—but of a wagon that says "Doyle and Fletcher" or "Fletcher and Doyle."

Woody: Yeah. So I know they were partners.

I think the Doyle-Barnes partnership lasted up until around 1928, and was begun somewhere between 1908 and 1909. I suspect it was around 1908. That would fit with Bope being in business with Doyle for 20 years.

Jo: It would also fit in the time zone of when Barneses moved from Pacific Beach to Fourth and Upas, which was about 1908 or 9. Because Daddy said he was about nine years old when they moved up there.

· · ·

Woody: So that's a little bit of information that I think is probably factual. We never knew where their location was but my understanding was that Fletcher's thing was on 5th Street.[8] So it might be they used the same building, although you don't have any idea if that was true. Also, Bope had a former employee, oh boy, whose name momentarily escapes me.[9]

Jo: The skinny guy?

Woody: Yeah. Used to come up to the old cider house and Bope always insisted that he get a jug of cider. He had been one of their runners that had gone around the county on a bicycle taking orders.

Scott: Oh wow.

Woody: Charlotte Holcomb, who is out there in Delzura, her family had had a store and she still remembered that Doyle-Barnes was their supplier for their little store. That was an interesting item that popped back into my head.

Scott: So he'd ride around on probably solid tire bikes.

Woody: I imagine it must have been. Fletcher himself did bike tours—Ed Fletcher. At least he claimed he did and I'm sure he did, because cars really didn't get popular until around 1909 or 10.

So that's one little vignette that I was thinking about. These things will not all fit in straight orders.

. . .

Scott: Obviously. We have a couple of years of interviews ahead of us, I think, at the speed that we're going.[10]

Woody: Which is fine. Let's see, we're up to 1908, which we both remember well because we were both fully mature at the time.

Scott: Yeah. I do want to concentrate on things that you actually remember rather than hearsay, but it's interesting. [laughs]

Now these people were all still alive when you can remember, though.

Woody: Absolutely. Colonel Ed used to come up to the store.

Scott: Colonel Ed Fletcher.

Woody: Bope was alive 'til 48. I was about 13 when he died. Wasn't that about 48? I think it was.

The former Doyle-Barnes employee that used to come by was Johnny Dexter. Apparently they were very fond of each other because it was a big event. He was a little tiny guy. He'd done a lot of their bicycle riding around the county to take orders.

Uncle Theodore Barnes was also a bike rider. (E.Y. Barnes' (Bope's) brother.) There was so much bike riding that you can hardly imagine it. Theodore was quite an athlete at U.C. Berkeley in track and stuff. But he also rode a bicycle from San Diego to Corona to watch the car races.

· · ·

Scott: Oh really?

Woody: Yeah. Now, if you think about what the roads were like and riding a bike like—that's something else. Those guys were tough cookies.

Scott: The roads probably weren't paved.

Woody: No, none of them were paved.

Scott: Probably a one-speed bike.

Woody: Oh yeah. They were used to misery and hard work. A bicycle was a great improvement over walking that far. And 20 years before everybody had had to walk that far. Or ride a horse.

Scott: Amazing.

Woody: But they rode bicycles as far as Julian and Palomar. Not often, but they did it enough to make these sales at these little stores.

Scott: Wow.
     You have a chair that Bope got for cigar rings, when he

was smoking cigars?

Woody: Mm-hmm. My grandfather was a smoker, but he knew smoking was bad for you. He offered my dad and his brother and his sister $100 a piece if they didn't smoke till they were 18. My dad and Hark never smoked, and got their $100. These guys both lived to be right around 90. His daughter smoked, and died young.

There used to be a little ring on the cigars, and you'd get so many of them and send them in for a prize. That chair is in the old cider house. We had it reupholstered, it was leather, and the leather went out. But it's got fairly decent upholstery. It's not the greatest chair in the world, except that it's probably one of the very few that was ever won or given as a prize for cigars—which eventually killed my granddad with lip and tongue cancer.

So a pretty good lesson right here in our family is to stay away from tobacco. They knew it back around the time my dad and uncle were little kids. I mean, my granddad knew it. So it's not something that came along in the '50s when we finally figured out that cancer was coming from those. They knew it years, and years, and years before that.

Scott: They used to call them cancer sticks.

Woody: Cancer sticks, yeah. Exactly.

Jo: While we're on that subject, refresh our memory about the people who always came from Lake Hodges while we were still selling at the ranch.

· · ·

Woody: Oh, gosh. The dam keeper. He had two daughters. I think the daughters were a little older than we were.

Cut Flowers

Jo: The other thing that we did a lot of at the ranch, before moving to Wynola, was selling cut flowers in the spring. We'd put a sign or two that there were lilac out at the gate and lots of people would drive in and buy a dozen tulips—

Woody: We even had a sign out on the corner of Pine Hills Road at times saying "lilacs-tulips."

Jo: Sometimes I would get to go with the customer and they would point at each tulip that they wanted. I'd pick it for them and make it a dozen, if they wanted a dozen mixed or a dozen something. That was a big treat for me, too!

Woody: When we were first doing that, Grampy Barnes was still working for the Farm Security Administration. He would start out on Sunday afternoon and drive to San Francisco and work his way south and end up in Yuma on Friday afternoon and then drive home and work (on the ranch) all day Saturday until Sunday noon. Then we'd have Sunday dinner and he'd take off. I don't know exactly what he did but he gave guaranteed loans to farmers who were going broke. He was so proud because none of the loans he made ever defaulted.

Jo: That was one of the times when we were put on flower duty, when they were having their Sunday dinner. We'd walk all over the place. A lot of the times the people would want the tulips that were wide open and big. Of course, that means that they're going to fall apart in about two minutes. But whatever they wanted, we'd get 'em.

Scott: It seems amazing now with all the gophers that we have that you could grow tulips.

Woody: It was a constant fight. Agriculture was a lot more profitable in those days. And so we had permanent employees in addition to Grampy and Grampy. Bill Loux, Sterling's dad, worked for us for several years. He had formerly worked for the Clarks on the Clark Ranch, which is what we call the Cauzza Ranch and the Cauzza barn. When the Clark's sold we ended up with Bill for a number of years. We had Jimmy Brand, who later ended up working for the County Roads. Jimmy had been badly burned in a fire somewhere. He had scars all over his face.

We had a hundred pair of gopher traps. Every day Jimmy would walk around and check these gopher traps out in the (gopher) tunnels. That kept the gophers down. The traps weren't all on our home place because at that time we had Timms, Wynola, Hawkins, Pluggers, and Drurys, and Websters. At that time we had all of Websters. We owned most of the property up Van Duesen Road—all of it, with Uncle Ted. It went clear over to Julian from the Van Duesen side.

Jo: Another thing about Jimmy Brand is that we got a pinball machine from him. It was down in the basement for a while. He fixed it so that you didn't have to put your quarters in it to play but you could pull the knobs and it would shoot balls around. Oh, that was fun.

·   ·   ·

Woody: The ball would go up and bounce around and if you were lucky it ended up in a place where you got points. I don't think we ever had it hooked up electrically. It was just roll up the hill and came down and 'ping, ping, ping' as it hit the various things. If you were real lucky it would go back in the same slot and you could fire it again.

Jo: The basement was a great place. It's where Grammy hung all the clothes in the winter. It was warm because of the furnace. We would play down there in the winter and roller skate even. Grammy always wished that somehow they'd have been able to get to the downstairs from inside the house rather than going outside, but it just didn't work.

Woody: They had, originally, a metal tube that went up from the basement between two of the rafters into the kitchen cupboard. It kept it cooler in one of the kitchen cupboards.

Another thing that happened about the time that Jo was born was we got a furnace. Previous to that, when I was born, we just had fireplace and a wood stove. And then we had a tank behind in the closet in what was called my room where the water would go through. If we were lucky it would be hot so you could take a hot shower.

Scott: So that's basically where the living room—

Woody: —stopped. They cut a hole in there (in the wall) for the hallway.

They were really frustrated because every once in a while

Grampy wouldn't be here [during building and construction] and it always went wrong.

The tractor shed: they put the posts in the wrong place, so they could never put doors on.

In the rock house addition, when they put the hole for a door through—and I can remember them punching the hole through the wall to go in the back, well, they put it at the wrong level. There was a tree stump that they should have dug out, but they didn't. So the wall in the bathroom and the other room still has a ding in it. If you go outside you'll see that the wall goes around the stump; the stump's still there. It would have been a major thing to dig out.

When they were doing the patio there was a big rock. They wanted to shoot it. In those days everybody used dynamite for everything. Grampy wouldn't let 'em shoot it because he knew they'd blow all the windows out.

The folks had some really good friends called the Websters. Mother, Dad, Len (Leonard) and Edna Webster played bridge about once a week. The ladies played the boys. They kept track for a whole year, and at the end of the year if the boys won the girls had to fix dinner. If the girls won the boys had to take them out to dinner.

Len and Edna's place was one of the places where we occasionally got babysat. One time I was up there, they had a fellow staying with them whose name was George Foot, and George had bought a piece of property and some dynamite from 'em or gotten a piece from 'em and he was blasting out a place to make a cabin. 'Dynamite' is what made me think of George. One day we went up there and George was getting ready to blast. He lit the fuses. We ran over behind a tree. And these rocks just rained down. I mean, it was like a thunderstorm of rocks. It was kind of exciting. George looked really white and we quietly left that area. [laughs] He'd obviously way over charged this sucker and it blew rocks all over the place.

.   .   .

Scott: Wow.

Woody: In those days a lot of people still used dynamite for everything, because there weren't as many powerful mechanical things. And really, rocks, about the only way you could get 'em was to drill a hole in 'em and blow 'em. They didn't have tractors as powerful as they have now. Within just a few years the tractors became incredibly more powerful.

Jo: Even the road workers. Whenever they were building a road or working on the highway they would blast stuff. Cars would be held back for awhile while the blasts were being conducted.

Woody: And then they'd push the rocks off the road and cars would go through.

Scott: I remember some of that when I was a kid on Santa Ysabel Grade.

Woody: Well, that was after they had the slide. It was in '80, wasn't it, the flood year that the rocks all slid down and closed the grade? How old were you in '80?

Scott: Eighty was the flood year and I was 12.

.   .   .

Woody: That'd have been a good memory age.

Scott: I guess that's right.

Woody: When they dug the peach tree hill up there on the way in [to the ranch], they put in a quarter of a stick of dynamite in a lot of those holes and blasted 'em because they were too hard to dig by hand.

Scott: Just to dig holes to plant trees? [laughs]

Woody: Yeah. Not all of the holes, but all the hard ones up on the top of the hill. It'd all been grapes before. I can remember the vines, big piles of them which we burned for wood. They'd pulled 'em out with the D2. At that time we didn't have a dozer.

Jo: Another thing that we did that was really exciting was the 'Thunderbolt' blasting up of the wood down by the pond.

Woody: Oh yeah. That was much later. That was when [Edward T.] Van Duesen[11] bought the Thunderbolt. A Thunderbolt Wood Splitter was a heavy steel hollow tube with one end open and a fuse out the other end. You filled it with black powder, drove it into a log, butt up another log against it, and then set it off. It would explode and blow the log open. This was before they had wood splitters. Of course if you didn't have a big enough log, it would go off like a rocket the other way. So you had to have a big log for a butt log.

.   .   .

Scott: You probably had no goggles or helmets or anything in those days.

Jo: No. We ran and hid behind a big tree. [laughs]

Woody: You know, they worry today about people blasting, dynamiting and killing people and everything. Heck, we were just using them for tools in those days.

The Thunderbolt was probably when we were in our teens, wouldn't you think?

Jo: Yeah. At least.

Woody: You may not have been [a teenager], but I probably was. We used it down there on the straight stretch of the driveway by the ponds on the way in. It wasn't very practical. But it was a lot of fun. [laughs]

Jo: And a lot of noise.

One day, Grammy was vacuuming Woody's room and vacuumed up a 22 bullet that was on the floor and it went off in the vacuum.

Woody: Blew the housing all to pieces in the vacuum. I think it was suggested after that that I was a little more careful where I left the bullets.

.   .   .

Scott: Did you go hunting, both of you?

Jo: I was never a big hunter except I used the pellet gun some just for fun. Woody hunted a lot more than I did.

Woody: Grampy had a high school friend whose friend was Frank Cluff. Frank Cluff and his two sons used to come down —they were a little older than we were. My early hunting was going out with Frank Cluff.

   The other early hunting, which is kind of an interesting story, is that we had the friends the Jacksons who lived right below where Jo's Archer Street house is. Right on Holiday Hill, they used to call it. (I.e. The Jacksons called their property "Holiday Hill.")

Jo: In Pacific Beach on Noyes. (From Beryl Street to Chalcedony Street).

Woody: They had four or five acres; there were no houses up there at that time.[12] I can remember going up with the two older brothers Remy and Demp and hunting rabbits on top of the hill. I don't think we ever got any rabbits but we walked clear up to where you could look down in Rose Canyon and see the Rice's brickyard.[13] You can imagine what would happen with a couple of kids wandering around there with guns now. We'd all be in jail. So would our parents.

   Jacksons had the cabin (on the ranch by the pond). Richmond Jackson had been one of Grampy Barnes's grammar school friends. His parents lived right across the street at Fourth and Upas from your great grandparents. Richmond's father was a dentist. When we needed a dentist the one thing our parents told us was never to do was never to go to Jackson the dentist. [laughs] He apparently was a 'look at your tooth and pull it out' dentist. He was not in the modern era.[14]

Richmond had four kids. Remy was the oldest, and Remy and I are still friends and he lives in Del Mar or somewhere down there.

Scott: R-E-M-Y?

Woody: Yeah. It's actually Remington. Richmond Jackson was his Dad's name. His wife was Ruth Remington Jackson. So that's where the 'Remington' came from, was Ruth. Ruth was a wonderful, conservative lady. Worked like crazy for the Republican party. It's part of the reason, in all probability, that I got the job at the University of San Diego, because she was a good Catholic supporter. I suspect that she wrote a letter of recommendation that had a lot of influence down there at that time.

Remy was the oldest one. I don't remember what all Remy did in his life but he's retired.

Demp was a lifeguard and then went into the Navy, and Demp... Dempster was his name. Not Dumpster, just for clarity. He retired in Washington DC, and he was fairly well up in the Naval ranks. Not an Admiral but pretty well up. He came here one day and we had a 48-stared flag. "You God damned son of bitches." So he sent us a flag that had flown over the White House with 50 stars. Of course they run hundreds of them every day. It's in the sleeping porch.

Scott: I hope you kept the 48 one.

. . .

Woody: Oh it's probably in the sleeping porch somewhere. Jo wouldn't have let that disappear.

Marcia was the next one. Marcia was about two years older than I was. She married Buzz Mackey, and the Mackeys had five girls.

Lucia was the youngest one (of Richmond Jackson's children); she was about Jo's age. She became a Catholic nun, and lived down in South Bay. Marcia now has something resembling Alzheimer's, and Remy, the oldest one, is still sharp. He had a sensible letter to the editor in the San Diego Union last year, and I talk to him every few months. His wife passed away. Nice guy. If you talk to him you'd think he's kind of a rough guy, but he's not.

So anyhow, that family grew up across the street from the folks, then the Jacksons bought the property and built the cabin down by the small lake. Well, they had the agreement that if they ever sold it, we could buy it back. Well, they got ready to sell it, and we were really squeaked by enough money to do it. We tried to negotiate with him, he said "Nope, I'm gonna put it on the market." So we paid for it. Which was a smart move on our part. It was a terrible cabin, but we gradually fixed it up.

And the Jacksons bought 80 acres up Van Duesen road when Ted and the folks subdivided the property up there. The Jacksons built a house up there. But they had, and still have, a wonderful piece of property in Pacific Beach. Probably three, four acres left. Marcia lives there. They used to have milk goats, because Lucia was allergic to cow milk—and that's a pain in the butt. Imagine a milk goat in Pacific Beach! Probably is one now, but—

Scott: Now you can buy goat milk, and other kinds of strange things.

·   ·   ·

Jo: Years later, I guess it was after the dentist had passed away, the Jacksons had his dental cabinet in the hallway between their living room and going down either way to the bedrooms. I always thought that was fascinating that that big black, mahogany fancy thing with the glass knobs and all the drawers for all the equipment was out of a dentist office.

Woody: That was up on Holiday Hill.

Scott: This is skipping around a bit but how does Ray Burnand fit into the family?

Jo: Ray Burnand's grandfather was one of Grammy Barnes's brothers (Raymond W. Jacobs, 1899-1983). Ray Jacobs married Thelma Crawford and they had one daughter, Beverly Ann. Beverly Ann grew up in Julian and graduated high school and went to Stanford. When she graduated from Stanford she moved back down and lived and taught school in Borrego. The Burnands were farmers in Borrego. She met Perry, they got married and they had two boys, one of which is Ray Burnand. The other is Perry Burnand Junior. Perry now lives in the La Costa area near Carlsbad.

   Ray Burnand got married and he and his wife went to join the Peace Corps. They were in Costa Rica for quite a while. Then they came back and they had one daughter named Raechel. Then they got divorced.

Farming and Cider Making

Woody: Milton Angel was one of the people who made cider at the cider house. He later became a very successful contractor. He was one of I think 12 in the Angel family. When I used irritate 'em when I was a little kid he used to say he was going to grind me up in the cider. Mother made him quit doing that.[15] The cider was made up in that upper, highest floor [of the cider house] and went by gravity down into wooden tanks. Most of the boards that are used for shelves in the tractor shed are out of the wooden cider tanks.

Scott: Right. They were vertical slats in the tank.

Woody: They were vertical at that time. They're now horizontal as shelves. We used them as shelving because the tanks were pretty well worn out. The cider sat overnight and they put in what they call Pectinol which was an enzyme which broke down the pectins that make the cider cloudy. Eventually we put in a tank that came out of Bill Edic's jam factory that warmed the cider (so the Pectinol worked more efficiently). Then we would pasteurize it: we would pump it into bottles and the bottles were then put into this oven and heated at I think 160 degrees for 30 minutes. I still have the thermometer in the cupboard behind my desk that goes in there. And then it went out on wooden racks until it cooled. The wooden racks are where all that insulation is piled now. If you were lucky when it cooled it didn't get cloudy again—if you'd gotten rid of all the pectins.

And then Grammy used to go down there and label all those things by hand. When we would try to help it always was frustrating cause we'd get the glue where the glue would show on the bottles. They weren't pre-glued labels.

Jo: You had to paste them.

. . .

Woody: You had to do it just right so it didn't show and the labels had to be straight. Then you had to put them in the box while they were straight. Then we used to load them on trucks by hand and after a while we got fancy. We got rollers that you could roll 'em down. Some of the rollers are still upstairs (in the eastern building), the three-track rollers. The two-track rollers we used in Wynola around the packing machinery, after they built the cement building in Wynola in 46. We still made cider on our home ranch until 56.

About 20 years later Pedro Mireles[16] and I were cleaning out the cider house, just before you and Barney built that apartment thing, and we found some old cider that had been there all that time. And so we sampled 'em all. About five or six of 'em still tasted pretty good. None of 'em killed us.

Jo: Upstairs in that same room was where they stored all the cartons of empty bottles. They'd buy the bottles and have a place to put 'em before you filled 'em. We used to play up there in those cartons full of empty bottles. We made tunnels through them. Sometimes we'd make a little room down in the middle. We'd hold them up with box shook so that we could tunnel and go through. Great hours of play time.

Woody: We did that primarily off season when they weren't making cider.

Even back in the early days they used more cider apples than were raised in Julian. The cider was sold by Pacific Coast Packing Company owned by the Edic family. The Edics were longtime family friends, rented houses from us up there for a number of years. They distributed as far as Long Beach and Phoenix and Southern California. They were a jam making factory primarily but they sold our cider along with their jam.

Bill died at what, 102 or 3. He was pretty well along. His wife died at 92 or 3. The three boys are still around.

During World War II we couldn't buy new bottles so we bought lots of Coke syrup [bottles], for making Coke. They used to come in one gallon jugs. And they had a little metal rim, in addition to the screw tops, that would break off. We'd have to take that metal rim off and then they were washed.

The house on the east side of Pine Hills Road, before the Orinoco Creek bridge, at that time there was a family living there by the name of Elder. Jackie Elder used to come over— he was a high school kid—and wash bottles. In later years we had a fellow who stayed with us whose name was Eric Davis. Eric's mother had worked with Grampy Barnes in the Farm Security Administration. Eric's dad died and his mom needed someone to take care of him. He lived with us for a year and washed bottles. We all washed bottles, but we were pretty little to do a good job. They hung 'em upside down on wooden pegs to drain.

Jo: There were boards between the pillars, one by sixes, and then pegs, and you hooked the glass bottles upside down.

Scott: Luckily there was no big earthquake.

Woody: Well, they probably would have stayed up. The building would have fallen down but the bottles would have stayed up.

Jo: All of these things could never be done now.

·   ·   ·

Woody: You couldn't use the building.

Jo: I don't believe that anyone perished from the use of any of those products.

Woody: Nope. Never did.

Jo: They're probably healthier because of the bacteria. [laughs]

Woody: At the beginning of World War II Grampy did a number of things which were fortunate. In the first place he bought two Nash cars.[17] He had always been buying one a year because he was traveling so much for the Farm Security Administration. He worked for them for about eight years.[18] He also bought a truck from International Truck. Ton and a half, kind of a light green truck, a twelve foot bed on it, it had a two-speed axle.[19] The first trip we got it we went up to Oak Glen to bring down cider apples. We were buying a lot of cider apples from Oak Glen. Across from Hemet to Sage there's a place called Saint John's Grade. We had a big load. Everybody always loaded things as high as they could. We barely made it up that hill. I remember Grampy telling me, "If it stops, jump!" [laughs] We didn't quite stop, but we never came up that way again. We always came up through Winchester and Temecula because you didn't have that terrible grade. But we just...barely...made it. It was in the low speed and the low gear. It was terrible trying to shift that thing. We kept it 'til the end of World War II. When I was old enough to drive—not old enough to drive, but I was driving— why, you could hardly shift the stupid thing. But we got it in low gear and made it up that hill just barely. Course the trucks didn't have near the power they do now.

In addition to Oak Glen, we used to get cider apples from Hood River, Oregon. They would come in a railroad car, loose, to Escondido. You only had two or three days before they charged you demurrage for not having the car empty. We'd have to go down there and push all of the apples out onto boxes, load 'em onto trucks, and haul 'em up to Julian. They were beautiful Pippins, far prettier than anything we could ever grow. And yet they were bruised up (from the transportation) and just good for cider apples.

I can also remember when the train still went to Lakeside, the freight train, going down there with Bope, my grandfather, and picking up fruit trees in boxes. They used to come from Starks (Stark Brothers Nurseries in the town of Louisiana, Missouri) in a rectangular box about six feet long. About two to four feet wide, depending on how many trees you bought, on the ends, wrapped with moist, stringy sawdust inside.

Mr. Paul Stark was in the Navy in World War II in San Diego and became a family friend.

Jo: I remember the boxes but I guess I never got to go on the trip.

Woody: One of the things that really impressed me, there were posts alongside the road and as you'd go by the posts the pickup would make a different sound. It would go phew, phew, phew. This was an old, 30s pickup, International, from Alessio Motors, which was out on El Cajon Boulevard. Alessios were a prominent family in San Diego. Mister A's building is some of the Alessio family's.[20]

.   .   .

Jo: Mister A's restaurant.

Woody: They also ran the racetrack in Tijuana for a while.
Which is another series of stories.

Scott: I've never eaten at Mister A's. I've heard a lot of things
about it.

Woody: At the beginning of World War II, all of Grampy's
Japanese friends were interred. One of the things that
happened was that their property was at risk, to say the least. I
can remember going up to San Juan Capistrano with Grampy
in the truck and taking down a building or two up there that
had belonged to these Japanese people, because you couldn't
buy any building materials. We hauled these old, used building
materials down to Julian. I'm sure some of that material was
used around Capistrano, but there was some left.[21]

They also took down a bunch of barns because the tax
people decided that these old barns were valuable. (To avoid
paying property taxes on a building they were not using.)
There was a barn on the Drury place and a barn on the
Hawkins place and I don't know how many other barns they
took down. So there was quite a bit of lumber around. Jo and
I took full advantage of that lumber.

Grampy built our tree house when the lumber was still
pretty good. But then with the leftover lumber Jo and I would
go out and build great buildings (forts and tree-houses around
the ranch). Some of them were up to four feet high that we
could stand up in. Out behind Grammy's house they had
some sandy ground and we dug tunnels and made covers on
them with the wood.

· · ·

Scott: Oh really?

Woody: I don't know if they were bomb shelters or what. They were some of our forts. And we cut miles of trails in the brush. Where you sprayed all that brush after the fire (to keep the chaparral from returning to the canyon between the ranch and Pine Hills after the Cedar Fire of 2003) we had trails all through there and clear down to the front lake. Of course, we'd make crooked trails cause it was easier than cutting big brush. We must have had several miles of trails scattered through that stuff. Most of them you could walk in, some of them you had to crawl in.

Why we didn't get killed in that stuff...

We used to go exploring down the big canyon, way beyond our properties. One or two times we got as far as looking down John Tellam's falls. We never went down them; that was rough country.

Now Rosemary, who is our cousin, used to come up and spend the summers at the house, and frequently she would help pack fruit in the fall for a while. She lives in Joseph, Oregon. There was a pothole in the creek over on the south side of our place where the water stayed in the summer in most years. And she'd go down there and go swimming. One time she went down and went swimming and looked up and here was a bar of soap that was still wet. Of course, this was swimming without the benefit of suits and so on. So she grabbed her clothes, got her clothes on, and left.

I can remember her telling us that story.

Jo: I do too.

Scott: Someone was spying on her, probably.

. . .

Woody: Possibly. Very possibly. Although it was never anyone that they found or saw or anything. But that was rough country, and we were lucky that we didn't get killed. Because the brush was so thick down there before the fire (the Cedar Fire in 2003), we used to jump from one rock to another.

(To Jo) Maybe that's why your joints are sore now, because we jumped all over these crazy rocks. Why we didn't get killed, or get rattlesnaked or something else, I don't know, but we never did.

Jo: I'd never do it now. Well, I couldn't anyway, but I'd never go down there in snake-ville.

Woody: I think I could walk down there but I don't think I could walk back up... laughs. It's pretty rough country.

Scott: I never made it that far in my exploring. I always went to where the canyons met and then came back the other side. (The joining of Orinoco Creek and an unnamed tributary between Pine Hills and Manzanita Ranch.)

Woody: That was where we usually went, but once or twice we went on down. We used to lease that Strick place (property down-canyon from the ranch) so we had cows down there. Once in a while the cows would disappear and you'd go down the canyon, and you'd have to climb up the far side. That came out close to where the Webbs (Robert and Yvonne) live on Eagle Peak road. And that was tough country. The fence was poor in there but the cows usually didn't go through. But once in a while you'd have to go and chase cows out.

Grammy was down there one time chasing cows and she went around one of those big rocks and came upon a mountain lion looking at her. She backed up and the mountain lion disappeared and nothing happened. That was one of her adventures. She was just about the right size for a mountain lion to gobble. [laughs]

Rosemary told me an interesting story about her grandfather, Charles Chapman. Charles was doing the construction on the Bank of America building in San Diego, and Walter, his son, convinced him to take a motorcycle ride to Los Angeles. They had been doing quite well economically, but they went up there and had an accident and Charles was injured badly. He was never able to return to this construction job. That was a life-changing incident; their economics were never terribly good after that.

Rosemary also told me that her parents Hartwick and Wilmeth Barnes very much wanted to have a larger family but after Rosemary was born Wilmeth had an ectopic pregnancy: they had to remove uterus and ovaries and everything else to save her life. That's why there was only one in that family.

School Days

Another thing that we used to do—we were a little older when this happened—they didn't used to have absence slips at school. We're probably the reason they have 'em.

Jo: Shhhh. Don't tell everything. [laughs]

Woody: Well, sometimes Jo and I would take our lunch and go off to school. We'd get about three quarters of the way to the bus stop and decide it was too nice a day—this was usually in the fall—and we would decide not to go to school.

Scott: Really!

Woody: We would sit under the big walnut tree that's still there until noon. And then when Bope would go over to the house, 'cause he was always gardening, when he'd go over to the house at noon we'd go on up to the garden and eat strawberries. Then we'd run back to the walnut tree and wait 'til school ended and we'd come marching home.

Scott: That was a long time to sit under a tree. I think I'd rather go to school.

Woody: We didn't do it very often.

Jo: There were times too when we'd get tired of that and go home early. We'd just tell 'em it was a minimum day. [laughs] But when I was in about sixth grade they started absent slips. If you were ever absent then you had to take this little blue slip home and have it signed because they still got paid for you if you were sick when you were absent. That sure ruined a lot of fun.

Woody: Terrible thing! But we were probably too old to do that anyway. I think that grammar school was sufficiently boring that we were more tempted. I was never really tempted in high school because there was always something interesting.

Late grammar school even, when we had Fox and Duermit, they were more interesting teachers.

I think the name of the lady (grammar school teacher) was Medford or something, she was dreadful.

Jo: You had Medford, I had Meskamin. Meskamin was from Lubbock Texas, and by the end of that year we all had such a Texan accent. That was the year we went to Saint Louis after you graduated (the Barnes family visited Saint Louis, Missouri), and going through Texas I think everybody thought our parents kidnapped me because I sounded more like a Texan than the Texans did. And that was the year in Lubbock, Texas that some youngster fell down a well and it was world-wide news of getting this toddler out of this ten inch well or something. In fact, Mrs. Meskamin was so upset about it that I'm not so sure that it wasn't one of her grandchildren. It was a real big thing in our classroom. I'm pretty sure it was one of her grandchildren that had fallen in this well.[22]

Woody: Did I tell you, the other day we couldn't find Pesty (Woody and Jane's cat, also known as Puzzle). It wasn't outside, it wasn't inside. I'd call around the house and everything. Finally about five o'clock I heard a meow. Heriberto had opened the door where the brooms are; I could hear this meow and pretty soon I found orange kitty who came in the house through the furnace room.

So I got orange kitty out. And then I thought, 'You know, it's really strange. Orange kitty just doesn't come over when our cat's around.' [The two cats hate each other. Or more accurately, Puzzle hates all other cats. And at 22 pounds, he pretty much gets his way].

It turned out that Pesty was in our bedroom and had been there all day. It had pooped on the brown comforter that's mother's pride and joy. I was able to clean it up before she got home. Puzzle would have been killed!

Jo: Getting back to what we were talking about, when we we were in elementary school it was only three rooms. There was one telephone in the supply closet behind the stage, or the 'ante room' that's behind the stage, connected to one of the classrooms. That was the only telephone in the whole school. Each classroom had an oil heater in it. The middle classroom had a collapsible wall and a stage at one end and a collapsible wall at the other end which would open it up into the entryway so that you could set up chairs for the auditorium at graduation or a performance or something.[23]

Woody: The folding thing didn't work very well.

Jo: But it sufficed.
   One of my favorite memories of that classroom was going in the closet and closing the door and eating paste.

Woody: Everybody used to eat that paste.

Jo: Stick a 'tongue blade' in there—because they always had tongue blades so that if you said you had a sore throat the teacher looked down your throat—if it was red she believed you, if it wasn't... But anyway, the tongue blades were readily available so you could go in there, take one and dig out the paste. [laughs]

·   ·   ·

Woody: The principal there part of the time was Minnie A. Woodard (teacher and principal.)

Jo: I think she lived in the house where your bookstore is.[24]

Woody: Yep. I think so. Manuel Woodard, her husband, was the bus driver for many years. Those houses were built by Minnie Woodard's father.

Jo: Mister (Joseph) McGowan.

Woody: And Mrs. McGowan, after he passed away, was the post mistress (Edythe C. McGowan).

Jo: Later on the Woodards built a house out in Whispering Pines and moved out there.

When you were talking about picking up the fruit trees in Lakeside reminded me of the last trip we made through San Diego going through by the dam and then coming back on the new road.

Woody: That's right. When they built San Vicente Dam there was a hole through the dam and the road, which is what we now call Highway 67, actually went through where the dam is, went right up Mussey Grade. The night that they closed it we were one of the last cars through. They had lights all over the place and water running everywhere and they were getting ready to plug it up so they could catch this water. And then for quite a while we had to use Wildcat Canyon because the new road (current road through Ramona and Lakeside-or-Poway) wasn't completed yet. They were working on it but they hadn't completed it.

Man that's a long time ago.[25] [laughs]

Jo's Marriage, College and Bridge…Or Not

Scott: So Jo, you got married when you were 18, 19?

Jo: I got married when I was 20, like 20 and three weeks. August 24th, 1948.

Scott: When did you meet Carlyn?

Jo: Carlyn and his friend Jim Howat each had MGs[26] and one day they decided to go for a ride to have a cup of coffee and they went to Julian from La Jolla to have a cup of coffee (a drive of 60 very curvy miles). I believe it was a Tuesday evening, and every Tuesday in the summer we had a square dance. So they wandered up to the town hall to see what was going on and fooled around a while. The following Saturday they decided to go up to Julian for another cup of coffee. On Saturdays they had Saturday night dances where the entire community came in to have fun. Apparently I was dancing with Dick Whitmore, the lifeguard at Camp Cedar Glen, who was about five feet tall. And Carlyn decided that he'd give that 'country bumpkin' a chance to dance with somebody taller than she was. (Jo is 5'11" tall.) That was his biggest mistake. [laughs]

Scott: Because Carlyn was six-three or something.

. . .

Jo: Six-four. I was a junior in high school.

Scott: So you dated him quite a while.

Jo: Well, we knew each other for quite a while. When he got out of the Navy I was a sophomore in college and that's when we started dating.

Woody: Where did you go to college?

Jo: My first year I went to College of Pacific in Stockton, which is now University of Pacific. And then I transferred to University of California Santa Barbara. And then I quit and got married. After I got married I went to San Diego State. And then I got pregnant, and then I quit again! [laughs] I—unfortunately—never finished.

Two things that I never did that would have pleased my mother very, very much. The first one was to graduate from college, and the second one was to learn how to play bridge. I think maybe learning how to play bridge would've pleased her more than getting my degree.

Woody: Grammy was a pretty good bridge player and played a lot. And so was Grampy. But he lost interest in it about the time we were in high school.

. . .

Jo: He lost interest in it when it became a death march rather than a fun evening. When people began to play for blood rather than to play for the enjoyment of the camaraderie. And that is how my image of bridge playing is—and one of the reasons I was never interested in it. I love to play games, but I don't like to play games where it isn't fun. Where it's work.

Woody: Grammy really loved her bridge and she had a really wonderful group of friends. I don't think they were quite so bloodthirsty.

Jo: No, they played for fun. But they really—

Woody: They were serious.

Jo: They had quarters on each corner and it was pretty important to play well enough to get those three or four quarters each game.

Woody: Grammy tried to teach me how to play bridge.

Jane and I joined a group. Give you an idea how bloodthirsty they were, we played with them for maybe three months and by that time there was nothing but wars and divorces going on. Two of the couples got divorced. One of them was Harvey Bisher.[27] The other one was Texiera.

Jo: Kate and George Texiera?

· · ·

Woody: I think it was. It was somebody else who ended up getting divorced. We decided bridge was not for us for the same reason that Jo did: too much out-for-blood.

And it ate up... We didn't have the time. I mean, these guys read the Goren on Bridge every week, studied all the strategies.[28] We weren't that serious. I couldn't have memorized the cards anyhow.

Jo: We had another couple of friends, the Kinzers, that are avid bridge players. John is another one that everything had to be absolutely perfect and competitive. For years Margaret was in tears over their bridge games because it was such a do-it-or-die sort of a situation.

Woody: John was one of the most competitive people I've ever met. We knew him from when his dad retired from the Navy and decided to raise turkeys in Ramona. Ramona used to have the Turkey Capital of the World.[29] There were six million turkeys at one time in Ramona. I don't think there's six turkeys left except—

Jo: The ones at the Turkey Inn![30] (laughs)

Woody: John had two sisters, Peggy and Sally. One time Sally ran through a plate glass window. Cut the heck out of herself. The Kinzers used to come up and square danced.

There was Jack Steffe and another big, tall guy came up from Ramona and square danced for years. We were always a little short of fellows, and we were awful glad they came up.

· · ·

Jo: Um ha. Peggy Kinzer and Margaret Wells went to Scripps College.[31] But before that they were roommates at Bishops and that's how John met Margaret.

Woody: Movies were a big deal during World War II. In the front of the town hall they put a projector. They had little square holes cut through the wall. I don't know if the square holes are still there but they probably are. They would project on a screen and we'd get to go watch a movie. I think they charged a quarter. Does that seem reasonable? I didn't go very often.

Jo: I don't remember the movies at the town hall. I remember the big deal of getting a movie once a month or maybe once every two months at the high school. It included the news reels.

Woody: Yup. If you were lucky you got a comedy. But usually didn't.

Jo: The only movie that I ever went to in Ramona with our Dad was Pale Face.

Scott: Oh yeah, Bob Hope.[32]

Jo: That's to my knowledge the only time my Dad ever went to that theater.

· · ·

Woody: That theater was built right after the war by Robert Bivens. He had two sons, one of whom was a really good basketball player and the other one who was not as good a basketball player.

Another basketball player from Ramona of that era was Darrell Beck. Darrell was just a short guy and if you see him you'd never believe he was an athlete, but he was really a good athlete. A good mid-distance runner and a good basketball player and a good football player.

Jo: He has become a local historian for Ramona.

Scott: So Jo, when did you join the Park Service?

Jo: I started to work with the State Parks in 1978 out at Cuya-maca as a part-time, seasonal person, and then eventually became permanent full time.[33]

Scott: That was later than I thought.

Jo: In 1974 we moved to Silverwood Lake from Pacific Beach because Carlyn had gotten the job as manager of a new marina that was opened up at Silverwood Lake State Recreational Area. Carlyn started in March and they wanted me to start in April because I was outfitting the snack bars and what-have-you and managing that end of it. And so your mother came down with you and Barney and stayed at our house with the girls[34] and you went to school in Pacific Beach for a couple months. When school was out we all moved up to Silverwood Lake. We were supposed to have a mobile home on the lake property, but it wasn't ready yet and so we rented a house up at Crestline and lived there that summer. And then unexpectedly the concessionaires changed from the people that hired us to another another company, and they had their own manager and so we lost our jobs. We were only there eight months.

In the meantime we'd leased our house out in Pacific Beach so that's when we moved to Julian, 1974, just before Christmas.

Scott: Orchard Lane?

Jo: Yes. Well, first we stayed at the ranch in Pine Hills with Mother and Dad and put everything in the garage because that ranch on Orchard Lane was rented. But then those tenants moved out a couple months later and we moved in and stayed there until they sold that property. And then we moved out and bought the place in Pine Hills.

The day after I moved to Julian I started work at the hardware store for Gary Coleman. He owned the hardware store along with a couple of other fellows until they sold it to John Lofgreen, who still owns it. After John bought it he let me go so that he could have my job, which is understandable. I immediately went to work at Sears.

Scott: I remember going out to the Sears catalog store. We got the big Sears catalog every year and I would go through it and make my Christmas list. I don't think I ever got anything that was on my Christmas list. [laughs]

Jo: We used to get, when we were kids, the Sears catalog and the Wards catalog. They were probably the most exciting mail that any two kids could ever have. Every summer we got to order one toy and I always had to order a truck or a car or something. I was never allowed to order a girly toy!

Which I probably didn't want anyway.

Woody: Was I a mean brother? [laughs]

Jo: It was so exciting to get to order. We always ordered toy cars or toy trucks for our toy roads. Which we should talk about: our toy roads. Waiting for that package to come was almost better than waiting for Santa Claus. Because we didn't go to the stores on a daily basis and get some crappy little Made-In-Taiwan piece of plastic full-of-toxic-material-type toys. [laughs] It was a big deal to get something in the middle of the year. I remember that vividly.

But anyway, I ran the Sears catalog store until 1978 and they had a vacancy at Cuyamaca State Park and I applied for it and got it and that's when I started with State Parks.

Woody: What year did Carlyn die in?

Jo: He got sick in 84 and died in 86.

Woody: Were you still at Cuyamaca when he died or were you in Old Town San Diego?[35]

Jo: I bounced back and forth because at that time in order to promote you had to change parks. But with kids I didn't want to go too far away. So I took a job in Old Town and that was my first permanent position. And then there was a position in Cuyamaca again and so I moved back there. When I was first in Old Town I was commuting (to her house in Pine Hills, about 60 miles each way). Julie was still in high school and I would leave before she got up in the morning and get back about the time she was going to bed at night. I felt like it was the motherly thing to do even though I never saw her. [laughs]

When Carlyn was sick I was working in Old Town San Diego. They were extremely helpful. I would go to the hospital every morning on my way to work, I'd go every day at noon, and I'd go every day on my way home from work. The last two years of his life Carlyn was in the hospital, I believe, 489 days. Multiply that times three and that's how many trips I made to the hospital. It was... It was not a very good quality of life. I have always wondered that if I got a diagnosis such as he did whether I would fight it and go through that awful life he had for two years—or not.

Woody: What kind of cancer did he have?

Jo: He had cancer of the colon. Before he was diagnosed it had metastasized and completely surrounded one kidney. His only complaint was that he had such a backache. He went to the doctor several times and was told, "Oh, you've just had a cold and it's settled in your back." Well, it wasn't a cold that settled in his back.

We were up in Julian one night, Susan and Dewey Degn were coming for dinner. We were having steaks, which was a big treat for all of us, and Carlyn got so bad with his backache that we left the Degns there to cook their own steak and went down to Pacific Beach to go to the emergency room. But by the time we got down the hill he was better so we didn't go to the hospital that night. We went the next morning to Pacific

Beach Urgent Care. That's where we met Doctor Nathaniel Rose. Doctor Rose took him in, X-rayed him, and sent him immediately to Sharp hospital and he was in surgery the next day.

Woody: Too late.

Jo: Too late. Yes it was.

Scott: I had always thought it was lung cancer because he smoked.

Jo: That's what a lot of people thought. We figured smoking probably had not hurt him because we don't think he inhaled that much—to get it in the colon.

My theory is that for over ten years Carlyn worked with the Flying Samaritans, which was a volunteer group of primarily medical people who operated medical clinics on the weekends in Mexico. And since he was not a pilot, and he was not a medical person, but he loved this organization, and we had a van, every other weekend for close to ten years he drove a group of medical professionals to a clinic in Punta Colonet.[36]

Scott: That's where Heriberto Obeso lives (a long-time employee of Manzanita Ranch).

Jo:. Yes. It's below Ensenada about 90 miles or something. They went there every weekend. Carlyn'd drive to the (San

Diego) airport and pick 'em up, usually. Sometimes they would rendezvous at Balboa Park where a lot of their supplies were warehoused. Pick up these doctors and nurses and dentists and what-have-you and drive to Colonet. But while he was there he operated the X-ray machines that were donated to the clinics, with no protection, no shields, no anything. We will never know and it really doesn't make a lot of difference at this point in time. But I wouldn't be surprised if that exposure could have initiated his problems.

Scott: I remember him complaining about his back. I don't know if it was from that—or maybe he always had back troubles.

Woody: Tall people tend to have back troubles.

Jo: Tall people do, and he worked over a drafting board all his life because he was a draftsman-designer. Anyway, we'll never know. But his last two years were pretty darn miserable for him.

Woody: What year did Carlyn die in?

Jo: Eighty six. Dad died in 89. Roe died in 90, and Shirley died in 99 (Carlyn's father and mother).

Woody: Mother (Alice Barnes) died in 96.

. . .

Jo: Yes. Which gets us to: Who's next? [laughs]

Woody: Holy-o Bolly-o, let's not think about that.

Family and Friends

(Jim Geary, Jo's husband, participated in the following interview.)

Incidentally, if you look at that lamp behind Jo, I think that's one of the lamps that Gramma Barnes made. She was an interesting person, kind of an unprofessional draftsman, an unprofessional house remodeler, and an unprofessional worker of metal. She did a lot of metal ashtrays that we still have some of around. Copper things.

One of the interesting, kind of ironical things in today's world, is that she had a friend. I don't know what his real name was, but they called him The Chinaman. He ran a store where he sold trinkets. Gramma Barnes[37] used to make trinkets to sell at the Chinaman's store. Made-to-order Chinese 'antiques.' If that isn't ironical in today's world.

She remodeled Fourth and Upas into apartments. Rosemary said that she thinks Bope and she were just the most in love people that she ever saw. The reason that Bope moved up to Julian and Gramma didn't was she felt terrible in Julian. They probably needed Bope's help from the 20s 'til he died to make the ranch work.

Jo: Because Dad (Franklin Barnes) was gone so much.

· · ·

Woody: For eight years Dad was gone practically all the time (to the Farm Security Administration). To make things more complicated, Grammy Barnes used to take in people to live there (in her house in Pine Hills). George McCain lived there for a year and there was somebody else. And then Eric Davis lived there for a year. But Eric was sort of to help Eric's mom out. George McCain was from over at McCain Valley, off of highway 8. He lived there for a full year.

Jo: I remember Eric.

Woody: I was in first or second grade when Eric was there.

Jo: Didn't Eric have a wood lathe or something?

Woody: Yeah, he had a lathe in the little basement. Mother always said that her kids were complicated enough, but she spent much more time over there straightening out Eric's problems with the school. [laughs] Eric must have been in about the eighth grade or a freshman in high school. He slept in the sleeping porch, including all winter. (Where there were screens but no glass in the windows and no insulation.) So we know it was after the sleeping porch was built.

Eric went to work for the telephone company and years later he rebuilt our entire phone line, free to us, from our house up to the junction at the town hall. He was very grateful.

Eric's mom was an artist and she painted the daffodil picture in our room and a picture of pansies.

. . .

Scott: Oh, I didn't realize that was her.

Woody: That was Mary Elsie Davis. She felt that the pansies reminded her of young men. [laughs] I'm just telling you the history, I am not commenting on it.

Scott: That's pretty funny.

Jo: We slept out there [in the sleeping porch] many summers.
   Woody: After Eric Davis left.

Jo: Yes. Right. Your comic books were on your side of the windows and my comic books were on my side of the windows.

Woody: I wouldn't have been able to sleep out there in the winter like Eric did. I still have Eric's (business) card sitting on the desk. I was going to call him. I ran into him at the airport in Sacramento.

Jo: You told me that.

Woody: Walking in there and looking at a guy and here, "That's Eric Davis." He was just as surprised. I don't think he would have recognized me, but I recognized him.

Scott: What kind of comic books were there back then?

. . .

Jo: Good ones. They were funny ones, too.

Jim: All the Disney ones, Donald Duck, Mickey Mouse.

Jo: Dagwood and Blondie, Archie and Superman and Dick Tracey and a couple westerns. Little LuLu and Sluggo. I can remember mine.

Jim: Captain Marvel.

Scott: Where did you get them? At the drugstore?

Jo: Drugstore. Five cents each. It really hurt when they went up to a dime and we slowed our purchasing.

Woody: They used to have them where you come into the drugstore in the back of the ice cream machine, and then there was the soda fountain, over at the right there were a bunch of comic books.[38]

Scott: They doubled the price. That's a big deal.

Jo: It was a big deal.

. . .

Woody: Most of the ones I had were dime ones. I don't remember many nickel ones.

Jo: Yeah, well you bought the high priced ones. I bought the kiddie ones.

Woody: We were really amazingly lucky to have the life we lived and the friends we had. I keep thinking over and over again, you run into people we had for friends in those days when we were just little kids and we are still friends. That's pretty unusual in the modern world.

Jo: Oh yeah. Every time I meet anybody, and they say, "Where are you from?" "Julian. My mother was born in Julian and my father was born in Pacific Beach." They just can't believe that somebody actually has roots around here.

Woody: I was reading the other day that the population in 1920 was 100,000 in the San Diego area. I thought the County has around 200,000 when dad was born, but it was in the paper the other day that in 1920 it got to 100,000. It must have been the city limits.[39]

Do you remember how high-tone we thought it was when we had the phone in the garage we could hook up...the crank phone with the batteries we could hook up and call the house? Finally we got it where we had the wires along the electric line down to the old cider house and we could hook it up down there during fruit season.

. . .

Jo: I also remember when we'd get in trouble and you'd get sent to your room and I'd get sent to my room and we had two tin cans with string on them. [laughs] We'd talk to each other through our built-in telephone.

Now, we could hear what we were saying out the window anyway...but we had to use a phone. [laughs]

Woody: We thought that was a great invention. You look at the toys that we had: We had stuffed animals, dolls, a couple of trucks or so—in later years quite a few, and an Erector Set. That was one thing that I had. And we had alphabet blocks.

Jo: You had a chemistry set.

Woody: That was when I got to be big stuff. Remember, I almost burned the house down?

Jo: Your red waste basket is still around here somewhere with all the burn marks. [laughs]

Woody: You know what I was doing? I decided that if I melted my shoe polish it would polish the shoes better. So I was melting the shoe polish in one of those tin cans, using my alcohol burner to heat the thing, and it caught fire. I ran to the door with it, and I burned the curtain.

Mom cut the curtain in half.

I think it probably still only fits half the window. [laughs] Oooohhhh, was that a mistake.

·   ·   ·

(Jane and Scott's wife Grace and children Ellie (Elizabeth) and Kaylynn join the conversation.)

Grace: So are you guys picking a lot [of lilacs] this week?

Woody: We're picking every day but there is mostly crummy stuff. The weather didn't cooperate.

Jo: Kaylynn looks very different from Ellie, doesn't she?

Scott: Sometimes I think they look very different and sometimes I think they look similar. She's very smiley.

Woody: You know, one of the best things in life you can have is a smile. It makes the rest of the world easier to get along with.

Grace: She's very well mannered. At least right now. [laughs]

Jo: Well (to Jim), shall we toodle?

Jim: Okay.

Woody: Why don't you come on down (to Wynola Pizza Express), have lasagna, tolerate us freaks?

.   .   .

Jo: I sat next to you three times and had my picture taken. Isn't that enough? [laughs]

Woody: It probably did spoil your appetite. [laughs] I hadn't thought of that. We're paying, so... That's another positive thing.

Grace: How often do you come [to Julian] now?

Jo: Not very often lately. About once a month. Used to be twice a month. Before that it was once a week.

Grace: Oh. Pretty soon it will be not at all.

Jo: In our house in Pacific Beach the tenants are leaving May first and we have quite a bit of work to do. So we're taking the air mattress and are going to camp down there for a while rather than run back and forth [to Carlsbad] with the five dollar a gallon gas looming at us. Try to get it fixed up so that we can get it rented.

Woody: How much stuff do you have to do?

Jo: We don't really know yet because we haven't seen how much damage has been done. There are still two [tenants] there. So the thirtieth, next Saturday, we go down and meet them and see what they've done to it.

.   .   .

Grace: I hope it's not as bad as what they've done to my place [a condo in Rancho Santa Margarita]. [laughs]

Jo: This is partly our fault because we've been somewhat negligent about checking things between tenants. We've had revolving door tenants, four single people there for six years or so.

Woody: Not the same four.

Jo: Different ones. It's a four bedroom house. Everybody has left stuff they didn't want. They just left it. Everybody says, "I don't know who that belongs to. That's not mine."

The fellow that's been there the longest and has been a great tenant says he's trying to get rid of everything—but we'll see. They took the doors off the closets because the rooms are small and they wanted more space.

Woody: Did they leave the doors?

Jo: It looks like they are all up in the rafters in the garage. Things need painting. We have bookshelves and a desk built in in Julie's old room and one girl painted the room kind of a fern green and all the shelves and all the woodwork a dark olive drab. They are so ugly. We'll probably take those shelves out and ditch them. Patch the wall and paint this dark, dark green out. Carlyn built the shelves in there. It was a beast of a job to paint. We didn't have our own furniture; that's why he built the stuff in.

The other two rooms had built-in furniture when we

bought the house, built-in drawers and built-in desk and built-in bookcase. So all the kids needed was a bed. It was great. But now the tenants have taken out the built-in furniture so there's no carpet underneath where the built-in furniture was. So there are some things that need to be taken care of.

Scott: That last I remember that place it looked great. You had just done all kinds of work.

Jo: Jim redid that house, and then we moved up here. And then we remodeled this kitchen (in Julian) and did a bunch of things, and then moved down to Carlsbad. Now we've remodeled that one so I don't know where we're going to move next. [laughs]

(Kaylynn, age one, arrives.)

Jo: Hi Kaylynn.
    How did you come up with Kaylynn? The name, not the baby.

Grace: I was thinking of Caitlin, but I already have a friend who has a daughter named Caitlin. Then when we went to the Elephant Bar, our serving person said, "Oh, my name is Kaylynn." I looked at Scott, I said, "Kaylynn, that sounds really nice. We can do that instead of Caitlin." So we just decided.

. . .

Jo: That's as good a reason as any. She [Kaylynn] says, 'It's not going to be very long and I'm going to be motoring around here. There are too many things to see.'

Woody: 'We could have fun pulling things off the shelf...'

Grace: We were talking about when she's old enough to start walking and terrorizing people... Our house will be a real mess.

Jo: Oh, just enjoy them. You'll have many years ahead of you when you'll be able to keep a clean house and wonder why because nobody comes around to look at it. [laughs]

Woody: Nobody cares. [laughs]

Jo: Now I'm going to have two clean houses and I'm never going to have company.

Woody: How's Abby [the cat in Lake Forest]? Is Abby okay?

Grace: Oh, Abby caught a mouse. I was upstairs with Kaylynn changing her, and here Ellie comes walking up the stairs. In her hand was a mouse. She said, "Look mommy, Abby brought me a squeak." And she gives it to me. Ahhh-hhh! I thought it was still alive! But it was dead. It was still warm so it had just got killed. [laughs]

· · ·

Ellie: (age 3) It didn't squeak very well. Because it was dead.

Jo: We better toodle. Thanks for the photo op. Bye.

Ellie: Bye bye.

Woody: (to Grace) Your kids are both pretty good kids, as kids go, I mean.

Grace: Yeah. She cries, but it's not very often. I was telling Scott maybe because we get them right away when they start crying.

Woody: Well, it helps. Dispositions vary. You can take some kids, there's nothing you can do, I don't care how good a parent you are.

Grace: Kaylynn we're starting to see is very smiley. It seems like she's such a happy baby.

Woody: Ellie's pretty good.

Grace: Oh, she's great.

.   .   .

Woody: That's a wonderful thing. Every once in a while you see someone who is a pouter. They are going to have a tough time in life. Nobody likes that.

Grace: And even when she gets mad it takes her a very short time to get over it. So it's good. I think their personalities are similar so we're hoping they'll be good friends.

Woody: You and Scott have pretty mellow personalities, which helps. A certain amount of that is genetic. You can't regulate what genes happen to pop up.

Grace: We're very happy because they seem to be good kids. So far. Until they turn into teenagers. [laughs] Then we'll see what happens.

Woody: That's right. Then when they turn about 22 all of a sudden they straighten out again. The long-term friends we have—almost every one of the long-term friends we have— was a moderate person. They didn't get mad. They didn't do extreme whatevers.

   We went to dinner at the Legion the other night, Martha Gwen and Larry Thum came in, and we've been friends since I was about a year old.[40]

Grace: Oh really?

· · ·

Woody: It was fun to be with them. They have lived very different lives to ours. She's a nurse; he was an M.D. They're very nice people.

Grace: I think of all the friends that I keep in touch with; we're all very similar too.

Woody: Keep in touch with them. Like this botany group we're going to go up with, it was 50 years ago when we were in class, or more.

Grace: I was here one time when you had them over.

Woody: The professor (Edwin Phillips) is now 97. Obviously he's not going to be around much longer. What will happen when he dies? Maybe we'll fall apart. But it's fun to see them. The little disagreements you might have had have vanished and the friendships have held on.[41]

Grace: Those are classmates?

Woody: They were all students of Professor Phillips at different times. I got there as a freshman about the time his first students were seniors. So I know most of them. He taught for another 20 years. The bond we have is having the same professor and the same subject. It works out pretty well.

We're reaching the point where age and decrepit-ness... The bodies are getting to the point where they don't want to camp on the ground. They don't really want to look at plants, they just want to visit a little bit. I wouldn't be surprised if this is our last reunion.

Grace: Do they live close by or are they from all over?

Woody: All over the country. There's one gal that lives in Ohio that comes every year. Her brother was a botany major in Santa Barbara. One of the organizers is from Seattle.

Ellie: Did you see the kitty?

Woody: I know where he was.

Grace: She really loves to see him.

Woody: He's outside somewhere. I'll bring him in.

Ellie: No, he's in there. Puzzle in the bed.

Woody: [To Scott recording the conversation.] Well, you can shut your machine down for a while. We've put enough lies on there for one day.

*Franklin L. Barnes on a Doyle-Barnes company buckboard
preparing to load boxes with fruit from Julian, 1918.*

*Rose Hartwick Thorpe weaving tales of adventure for Franklin
L. Barnes (left) and his siblings, Hartwick and Peggy at Fourth
and Upas in San Diego. Ca 1911. Rose wrote many poems and
tales, the most famous of which was "Curfew Must Not Ring
Tonight" written in 1867 when she was 16.*

*Woody and Jo goofing around on a Ford tractor borrowed from the
Hawkins family.*

Jo prepares the way to using the Thunderbolt Wood Splitter.

Jo enjoying the snow in front of the rock house with Butch.

Mary Alice "Jo" Barnes marrying Carlyn Roe Tuttle on the patio of the rock house, August 24, 1958.

Four generations enjoy the ranch patio: Jo holding Mary Lynn,
Gramma Jacobs (Alice's mother), Alice.

The family taking a break from farming. From left to right:
Woody, Karen Tuttle, Barney, Franklin L., Julie Tuttle, Scott,
Mary Lynn Tuttle, Alice. July 7, 1973.

1. Bill (whose name was Willard, not William) was famous for saying, "Never hang a door after two in the afternoon," and "Measure twice, cut once."
2. Today the gas pumps are on display in the Groskoff building in downtown Julian.
3. Lucy (Sawday) Cumming
4. T.L. Barnes (Theodore Lockwood) was Bope's brother.
5. Lower Otay Dam was first completed in 1897 by the Southern California Mountain Water Company. It burst in 1916 and flooded the Otay Valley, detroying most of the town of Otay. The dam was rebuilt in 1918, and renamed the Savage Dam. Today, the town of Otay has been annexed into Chula Vista.
6. The Doyle-Barnes Company's first location was the corner of 5th and J street. The second address was the corner of 7th and J street in San Diego.The family taking a break from farming. From left to right: Woody, Karen Tuttle, Barney (outside), Franklin L., Julie Tuttle (holding rail), Scott, Mary Lynn Tuttle (standing), Alice. July 7, 1973.
7. Ed Fletcher (1872-1955) became a well-known San Diegan, a politician, and real estate developer. Among other things he helped develop water projects including San Vicente Dam and Lake Hodges. He earned the nickname "Colonel" when he was appointed lieutenant colonel of the California National Guard.
8. According to the *City of San Diego and San Diego County: The Birthplace of California, Volume 2* Jarvis Doyle became associated with Ed Fletcher and incorporated their business in 1901 as the Fletcher-Doyle Company. "After the retirement of Colonel Fletcher a few years later E.Y. Barnes became a parrtner and the business is now known as the Doyle-Barnes Company, with Mr. Doyle as president and Mr. Barnes as secretary and treasurer. This form, whose headquarters are at Seventh and J streets, is one of the leading houses of Southern California handling produce and provisions and grocer's specialties." p172
9. Jarvis Doyle and his wife Rebecca Kimball (Fletcher, sister of Colonel Ed) lived at 3427 Fourth Street, so they were literally neighbors to the Barnes' Fourth and Upas residence.
10. This particular interview with Jo and Woody was done on June, 2013 at Jo's house in Carlsbad, CA. Interviews between Scott and Woody continued off and on from 1995 through 2019.
11. Edward T. Van Duesen bought property from Franklin L. And Theodore L. Barnes (Woody's father and uncle). The road was subsequently named after Mr. Van Duesen.
12. In 1900 Pacific Beach counted 185 residents. Roughly half of these were involved in the lemon business. E.Y. Barnes and F.W. Barnes had ten acres of lemons next to College Campus (today their ranch is the location of Plaza Condominiums) between Emerald and Diamond, Jewel and Lamont Streets. According to *Originally Pacific Beach* by John Webster, the ten acres grossed $2,000 in 1901. Across Lamont Street was the lemon grove of Edmund Carson Thorpe and Rose (Hartwick) Thorpe, block 167. Edmund claimed to be the first resident of Pacific Beach. Their daughter

Lulo married Edward Y. "Bope" Barnes. Lulo and Bope were Woody Barnes' grandparents.

13. Franklin L. Barnes' (Woody's dad) first job outside the family was loading bricks onto railcars at the Rose Canyon brickyard. Three men standing beside the train would throw stacks of five bricks at a time. Franklin and the other man already on the flatbed would catch the bricks in a stack and set them on the railcar. The Union Brick Company ran the factory at a capacity of around 25,000 bricks a day. Most of the bricks were for use in burgeoning San Diego. John W. Rice was president of the Union Brick Company from 1910 until 1946 when he turned control over to his son, John W. Rice, Junior.

14. Richmond Jackson lived across the street from E. Y. "Bope" Barnes' Fourth and Upas house near Balboa Park, San Diego. Richmond's dad was a dentist. Richmond had four kids: Remy (oldest), Demp (from Dempster), Marcia (married to Buzz Mackie), and Lucia (youngest), Jo's age.

15. Milton Angel: (1921-2004) husband of Dorothy "Dot" (Dodge) Angel. Milton's grandparents James Newton and Henrietta (Haun) Angel settled in Mesa Grande in 1880 and developed a successful cattle ranch. Angel Mountain is named after the family. James Newton was among the first party to cross into the Central Valley, California over what is now known as Donner Pass after the Donner tragedy in 1846-47.

16. Pedro Mireles began working at Manzanita Ranch as part of the Bracero program in 1943 or 44. He came up permanently with his wife Sara in 1948.

17. Nash Motor Company based in Kenosha, Wisconsin. Likely the Nash 600 model.

18. Part of the federal Department of Agriculture, the Farm Security Administration (FSA) was a New Deal policy created to fight rural poverty during the Great Depression. Initially created as a scheme to create collective farms (resettling poor farmers on group farms owned by the federal government and supervised by bureaucrat 'experts'), when the "conservative coalition" took over Congress in 1939 they transformed the program to help poor farmers purchase their own land through low interest loans.

19. International trucks, built by International Harvester Company from 1914 to the present. Likely the K/KB model built between 1940-1948, it was available with two-speed rear axle and offered around 100 horsepower. The "two-speed rear axle" allows for shifting while moving and gives each gear a high and low range.

20. Owned by John S. Alessio. Mr. Alessio began his career in San Diego by shining shoes in seventh grade. One of his frequent customers was C. Arnholt Smith. Smith offered him a job as a messenger for Banco del Pacifico in Tijuana, a bank that Smith owned. Alessio rose to director of Banco del Pacifico by 1943. Alessio became a prominent force in San Diego and California. He owned such local properties as the Hotel del Coronado, the Kona Inn and the Kona Kai Club, and became assistant general manager of the Caliente race track in Tijuana. In 1965 he founded Mister A's in downtown San Diego on the top floor of his 12-

story building at 2550 5th Avenue. Accused of embezzlement along with the Tecate Brewing Company, he avoided conviction and became friends with the San Francisco District Attorney G. "Pat" Brown. Alessio subsequently financed Brown's political campaigns. John S. Alessio was convicted of tax evasion in 1970, nine years before his patron C. Arnholt Smith was convicted of the same crime.

21. U.S. participation in World War II began on December 8, 1941, the day after Japan bombed Pearl Harbor, Hawaii. The War itself began on September 1, 1939 when Germany and Russia (temporary allies) invaded Poland from opposite sides, although Axis action and maneuvering had begun in both Asia and Europe years before this.

22. Probably refers to the story of Kathy Fiscus, a three-year-old who fell down a well in San Marino, California on April 8, 1949. The attempted rescue was broadcast live on radio and television and has been cited as the beginning of long-form journalism in the United States. After two days, the rescuers found Kathy, dead, although she had reportedly spoken at least once after the 100-foot fall. The story prompted the "Kathy Fiscus law" that requires the capping of abandoned wells.

23. Julian Elementary School was first dedicated in 1887.

24. Woody and Jane own a house in Julian that is leased to the Old Julian Book House, 2230 Main St, Julian.

25. The concrete San Vicente Dam was built to a height of 220 feet in the canyon through which ran Mussey Grade Road, the primary horse, stage and auto road from the coast to Ramona. While the reservoir is fed by runoff, its primary source of water is a diversion of the Colorado River via the First San Diego Aqueduct. During construction, a tunnel allowed drivers to pass through the dam and continue to travel up Mussy Grade. According to the Coronado Eagle and Journal, the dam had filled to a depth of 43.8 feet by February 4, 1943; thus it is likely the road was plugged in 1942. San Vincete Dam was raised by 117 feet from 2009-2014 (dedicated on August 4, 2014).

26. The initials stand for Morris Granges, the founder. The auto company was part of the British Motor Corporation Limited at this time in its history.

27. Harvey's son runs Bisher Meat's butcher shop at 2330 Main Street, Ramona.

28. A column by world champion bridge player and writer Charles Henry Goren (March 4, 1901 – April 3, 1991).

29. Ramona was known as the Turkey Capital of the World in the 1920s through the 1940s, though the number of turkeys being raised there couldn't be verified. Ramona used to elect "Turkey Queens" to lead the Turkey Day Parade.

30. A bar at 716 Main Street, Ramona, the Inn's iconic turkey sign was erected in 1937 to indicate that fine turkey dinners could be had there.

31. Scripps College—at that time an all-female liberal arts college in Claremont, CA, founded in 1926 by Ellen Browning Scripps.

32. *The Pale Face*, a comedy-western released in 1948, staring Bob Hope and Jane Russell.

33. Cuyamaca Rancho State Park

34. Mary Lynn, Karen and Julie, Jo's daughters.
35. Old Town San Diego State Park.
36. Flying Samaritans is a volunteer organization which operates medical clinics in Baja California, Mexico. Doctors, dentists, nurses, translators, pilots and support personnel drive or fly to clinics in private aircraft. All treatment is offered free of charge.
37. Lulo May (Thorpe) Barnes, wife of Edward Young "Bope" Barnes.
38. Julian's first brick building—the drug store was originally built in 1886 by Joseph Marks and A. Levi. Over the years it had various uses and owners. A soda fountain was added in 1929, and Clayton Tozer bought the building in 1933. Half the building remained a store (with comic books) and pharmacy; the other became Nida's Pine Café. 2134 Main Street, Julian.
39. According to the U.S. Decennial Census, the population in San Diego County was 35,090 in 1900, the year after Franklin Barnes "Dad" was born. The population rose to 112,248 in 1920 and 209,659 in 1930. Today it is around 3.5 million.
40. Julian American Legion Post 468, 2503 Washington Street, Julian
41. Professor Edwin Phillips received the Wig Award from Pomona College in 1966. According to the Pomona College faculty page, the Wig Distinguished Professor award for excellence in teaching is the highest honor bestowed on Pomona faculty and recognizes exceptional teaching, concern for students and service to the College and the community. They were established by Mr. and Mrs. R.J. Wig in 1955.

5

RANCHING IN CALIFORNIA AND
OREGON

Scott: How did you and Mom get into the cattle business in
Corning and Oregon?

Woody: I should start out with the history of what our folks
did, which was minimal compared to what we did later. When
we were kids at the beginning of World War II we had a
couple of milk cows and Bill Loux, that we were talking about
before, did most of milking down there at the Hawkins Ranch
(in Wynola) and kept them down there. We had other properties that had waste land on them. We had the Julian Grade, we
had Drury's, which is up at the corner of Deer Lake Park Rd
and Frisius Rd, and we had the big piece in Wynola, couple
hundred acres there. At one time we had a partnership with
Len Webster on a couple hundred acres down where Fairbanks Ranch is in San Diego. They were raising lima beans
and barley down there. Bruno Denk was the farmer that did
that for us most of the time... There were a bunch of German
families that lived in Olivenhain.[1] Dad did some of it.

I'm getting off track, I know. We used to call it Del Mar,
but it was up the river a ways from Del Mar proper. Dad and

Len Webster had an agreement on that property that if it ever got to a thousand dollars an acre they would sell it. They sold it and the lady who bought it and her husband, it took them twenty five years before the property went above a thousand. So they did the right thing. Although looking back at it you think, 'God, that stuff would be worth a million an acre now.' But Len died a few years later, and we used the money we got out of it.

The rake over by the shed, the planter was one we used down there (to plant lima beans in Fairbanks Ranch).

Scott: Oh is that right? The one with the wood on it?

Woody: Yeah. Anyhow, that's water under the bridge.

When World War II came along, we bought a couple of milk cows. There was an antique dealer in El Cajon called Streeter Blaire, he had a few acres down in El Cajon. At that time everybody had a few acres. We bought two milk cows from him.

I can remember we had a '42 International ton and a half truck, right after World War II began. We were hauling them home—I got to ride with Dad, a big deal. Over at Cuyamaca the cow slipped and had a rope around its neck—because we didn't have a cattle rack at the time, we just had three or four foot sides. Grampy got out there and cut the rope, saved the cow, and we had milk cows.

Bill Loux did the milking most of the time; I was the emergency relief milker. Very bad emergency. We had a cream separator down there and Grammy (Alice, Woody's mom) used to make butter in our kitchen sink at our house... Anyhow, we started out with just a few. Originally we leased most of the property (in Wynola) to the Cauzza family, Elmo particularly. They were three brothers, Albino, Victor and

Elmo. Over time we started running cattle ourselves. We had up to about thirty five head on our various places.

Scott: Now those would be no longer milk cows—

Woody: They were no longer milk cows. They were gradually bred to whatever bull we could get. At first we were getting Herefords, then Uncle Ted (Jacobs) bought a place out in the desert and raised Charolais, so we had Charolais bulls because he gave us a free bull. Then eventually we sold those out when we sold some of the other property, we got down to where it wasn't worth fooling with.

But we had around thirty five head of cattle here. That was our Julian cattle business.

Edith Vedova's husband, Cleto Vedova, used to haul the calves up to auction in Chino to sell.

Anybody we could borrow a bull from to breed them, that was our beginning. We had the most primitive corrals, wire stuff and everything, but anyhow, that was it.

Then Glenn and Charlotte Mathis (Jane's parents), when they began to sell out their property in El Toro, they gave each of their kids a small piece of property located off La Paz Road just over the hill from Cabot Town Center, off of Freeway 5. They each had forty or fifty acres of bare ground. (By exchanging out of the Moulton Ranch in El Toro) Glenn and Charlotte bought cattle ranches and their kids exchanged into the various cattle ranches.

Scott: So you were a partner with Lewie and Deke Mathis (Jane's brothers)?

. . .

Woody: Everybody was partnered. Then, probably wisely, they could see it was good to split them up.

Scott: Were you partners with Glenn also?

Woody: I don't think we were at that time.

Scott: Just the kids.

Woody: I think Glenn gave us those 40 acre properties in El Toro and we switched into the ranches from those. Eventually they decided to split up the brothers' and sister's partnerships up there. In the meantime Glenn had arranged to get water on the place in Maxwell that later became Deke's, and he also arranged to get water on the Moulton ranch.[2] That was a Godsend for all of us. He was very farsighted.

Lewie got the ranch in the Central Valley (near Merced), Deke got that one in Maxwell.

Well, we were all partners. When they split it up Jane and I got cash to go buy our place. Deke and Lewie didn't want us to have the cattle, so we got money for our third of the cattle. So we looked around all over and found the places we ended up buying. The one you guys (Barney and Scott) own in Corning and then the Brown Road property (in Fort Klamath, Oregon). The Brown Road property was a really good irrigated pasture. Jane never liked it but it was wonderful; you grew so much for so little.[3]

·   ·   ·

Scott: That was a great piece of land. A lot of the people looked down on it because it was so boggy but I thought it was great.

Woody: One of the reasons we went up there was that Glenn had bought the ranch that they still have (on Loosley Road in Fort Klamath). We liked it so much, we thought it was the best valley west of the Rockies for cattle. I think it still is—if they don't take all the water away from them.

We were lucky. Another interesting thing is there was a fellow down here by the name of John Patuce and he had made some money and had eighty acres in Wynola and he bought a thousand acres up there right in that same area, the Weed Road, Fort Klamath area, on the edge of the lake. He eventually sold it to Fish and Wildlife, I think, or one of the conservation groups, just like we did. (Jane and Woody sold out their Brown Road property to The Nature Conservancy in 2006.)

That's how we got up to Oregon.

Then we had to buy the cattle. We learned more about them. The first I'd ever seen of Angus to amount to anything, Willie Tellam, when he was in high school, went up to Montana and bought an Angus calf and won the Del Mar Fair down here. Everybody said, "Wait, you didn't grow that, really," but he had the foresight to get that Angus calf. So that was another thing.

We looked around and decided in general that the Angus people, the genetics were improving so rapidly. When we were kids we thought Herefords were the best beef cow going, Stewart Hathaway had some over here (in Pine Hills)—they were really the best things going. Then when Uncle Ted got Charolais they were the best thing going.

They didn't have the genetic information that the Angus people did. The Angus people were the first ones ones to collect genetic information that would apply to the next generation of cows. Now everybody does it.

That's one reason we went to Angus, the other reason was no horns. We didn't have to de-horn them. There's a hornless heifer (also known as 'polled'), but they've never been quite as good as the horned heifers. We didn't want to get in the habit of cutting horns off them. In the first place it is painful (to the animal), in the second place it is a heck of a lot of work.

The first employee we had in Corning was Harvey Smith. He hated humans. He hated me; Jane was tolerable, but he quit and we were so lucky we got John Venable. You know, how about walking on water? John Venable's then mother-in-law still lives in Corning, her parents were great... Pitkin. She was working at the school and she heard Harvey was quitting because he was taking his kid out of school, and she got John lined up with us.

Again, fortuitous things happening over and over again. We are still thankful. John got divorced from his first wife and he has that much better wife now. We are still good friends and they're still taking care of stuff for you guys...

Scott: He manages the Corning ranch still.

Woody: He is a wonderful guy and so is his wife Lori.

Up in Oregon we had a guy, can't remember his name right now, a truck driver that managed the thing. One day we had a truck coming to load and I moved a colt from one pen to another, about fifty feet—he was gonna kill me. He got mad quickly. Rosemary was his wife's name. She was not as bad, but I can't remember his name. They left and we hired the Browns. They (the truck driver and his wife) had hired the Browns to do some of the work because they were too lazy to do it.

Dick and Sandy Brown turned out to be wonderful people. I had a phone call to Sandy yesterday because Jo and Jim (Geary) are gonna go on a vacation in May and I think they are gonna use our house up in Klamath Falls since the house is empty. Sandy takes care of the house for us and we pay her, of course.

We probably should sell it, I know, you don't have to tell me.

Scott: I haven't said a thing! I would love to go use it but...

Woody: I understand that perfectly.

Scott: I haven't even seen Barney's cabin, which is half mine, on the Sprague river up there.

Woody: It is much more scenic, although ours is plenty scenic.
     That's how we got in the cattle business.

Scott: And then you got out. Why did you—

Woody: We didn't really get out, we traded out because they were threatening to shut off our water over on Brown Road. We exchanged it for the property in Lakeview and for Fuddruckers. (A commercial building in Ontario rented by the Fuddruckers restaurant.)
     Fuddruckers has turned out to be a good deal, but scary now. They're closing Fuddruckers right and left. The nicest thing about Fuddruckers was that it was an absolutely triple

net lease. They pay everything. We keep a little extra insurance on it but basically the seventeen thousand (dollars a month) is net to us.

You and Barney own that now, I think 49 percent each of you.

Scott: It is in a trust but we control the trust.

Woody: One of the good things Bill Brinkloe (William B. Brinckloe, Jr., Woody and Jane's long-time attorney) did was negotiate a reduction in rent for an extension in rent. A triple net lease is rare. I mean, we pay a little bit.

That is one property that people keep hounding us to sell. The negative is, I do a counting, I'm a counter wherever I go. The building has no drive-through, and probably could never have one. It is not designed for it. Wherever I go, more than half the business in most restaurants is drive-through. I'm not talking about fancy, sit down restaurants; the "dinner trade," they call it.

One thing I'll give you for advice is if you ever buy anything, medium to fast food things, make sure it has a drive-through.

You may never want to buy another restaurant. That lease expires I think in '22, I'm not positive about that. In all probability they will not renew. We will be lucky if they last that long. They closed the one on your street there, El Toro Rd

Scott: They said they were going to close it, but they haven't. Whatever arrangement they have made, it is still open. I talked to a couple real estate brokers, and I don't think we are interested in selling. I talked to one broker who just wants to be the leasing agent on it and he thinks it is a great property.

.   .   .

Woody: They're doing a big development just diagonally across the street and I don't know how that will affect things, but I think it is a good location and like I say a triple net thing is rarer than hen's teeth.

One reason we sold the Brown Road thing, The Nature Conservancy has a little bit of influence. They got a bill passed through the U.S. Congress specifically to buy our property. That's one reason why we only had forty or thirty five days to do an exchange. We couldn't say no when it was all cash. We could have just paid taxes on the cash and sat back on our butt-inskis, but we traded it for properties.

Scott: Eventually you sold all of your cattle.

Woody: That was in 2006, several years later. We moved a bunch of them over there to Lakeview. We shipped them out there (in the summers) for several years.

Scott: Just a question of time and energy?

Woody: I don't remember exactly why, but we did. One of the reasons was we had to keep leasing other properties because that place wasn't big enough for all our cattle. We have two or three places on Sprague River Road that we leased. We leased the Klamath Agency Ranch, right near our house on Loosley Road for a couple years. You were always looking for a place to lease. The Klamath Agency thing, the corrals were built long enough ago that our cows were so big they couldn't go through it, and we had to buy panels and run the cows around the side of their corrals.

·   ·   ·

Scott: That's amazing how animals have gotten bigger.

A Year in the Life of a Cattle Ranch

The below was done to help Scott with a one-hour talk he gave on cattle ranching at the San Diego Fair in Del Mar on June 7, 2015. Recorded in Julian with Woody, Jane, and Scott's family present, Grace, Ellie and Kaylynn.

What time of year do you want your cows to calve (have their babies)?

Woody: You attempt to have your calves when the grass is the best because fresh, green grass helps the cows to produce milk. So in California you ordinarily want them to calve in say January because, particularly in the lower lands, the grass is good from February until May, if you're lucky.

It's 280 days, more or less from the time the cow is bred until the calf comes.

Usually your first-year calves you breed a month earlier because you want the cow to calve a month earlier so that they have a little more time to recover. Because it's very hard on a calf to be growing, and at the age of a year plus to have a calf. In our case, we had them calve in November for first-calf heifers and in December for second-calf heifers.

And then we started to breed them right around the first of February. That way the second-calf heifers and the older cows would all have their calves at a similar time.

Scott: So two months after they have their calves they are with the bulls?

· · ·

Woody: Yeah. We wanted our calves to be a tight calving season. Some people don't, and they have calves all year. We felt it was better to have a lot of calves at a given time so that you could do the various things you need to do all at once, to a similar age group.

Now the calves you want to vaccinate and identify—brand them, if that's what you're going to do—before they get to be four months old. Three months and under is ideal because they recover quicker from the vaccinations, and the antibodies that they inherit in the milk tend to drop off about that time so they become more susceptible to various diseases.

You want to vaccinate them to prevent them from getting any diseases, just like you do babies. We used several vaccines.

One of the things you want to be careful of is where you inject the needle because it always leaves a little hard place in the meat. So you vaccinate them right up here in the neck that is not used for human consumption so that that vaccine nodule is not put into the food chain two or three years later.

Ordinarily the bull calves, the male calves, are castrated at the same time. There are two or three reasons for that.

One of them is docility. It makes them more docile.

Another one is there tends to be a little better growth factor (among steer rather than bull calves).

And the other thing is from the standpoint of genetics, you want to bring in new genes. You don't want them to be breeding their sisters, which is what would happen if you didn't castrate them and you put them in the same field for six months. That way you are obligated to purchase outside bulls.

Bull breeding and development is a specialized field. A person in a cow-calf operation, which is what we were, tends to buy bulls, not raise their own. You tend to be able to buy better genetics than you can produce on your own. That is not always true but it's usually true. So we always bought bulls.

But that gets ahead of us.

Then comes summer and all of these animals are growing

and the food requirements go up. In California the quality of the feed deteriorates. So in the summer months we took them to Oregon where we could have nice green pasture around Fort Klamath, or in Lakeview. This involves loading them up and hauling them (on semi trucks), which is somewhat stressful, but a lot better for the animals than to spend four or five months on mediocre feed.

Also it saves the feed that you have in the ground for the next year, because the grass comes up better if there is a little bit of grass left. It kind of nurtures it, prevents it from drying when the grass is tiny and very susceptible to drying and dying. You always want to try to leave a significant amount of dry grass for the summer months which you are not using and take the cows and the calves to another pasture area. In our case, it happened to be in Oregon.

You can take them to irrigated pasture in California if you happen to have that, but with the drought there is very little of that available.

While they are in Oregon the cattle tend to get flies. Certain of the flies tend to be very irritating to the cows. So you frequently put an ear tag on there that has some sort of an insecticide. It doesn't actually get on the cow but it is there around the head so that the flies don't continually pester the cows.[4]

The flies can be very, very thick. With summer pasture and the warmth the flies have a very short breeding season. They can breed in roughly two weeks. So one fly that's mated and lays eggs can have a bunch of flies in two weeks.

Ideally you put the ear tags in the same time you vaccinate them in California—then you only have to touch them once. But sometimes that's more than you can actually accomplish. A lot of times you'll wait until you get to Oregon and do a second run-through (to put in ear tags).

You vaccinate only the calves. Both cows and the calves need ear tags.

You want to give the cattle the least possible stress. They live a very peaceful life up there in Oregon, usually. You move them maybe once or twice from one pasture to another so that the pastures have chance to grow back.

Then about August or so, when the grass is beginning to get tired in Oregon, the calves reach a weight of say six to seven hundred pounds. Then you decide what calves you are going to keep and what calves you are going to sell. You sell all of the bull or steer calves each year. But the heifer or girl calves you do what we call a pelvis check to see how their pelvis is developing, if they would have calves easily or not. Sometimes the pelvis's are such that they would not be able to have a calf very easily. The ones that are in that group you sell.

You check the cows (as opposed to heifers) to check if they are pregnant, do what you call a 'preg check.' If they are not pregnant (called 'open cows'), you sell them.

Not everybody does preg checks. We did. We wanted our calves to come in a lump so that we could load a truck with a bunch of calves. Load another truck. Five trucks or so, they were all gone.

Our calves we sold on a video auction. The buyers came up and took pictures of them and then had a video sale. The open cows went to a physical auction yard where the guy looked at each cow, because there's a lot of difference in old cows. The calves we were aiming for pretty much a uniform group.

We had one cow, I think she was called Buttercup, still having calves at nineteen years old. That's unheard of. Most of them, after five or six calves, you begin having open cows.

The other thing you check is the teeth. The teeth grind off and pretty soon you have what you call "broken-mouth." They just have no teeth. They can still eat, but they are not very efficient. They usually tend to be poor "keepers" (of weight) if they get that way. Some of them are smart and manage to keep eating for years without any teeth.

But anyhow, the open cows and the broken-mouth cows you ordinarily sell. That means that you have to replace them with those retained heifers, the ones whose pelvises were big enough and look like they would be able to have calves. It's a continuous replacement process.

Likewise with the bulls. You buy bulls every year but some bulls you keep for several years, if you are lucky. Some bulls die before you ever breed anything.

Bulls are not very easy to handle. They tend to be belligerent. They tend to get into fights with each other, break each other's hips. They also get a series of diseases that they now check for (STDs).

In September all through California there are bull sales. Bull selection has become much more scientific than it was 20 years ago. They have what they call EPDs, which is Expected Progeny Differences. There are many things you can select for. Just like in humans, no one bull is good in all characteristics. So you decide what characteristics are most important to you.

With us, we usually select low birth weight, so that they calve easily.

We usually select for fairly rapid gain. Which is expected weaning weight.

And we usually select for marbling, a relatively new thing.

One of the things which makes meat tender is how much marbling it has. They have recently learned to predict in bulls how much marbling that bull has and how much will tend to be transmitted to his children or calves. Marbling measures intra-muscular fat—not the fat on the outside of the cow. Theoretically you could get a cow with relatively thin fat on the outside and well marbled (tender) on the inside of the meat. We were making a lot of progress on that.

Almost all the characteristics are multiple genes. You don't get a "yes" or "no." You get a range.

Then you buy those bulls. You also keep bulls from the year before. You try to get maybe four years out of a bull.

During the summer you have a problem: Where do you keep your bulls where they won't be breeding cows? It's quite possible to leave the bulls on lesser feed, so frequently the bulls are left in California in areas where there is plenty of dry feed. That tends to work out pretty well and you don't get them breaking through the fence and breeding the cows at odd times.

Approximately in November it begins to rain in California. At that time, whether you have the cows on irrigated pasture in California or in Oregon as we did, you ship them back to the dry-land, non-irrigated pasture, because—if you are fortunate—it begins to have some grass from the early rains.

About the time you get to the first of December, or November in the case of heifers, they start having calves. This is a critical time in that calves, just like little babies, are very tender and susceptible to all kinds of things. One of the important things is that they need to get up and suck milk within just three or four hours from the time they are born. The milk that comes out early is full of antibodies. If you don't get them these antibodies in the first few hours the calves are going to be puny if you're lucky and dead if you're not.

In addition, the calves need that milk because their digestive system is still in formation. Cattle have four stomachs. One of them is a rumen, which is basically a fermentation sack. And you need to get them started on that, get the right bacteria in there. They are a big bag full of enzyme-producing bacteria and other critters that help digest the food.

Anyhow, if you have done your breeding right the first-calf heifers will start calving around November 15 and the second-calf cows around the first of December. You're back raising calves again.

That's the cycle.

In the mean time you have to do a lot of things like 'Who will buy your animals? How you are going to sell them?'

We sell our calves in the late summer at a video auction. But you can sell them to a private buyer. They go two ways from there.

These young calves, which are around 700 pounds, can either go to a feedlot and be fed directly or they can go to someone else's pasture who specializes in taking them from 700 pounds to say 850 before they go to a feedlot. Most animals go to a feedlot at one time in their lives.

There is a movement to take them directly from the grass and butcher them. That works fine if you have lush grass and can keep them on it all year until they get to an appropriate weight. So you can have grass fed beef. For most people, running them to a feedlot is a more practical answer.

Scott: That's because the feedlot has feed when you don't.

Woody: That's correct.

Scott: Does it also fattens the animals up, get the beef more tender?

Woody: You can argue about how much tenderness is added to it. We think quite a bit; some people think none. Feedlots have people who specialize in gaining them just right. We specialize in raising calves just right. We didn't go into the "feed-em ourselves" business.

Roger Nicholson a good friend of ours, feeds cattle all over the country. He's an expert.

There's another thing. Doing it the way we do is economically conservative in most years, not this last year.[5] You make a little bit but you don't make a lot.

Taking animals to feedlots (retaining ownership throughout the process) you can make all kinds of money one year; you can make nothing the next. Most of the people who put their animals in feedlots hedge their bets by buying insurance policies that say that if the calf comes out and weighs so much you get so much a pound, and if it weighs more you get a little penalty. The price is somewhat guaranteed.

For example, the insurance policy says you're going to get 70 cents a pound. If the guy who guaranteed it sells the animal for 75, he gets that nickel. If he gets 65 you still get 70. We never did that, so I'm not really familiar with all of the ins and outs.

Scott: Is that through a company like Farmers Insurance?

Woody: No. These are usually animal specialty companies. It's a gamble type thing: a very good deal if you know how to do it, and a very quick way to lose your tail if you don't.

I met a fellow by the name of Saul Brinker. Brinker Brothers were down in Bakersfield. Forty years ago, they made $2 million in one year, continuing to own their animals through the feedlot. The next year they lost $3 million doing the same program. When you do that you're gambling with the whole United States because your price varies nationally. The price swings can be surprising.

We were happy to take the money we got at the auction and not think about it. Go back into the next year.

. . .

Scott: How does the cattle industry in San Diego differ from what you did shipping cattle from northern California to Oregon?

Woody: The San Diego market... I don't know exactly how they do it; there are only a few who do. Most of the time the San Diego ranchers take their animals to sales. The nearest one is in Chino where they used to have a lot of dairy cattle. They take beef cattle and old cows up there.

If you are a gambler you can take them to the Imperial Valley and feed them. Or you can sell them to somebody in the Imperial Valley who will feed your calves.

Scott: In San Diego County we mostly have smaller ranches. It's mostly a hobby, right?

Woody: Well, if you take up here (in the Julian area) there is Cauzzas. There's Bugs Ponchetti. There's the Sawday family (and Tulloch family). There's Spike Alford (Arthur F. Alford, Jr.) over in Mesa Grande. Tellams. Feigels still have quite a few. There's one or two down in the southern part of the county.

The two biggest ones are Rancho Guejito[6] and the Warners Ranch.[7]

Guejito belonged to the descendants of the Coates family. The oldest Coates just died a year or two ago. They are trying to subdivide but they haven't.

The other is the Warner's Ranch, owned by the Vista Irrigation District. They usually lease that out for milk cows.

Beef cows and milk cows are two distinct breeds.

One of the interesting things which I've only learned recently is that Holstein (milk) cows are almost as tender as good Angus (beef) cows. Angus has been the leading breed, other than perhaps some of the rare Japanese breeds, for tenderness for quite a few years. We chose to use all Angus bulls because we felt that the Angus breed was large and had more statistics in their Expected Progeny Differences (EPDs) than did the others.

A lot of people like the concept of cross-breeding because they think they get vigor from cross breeding. There is some truth to that, too.

It's an interesting compromise that you make.

We chose to use all Angus. A lot of people choose to use one kind (of bull) for a few years then another kind. A lot of others don't care. They just use whatever bull they happen to find.

Many years ago Uncle Ted had Charolais. He'd loan us a Charolais bull for nothing when we were running just a few head of beef cattle here in Julian. That was a big economic boost for a small operation. Theodore Jacobs was a very clever cattleman—even though he was primarily in real estate and insurance.[8] So we got good bulls and they worked rather well. By the time we quit raising cattle (in Julian), we had almost a straight Charolais herd.

During World War II we had milk cows. We gradually turned those into beef cows as we quit doing milking for ourselves. We bred them with whatever bulls we could find— which at that time were largely Herefords. We had about five milk cows. That is not something I would recommend for anybody. But during World War II that was a very good deal.

That's a long time back.

Scott: Do most of the San Diego County ranchers take their animals to the Imperial Valley for irrigated pasture? Do they feed hay in the summer?

· · ·

Woody: They just live with the pasture they have. Many of the ranchers own a small area that's kind of green, like the bottom of the Santa Ysabel Valley.

Sawdays originally had property clear to the coast. Rancho Peñasquitos subdivision was their winter pasture, and then they came up to Ramona, and then they came to Witch Creek, and then they went to Laguna and Cuyamaca for the summer. The next year they would take them back down (to the coast). They used elevation to provide them with the feed that would accomplish what they wanted.

I think that some of the others did the same over towards Palomar Mountain. Going up and down.

Feigels' in Mesa Grande was part of the Santa Ysabel Ranch,[9] which was a very good ranch. It had some pasture that they reserved for summer grazing. So they didn't have to ship them like we did.

(Carrying a sheaf of notes, Jane Barnes joins in the conversation at this point.)

Jane: I wrote some things down as they came to me that we did up there in Oregon. *(Reading.) Quality insurance program.* Basically, if you want to advertise your animals as having been vaccinated and taken care of in a good way. The number of cattle we were selling. The brand. If they'd had any implants —which we didn't do. If they had brucellosis "bangs" vaccination. If they were wormed.

Were they de-horned?

Well no, because our cows didn't have any horns.

Castrated?

Yes.

We would fill out both sides of this and send it to the auction yard before they had their video auction sale. When we vaccinated them we kept a lot of records. We wrote down each ear tag and if there was any problem with the animal.

Another interesting thing is you can raise "grass fed" beef just on the grass that you grow at home. You can supplement them with grass hay, and you vaccinate them and worm them.

Beyond that there is the "natural beef." I forget all the requirements for natural beef, but I know you cannot have any vaccines or feed additives.

Scott: No vaccines? That almost seems cruel.

Jane: Yes, but those that get sick you take out, give them their medicine, then sell them as regular beef, not natural beef.

Scott: Okay.

Jane: Then for organic beef there are additional requirements.

The other thing are pests. Coyotes can be a big pest, and dogs that people let loose to run. They are even a bigger problem than coyotes.

Woody: Dogs are a much bigger problem than coyotes.

Scott: The problem is they kill calves and they run the cows and make them lose weight.

Woody: I remember that Deke (Glenn Mathis Jr., Jane's brother) had a dog that just laid around. Deke always thought he was a lazy, worthless dog.

One day a neighbor called him. "Do you have a dog—" Gave him the description.

"Yeah."

"Well, your dog keeps running out here and chasing my calves at night."

This guy was 10 miles away. The reason the dog slept all day was he was running ten miles up, chasing this guy's calves, and coming back and lying around all day.

Jane: Here's a file on our vaccination schedule. At birth the calves got BO-SE; I can't remember what BO-SE was for but it was probably to keep them healthier.[10] (laughs)

We didn't give the vaccines right at birth but a couple of months afterwords. Then at spring branding we gave it to those who hadn't received it. Just prior to leaving Corning to Oregon we gave them vaccines, like we (humans) get the smallpox vaccination, but the cattle had to have them every year. We put fly tags on. The anthrax vaccination. In early August we gave them a Bangs shot.[11] We selected the replacements at that time. Then we would weigh all those replacements. We vaccinated them three times.

Replacement heifers had a little different schedule. The bulls got spring and fall, and the calves more often.

Woody: One vaccine is 8-Way.[12] The other one is ivermectin. Ivermectin is a wormer; they pick up worms in the feed which wind up in the intestinal area.

Jane: Your vaccinations take care of respiratory or pelvic diseases.

(*Reading.*) *Bull Distribution.* Didn't we have about 20 cows to a bull, Woody?

Woody: Yeah. They say you should not have more than 30. We found 20 was much better for a short breeding season. And you always get one that is no good in spite of your semen check and everything else.

Jane: For the first-calf heifers we made sure that we had calving-ease bulls on them. For cows, we never got anything on the calving ease line above a 2.5 score. (I.e. The calf birthing weight would be low.) This is for Angus. Every breed has a different number.

Woody: Nowadays you would require lower.

Scott: You mentioned the spring branding?

Jane: We have to mark the animals to identify them if they get out or somebody steals them.

Woody: We put a year brand on most of them so we knew how old they were. (Each birth year was assigned a separate brand so the cowboy could tell the animal's age at a glance.) Theoretically, you could do all that with ear tags. But the problem is that the ear tags get wiped off. They don't stay on.[13]

Hot iron branding is going to be gone in a few years. They also do freeze branding which requires liquid nitrogen which is awkward to obtain in a lot of areas. It's less painful to the animal than hot iron branding, but not a whole lot. It turns the hair white. If you have a white colored calf, like a Charolais, it won't show. If you have a dark calf it works pretty well.

Scott: Researchers have spent a lot of money trying to develop micro chips and transmitters.

Woody: They have a lot of chips that work fine but most of them are limited to 26 inches or so, so you have to run them through a chute to read them. It's the coming technology, no doubt, but so far they don't work worth a darn in the field. If you are bouncing around in a four-wheeler or a horse and the calf is running around you are not going to get within 10 feet to identify the animal. Unless it's sick. If it's sick you already know it's sick. You can bring it in and do anything you want to with it. (Cattle tend to become very lethargic and docile when they are sick.)

Scott: Probably in 30 years you will be able to follow all of your calves from your living room. They will be tracked from a satellite and it'll keep track of the body temperatures, so you will know if they are sick or not.

Jane: The government wants trace-back, because if a person buys some beef in a store and gets sick they want to know who to blame it on. (Allowing all store sales to be traced back to the individual ranch.)

Woody: It's going to have to be an implant with a cow. They rub and scratch and fight each other.

. . .

Scott: What other jobs do the cowboys do?

Jane: John (Venable)[14] spent the whole year feeding hay up there in Corning this year (due to lack of rain). A lot of time and expense for the hay.

You have to maintain your wells and water-troughs and your ponds, dig them out every once in a while as they get silt in them. Fence repair. Barn and corral maintenance. Pulling calves during the calving season.

When we first started, and we didn't know much about calving, John had to pull about 25% of the calves. Towards the last John was only pulling 6-10 calves out of 600.[15]

Scott: One percent.

Woody: A lot of those you lose. They don't do very well because of the stress.

Jane: Every spring in our particular operation we had to haul these animals up to Oregon and then back to California in the fall. In the spring we'd take about 21 semi trucks up with cows and calves. We left the bulls down in Corning. In the fall there would be fewer trucks.

Woody: Because we sold them and somebody else hauled them.

. . .

Jane: Every year we kept about half of the heifer calves as replacements. And that would just about replace our herd, keep it about the same numbers.

Scott: Around 25% of the total the number. Okay.

Barnes Cattle Co. Annual Tickler[16]

January:
Order vaccines for branding time.
Decide which bulls for heifers (calving ease a primary criteria)
and which for cows. Send list to John Venable (manager).
Order calf ear tags, including "natural beef" tags when
applicable (later years).

February:
Order and Request forms for Age and Source tags (later
years).
Record number of cow-calves born and number of first and
second year heifer-calves born.
Check pasture for grass and pond water levels (manager does
on regular basis).

February-March:
Brand, ear-tag and vaccinate the calves. Manager prepares a
BBQ for the mostly volunteer crew. (Manager cooks the meat,
plus potluck.)

March-April:
Fill out "Pasture-to-Pasture" permits (California to Oregon)
Order vaccines for pre-shipping to Oregon
Remove bulls from cow pastures. (Manager takes care of.)

May:
Schedule an on-ranch video of the calves with cows and
heifers for June in Oregon.
Prepare info for the video (brief description of cows and
calves. I.e. brand, age of calves, etc.) and vaccines used.
Manager to vaccinate cows, calves, heifers and bulls, and
arrange for trucking all but the bulls to Oregon.

June:
Meet rep. from Shasta Livestock Auction Yard for the video of
the Oregon ranches.
Take cattle squeeze to Oregon.

July:
Order vaccines for August in Oregon.
Check the irrigation ditches and water distribution (manager
also does on a regular basis).

August:
Preg check the cows and heifers, and pelvic check the first-
year heifers.
Vaccinate cows, heifers and calves.
Keep a written record of pregnant and open cows and heifers,
and number of calves surviving to date.
Compare calving percentage and open cow and heifer rate to
national average.
Provide a BBQ for help.
Ship seller cows and heifers to the sale yard.

September:
Recover!!

October/November:
Order vaccines for November in California.
Ship retained cows and replacement heifers back to

California.
Record the first calf born.

*For several weeks in 1985 the Barnes hosted an exchange student
from Japan, Shiginobu Motishima. Here they are visiting the
Barnes herd of mostly Charolais cattle in Pine Hills. The ranch's
4-inch irrigation line from the "big lake" passes beneath Scott's
feet. It can run around 25 sprinkles at a time.*

*Spring of 1986, Woody shipping all the cattle from the ranch in
Pine Hills to the Chino auction, ending the Julian cattle business
for Manzanita Ranch.*

*Spring of 1995 in Fort Klamath, Oregon, Woody helps the
cowboys and veterinarian vaccinate the cattle. Not seen is the 4-
Wheeler ATV he's sitting on, which he used to gather the herd
from the swampy fields of this ranch bordering and nearly level
with Upper Klamath Lake.*

*Woody holding the vaccination gun on the ranch in Corning,
California at a roundup. To his right, in charge of castration, is
John Venable, their foreman. The little boy carries the "nut
bucket" and its dubious prize.*

*Woody cleaning out an irrigation canal on the ranch in Corning,
California.*

*In a barn in Corning, CA with John Venable and the all-
important "mousers." Woody is an irredeemable cat lover…
though Puzzle was the first feline he ever knowingly allowed in the
house, and the last cat they plan to own.*

August 22, 2007, Woody and Jane in front of a shed on Bill Nicholson's pasture which they rented in Fort Klamath, Oregon.

Barney and Woody looking over the irrigated pasture in Lakeview, Oregon, June 2012.

1. The Olivenhain colony is the eastern-most area of Encinitas. The name means "olive grove" in German. It was settled by German immigrants, among them Louie Denk, Bruno's father.

2. Glenn Mathis (Jane Barnes' father) was involved in forming the Moulton-Niguel Water District in 1960 and along with Louise (Moulton) Wineman (Jane's aunt) was on the first board of directors.

3. Woody and Jane purchased the ranches in Corning, California (6,000 acres) and Fort Klamath, Oregon (2,000 acres irrigated) in 1993. Later they added 2,000 acres in Henleyville. In 2006 they exchanged the Fort Klamath ranch for land in Lakeview. They could run approximately 600 head of cattle year round.

4. Ear tags are infused with an insecticide. Bloodsucking flies are a major pest for beef cattle, can reduce weight gain and transmit diseases.

5. Cattle prices reached $168 in November, 2014, the highest in history, a year before this interview took place. It had dropped to $126 in 2015 and $107 by 2016. As of publication the high price has not been matched.

6. The first recipient of the 13,298-acre Mexican land grant that became Rancho Guejito (pronounced wah-hee-toe) was Jose Maria Orozco in 1845. Various owners through the years purchased land until it comprised 21,400 acres. Benjamin Coates, Sr., bought the ranch in the early 1970s. The Los Angeles Times lists his business ventures as shipping, oil, and furniture production. Benjamin Coates, Sr. passed away in 2004, leaving the future of Rancho Guejito in question.

7. Juan Jose Warner (born John Trumbull Warner) received the 26,689-acre Rancho San Jose del Valle as a Mexican land grant in 1840. The Rancho was alternately called "Rancho Agua Caliente" for the hot springs located there or Warner's Rancho after the owner. Vista Irrigation District acquired the property (grown to 43,000 acres) in 1946, primarily because it included Lake Henshaw.

8. Theodore "Ted" Martin Jacobs, Dec 3, 1902-Oct 10, 1993, Woody's uncle.

9. Originally a land grant of 17,719-acres to Jose Juaquin Ortega and his son-in-law Edward Stokes in 1844, Rancho Santa Ysabel lies between Mesa Grande, Mount Palomar, and Julian.

10. BO-SE (selenium, vitamin E) is an emulsion of selenium-tocopherol for the prevention and treatment of white muscle disease (Selenium-Tocopherol Deficiency) syndrome.

11. Bangs is to prevent brucellosis, a bacteria that infected as much as 10% of American cattle before the development of the "Bangs" vaccine, caused pregnancy loss and reproductive failure.

12. Clostridal 8-Way prevents such bacterial diseases as blackleg and tetanus.

13. Manzanita Ranch used the brand "horseshoe F." Barnes Cattle Company used the brands "shining B" and "rocking JW."

14. John Venable managed Jane and Woody's ranch in Corning for many years. He now leases it for his own cattle.

15. To "pull" the calf means helping in the birthing process, generally by making sure the calf is oriented correctly and then, if necessary, putting a chain around its legs and pulling it out.

16. Written by Jane Barnes.

6

CONTOUR DITCHES AND HAY MAKING

This interview took place as Woody and Scott traveled around Manzanita Ranch in a 1985 Chevrolet S-10 pickup in July, 2012. They begin with a discussion of the contour ditches used in early years to direct water runoff, and then inspect some brush that had been cleared by a tractor operator and look at where the fence had been moved after a survey showed it to be off the property line.

Woody and Scott climb into the blue S-10 after talking with the bulldozer operator, Dave McCoy, who has a ranch down in Boulder Creek.

Woody: (Looking at some large trees over the hill, toward the lake from the tractor shed.) These two trees here on the end are the oldest apple trees on the ranch. I think these two were here when Grampy and the crew started in 1916. Just those two. Everything else has been replanted.

Before they irrigated they did what they called 'clean culti-vation.' They disked everything. Then you had to be very careful for erosion. A contour ditch ran about the edge of that oak tree, came through here, and dumped the water out in the sand patch there. These ditches used to flow a lot when I was a kid. One of my jobs was to walk along them and patch the gopher holes. There was one [ditch] that went through here and then it went over by our place. I can show you the other end of it when we get over there. (Driving to the bottom of the 'corn patch' on the east side.) These guys did a lot of contour work. It came right through here and went across here. There's still a culvert that goes under the road here, and there was a lake that I used to call 'Lake Bopo' which was a little pond right in there that stored water. Then the ditch went right on across from there over to where that dead oak tree is there, around the end of that. That was all to prevent erosion in the dirt.

The next contour ditch, see where the electric pole is now? There was no culvert there, they just ditched it.

Scott: We had a couple of years when these ditches ran quite a bit.

Woody: Oh yeah. You were here in '80. We still had a dirt road from the tractor shed down. The flood ate a four or five foot deep hole there. We put a hundred yards of rock in it to fill it up. When they tell you that it's now required that you have zero anything except pure water leave your place, a fool had to have thought of the rule.

Scott: I think Matt Feigel (the truck driver) brought over the pavement grindings, and we paved the road from the shed down.

·   ·   ·

Woody: Five hundred tons of pavement grindings from the shed down to the to the pump station at the lake. And then few years later we spread oil on them to glue them down, which was a good idea.

Scott: That really improved things. I was trying to guess what year that might have been.

Woody: That would be buried in my daily journals.

Scott: I'll have to go through all of those.

Woody: You'll go crazy if you do. Well, many of the major things I listed on the back pages with just a brief line. I didn't list who I was eating breakfast with or anything like that, but things like 'fixed the dam' are in the back and have the dates on them. They go back to 62. I think you'd find that my list of factual information is more factual than you'll get almost anywhere else about about Manzanita Ranch. There will be some mistakes, no doubt about it.

(Driving past the cider house to a flat area above the corrals.)

We had a ridge along here to catch any silt that came down, and we used a lot of that silt to fill holes with over the years.

When I was a kid on the Strick place there were two remnants of houses. One of them, you see that little piece of cement there? That was one of them.

. . .

Scott: About 20 feet on the west side of the fence, from the oak trees.

Woody: This is one of the lines that the Stricks had moved over 50 feet or so, when we got it surveyed. (They had moved the fence onto the Barnes' property.) Nobody really cared in those days very much. In most cases.

Scott: Except the people taking it. They obviously had a care or they wouldn't have done it. [laughs]

(Scott opens the gate that leads to the corral, the "big lake" and the pastures across the canyon. Woody drives through. They park and begin walking along the ridge on the south side of the lake.)

Woody: You can just chain this open.

The horse era really stopped around 1924. Grampy bought a tractor the day he got married—he was almost late for his wedding because he bought a tractor because he didn't want to use horses in farming. So that's roughly when the horse era ended here.[1]

They used to make hay in these little meadows across [Orinoco] creek, which is across the lake now. They hauled the hay over in wagons, primarily for their horses, because horses were their motor power.

I'll just show you where the road went. You also see where the erosion went.

Scott: We're walking parallel to the dam on the near side.

. . .

Woody: You see this draw here? That's where they used to bring the hay out. They used to take the hay up and store it in what we now call the 'poison room' [stacked rock building]. It went across here. There's a little jig in it, and went across there where the lake is now. That used to be what we called 'buttercup meadow' when I was a kid. It used to have buttercups in the spring. All of that happened before we built the dam in 1954.

Scott: This is where we now have pipes crossing with solar powered well water.

Woody: Exactly. We put that pipe in when the lake was low one year, when Chuck Martin was down in the cabin (the cabin by the little pond). That was a good move. Then Roman (Gutierrez) and Harry (Obeso) and I put the rest of it in, both ways, later.

Scott: Don't forget me.

Woody: And you. That's right, you were here all that time, weren't you?

Scott: Oh yeah. I did a lot of that work.

Woody: The government now wants us to measure how much water we use and how much we store and send the information in every three years. I did the initial one in '09. And I've done the measurement work in '10 and '11. We took a 50-gallon barrel and held the four inch pipe over it, and then figured the flow from that. That exaggerates the flow a little bit because when you put pressure and flow it through nozzles you get less. But it's a pretty safe amount.

This year I have a meter that we're going to put in this pipe down here. It was one of the things I learned at the Farm and Equipment show in Tulare.[2] It's in the garage waiting for us to install it. The meter is supposed to be accurate between one to two percent, which is pretty accurate. Before I had to write down each time I turned the pump on, like if I turned it on at 10 o'clock in the morning and turned it off at noon, I got two hours.

Scott: The time consumption for government paperwork is unbelievable. That's what people don't understand that don't have to deal with it themselves.

Woody: Well, and the government doesn't care because they want to control everything anyhow.

Scott: It doesn't cost them anything. I mean, it does—but not directly.

Woody: It gives them a job. What would a guy do sitting around if he wasn't sitting around collecting all this stuff, getting ready to write a rule that tells you you can't do it?

Scott: It's insidious.

. . .

Woody: Barney did some of the report work for me this year (on irrigation water usage). I had Pat Brown survey the whole lake and mark the slide (where the pump is set for irrigation) as to how many acre feet was in the lake when it was at a certain point, and we did the same thing at the little lake. There's no pump slide but we measured this lake, had them survey the whole thing. What's the guy that used to live down in Eagle Peak in a tent?

Scott: Danny Lynch.

Woody: He did a lot of the survey work. That's why we put a little more dirt on top, because we also had him measure the spillway to be sure it was big enough for floods: That drainage area can produce, under the worst of circumstances, 1,000 cubic feet a second of water. So we had to build spillways big enough to handle 1,000 cubic feet a second, in case it happened.

Scott: Wow. That is a lot of water.

Woody: That's a lot of water. I think there's seven and a half gallons to cubic feet.
　　(They stop to look at the lake.)
　　Lots of ducks here again.
　　I counted 85 here a couple of days ago. See how many of them are on shore? And they get in those bushes and you can't see them.

. . .

Scott: (Spotting) A great blue heron.

Woody: I'm trying to get the planning group to put a pro-ponds policy in our charter. I gave them a rough draft this month. Hopefully they'll pass it next month, before the people we have there retire.

Scott: I count 104 ducks. And I think I skipped a few. As we go around the corner...

Woody: You'll see more way up there.

Scott: Three...six...ten...eleven. They're getting a little small for my eye to pick out now, but eleven more, so 115 at least.

Woody: I'm not smart enough to know the different kinds of ducks we have. I can tell there are two or three kinds. If they got a green head I call them a mallard. But teal also have green heads.

Scott: These have orange bodies.

Woody: That one there I think is a mallard with the orange body and the white flecks. And the females are dull. So those are probably female mallards.

Scott: Do you have any pictures of all of them?

. . .

Woody: I got a picture or two. Not of all of them. Last year I counted 120 one time and I thought, jeez, did I really count 120? It doesn't seem real. And I counted them two or three days in a row and they were always right around 115, 120.

(Scott and Woody return to the pickup and drive across the dam to the far side.)

Woody: Oh good, he opened this up again. (The steep mountain trek had been overgrown by chaparral and manzanita bushes) Let's just walk up here a little ways.

Scott: Let's gun it! [laughs]

Woody: No, I don't think so. I don't want to walk up to the house. (They descend the truck and begin walking.) It had gotten to where you couldn't really ride anything but maybe a horse or walk up here so I had him push it open enough to be able to drive through.

Scott: That's the road going towards the clay pit on the side of the hill. Oh, this is really open. I've never seen it like this.

Woody: Well it was, but it was covered in dead manzanita, this whole slope.

. . .

Scott: You could put a house in here now. This is some hard d.g. (decomposed granite).

Woody: This is where they got some of the dirt for the dam—that's why there's no topsoil here.

And we, years ago, made a little ridge in here to divert this water into the dam. Because on dry years you need to get every bit of water you can. And so I had him redo this. He did fabulous work. This is much neater and cleaner than I ever dreamed it would be.

The fence here was 20 or so feet off this way. (On the ranch property from Hoskings.) Up there it was off 50 feet. So it's on the [property] line now. And you can walk to it. This was an impossible brush pile. I told him to leave one or two of the oak trees but to take everything else out. And he did a great job.

This is totally luxury. It doesn't make any economic sense, but it's certainly a pleasure for me to be able to walk—and he's done a good enough job that I can drive my tractor here.

Scott: Those big tractors are so powerful.

Woody: This is a D-6 here. Rick is a perfectionist kind of a guy.

Now this pile of dirt here, we piled this up in case we ever needed dirt to repair the dam.

(After looking around, Woody and Scott return to the pickup.)

Scott: Are we going to drive up to the next section?

· · ·

Woody: Drive on up.

This dam was probably built in 1954. About 1955 or 6 they were doing some work over on that side. I have a picture of this. When they were building it, Smitty, who was a relative of [Rick] McCoy's here, the fellow who is doing the work for us, was pushing dirt in, and the lake had come up some, and the tractor and the dirt started going in. He didn't swim. So he jumped off. And the tractor, a D-7, went underneath the water. They had to get divers from Temecula to come up to even be able to hook a cable on, it was so deep in the mud. Because it was pushing mud and when it, you know, kuthhhh, loose mud underwater. They towed it up, put it up on top of the dam, rebuilt it, and went back to work.

And then of course there was a fellow by the name of Woody who was working, you see where that center, second pole is? He was working there planting reeds. And he got a little too close to the edge, and his tractor came down and turned one way, then rolled another way, and then went under water. Fortunately I had a seatbelt on. I was then underwater with one breath of air, trying to undo a seat belt. And incidentally, if you ever need to know, that seat belt undoes on the left side, not the right side. [laughs] Anyhow, I made it with nothing but a bruise. Went to a couple of parties that day.

Scott: That's amazing. That was that Mahindra loader that we pulled out, rebuilt, and are still using.

Woody: Yup. Robert Redding rebuilt it for us. And we're still using it. Roman Gutierrez and Robert pulled it out. Brought two backhoes over. We'd pull it six inches, and then the other backhoe would move back a little bit and pull it six inches. And then the other one would move it. We see-sawed it up over the hill and rebuilt it.

You'll notice here how steep that canyon is (below the dam). The boom went down the drain in 1980 and we didn't replace it thinking that there was not going to be erosion. (The "boom" was a line of wood electric poles chained together across lake in front of the earthen dam to reduce wind erosion.) But you can see how the wave erosion has been doing damage. A fellow may have to dump block or something in there. But we're trying to plant more of these reeds, and I hope to get some more planted this year because I think they will stop the erosion.

Scott: Well, carry them down by hand or something.

Woody: We're going to put them on a pickup and throw them off the pickup and then place them by hand. Because if you throw them when there's a little west wind they'll carry pretty far. You put them right in the mud out in the water.

And see, there's a very big pile growing right there (in a finger of the lake). They're very close to the dam but you can't get to them because it's too wet.

Scott: I got stuck out there with the tractor. The slope was about a two percent grade, but with that mud... [laughs]

Woody: It's just like grease.

(They begin drive to the "hay fields" which would have overlooked "buttercup meadow.")

Bret (Hutchinson) cut a tree up that was right in the road. He needed some wood. There's a culvert that goes under here and it usually runs quite a bit. It needs a new culvert—it isn't going to get one this year.

Have you seen our solar panels?

Scott: No.

Woody: Okay. This is going to get a little bumpy because I have to step on the gas.

You can see here how far the fence moved this way with the survey. We had the fence way over on the other people's side. This is where it belongs now. The Hosking's guy said, "Well how much did we lose?" Rick told him very correctly, "You don't lose anything, you don't gain anything, you just put the fence where it belongs." And that's true. Probably no net gain for either of us. It's just that the fence is where it belongs.

Scott: Here's the first well. (In the pasture across the lake, the west end.)

Woody: This is the well that's actually hooked up. This one, last year, artesianed—ran over—for about a month.

The electricity comes from those panels over there. Barney was here and helped me do that. We had done the primitive stuff but he helped get the wires in and get them hooked up.

(Walking further.) This is where the electricity comes from.

Scott: Just three solar panels.

Woody: Yeah. And it pumps the water clear over at the house quite nicely. The reason we put them here was because a) it didn't show and b) it's on a rock pile not wasting any good pasture grass.

I ought to come over and spray those weeds (thistles) right now.

Scott: That probably pumps less than a gallon a minute.

Woody: Two gallons a minute over at the house.

Scott: Wow. That's pretty good.

Woody: It pumps it with quite a bit of pressure. One of the things that we were able to find and learn about was that they make a pump that will take DC current directly without putting in an AC converter. So that's pretty efficient. And Grundfos makes the pump.

(Looking in the distance.) That's the other well that we don't have hooked up. The reason that we hooked this one up was that it looked like it flowed more water to begin with, and was right at the top.

I was skeptical when the guy told me how this would work. We have $2,500 in panels and $2,500 in pump and a couple thousand in hooking it up. So it's expensive but it doesn't cost you anything basically after you do this until the pump wears out or the panels wear out. We're hoping that'll be a long time.

These were the hay fields. After we built the dam we used to have irrigated pasture here for the cows in the summer. We fenced seven fields so we could move the cattle into one and the other six could grow. It was a pretty efficient deal. But the electricity got to be more expensive than the pasture was worth. So we quit.

You'll notice that all this fencing is new, and that they picked up all the wire, took up all the old rotten posts. Rick did a great job.

We split the cost with the Genesee Properties that owns the Hoskings. Genesee Properties is owned by the Blue Brothers[3]. Another one of their minor properties is General Atomics[4].

Scott: So this is just a line item on their spreadsheet.

Franklin (Woody's dad) cleans one of the erosion control ditches on the farm in Pine Hills, 1929.

"Lake Bopo" into which drained several contour ditches to control erosion and help recharge the water table. Woody's parents Alice (foreground) and Franklin in 1929.

*Mary Alice (Jo) rows between pine and oak trees they didn't have
time to clear when the newly constructed "big lake" filled faster
than expected, 1954. The boat was discarded at Lake Henshaw.
Woody and Red Brown salvaged and rebuilt it.*

Woody and Scott clean the second "overflow" spillway of the big lake to try to save the dam in the flood of 1980. The effort was successful and the dam survived, though many dams in Julian washed out.

Fourteen inches of rain in a week—and then seven inches of rain overnight—washed out the road from the Cider House to the big lake in 1980. It required 500 yards of material to fill in the holes in the road. Water filled up both spillways and ran over much of the dam. Since then the spillways have been deepened and improved and the top of the dam has been raised. Julian weather is unpredictable and often characterized by drought...with the occasional flood.

Full again, Woody by the primary big lake spillway in 1993.

Woody and Barney removing the irrigation pump from the big lake for winter, Dec 1996. Farming would not be possible on Manzanita Ranch without irrigation water from the lake.

---

1. Franklin Lockwood Barnes and Alice Genevieve Jacobs married on December 25, 1924.
2. Now called the World Ag Expo, the annual Central Valley agricultural exhibition (every second Tuesday in February since 1968) is the world's largest.
3. Linden and Neil Blue
4. The pristine Hoskings ranch is 1,416 acres adjacent and north of Manzanita Ranch farm. The land is being developed into 40 luxury homes by Genesee Properties Inc., a company owned by Linden Blue. Linden and his brother James Neal Blue own General Atomics, a defense contractor and one of the largest employers in San Diego County.

7

LILACS, WEBSTERS, AND WELLS

This section offers a nice overview of the historic community that developed along Pine Hills and Van Duesen Road. The interview took place while Woody and Scott were driving from Woody's home on Manzanita Ranch, down the driveway to turn north on Pine Hills Road, and later headed east up Van Duesen Road to its end.

(Woody and Scott climb into a blue, 1985 Chevrolet S-10 near the house. Through the dirty windshield they can see over a hundred pots—cedar trees mostly, and also rare local plants such as native tiger lilies—that have been potted over the years but never planted on the ranch. There is also a mound of dark earth as high as the pickup roof.)

Scott: Down here by the garage, you had salvaged some, were they tiger lilies from someone's ranch?

.   .   .

Woody: Bonnie Osuna, who has had several last names, dug a couple of those up off of the Indian reservation for us, native tiger lilies. Bonnie is a wonderful person, and I don't know where she got them or how she got them, but they came from the reservation. They also grow on Volcan and over at Cuyamaca.

Scott: Were you going to plant those out or...

Woody: I was going to, but I never have. I've got them in containers.

Scott: They seem to be surviving. As long as we keep that fence up, they'll probably be okay. Maybe drop a little fertilizer once a year.

Woody: We do and water them in summer. This is dirt that we brought down from Webster's. I have a couple hundred lilac being produced by Knight Hollow Nursery in Wisconsin: Deb McCown. They are all the Alice Franklin[1] dark purple ones. They were all tissue cultured from the wood here.
    Deb McCown's brother (I think, unless it's her sister) has a place down on Eagle Peak Road.

Scott: You said you were going to send Alice Franklin lilac to different gardens around to make sure they stay alive?

Woody: That's right. And I've got them registered with the International Lilac Society. I'm still dealing with them. We did it once before and it didn't pass... The guy was an irritant. He's become much more mellow in his old age.

As you know I try to do too many things.

Scott: For lilacs we have the Alice Franklin, the dark purple. Wasn't there another one?

Woody: I have two or three others that I think might be worth developing. But I don't really like the concept of... Historically people have named everything that they saw. We had a fellow by the name of Joel Margaretten, a dentist who had property up there in the Lancaster area. He named every seedling that he planted, five hundred or so lilacs. I went up and looked at them: there weren't two or three that were any good at all. People want to become famous or leave a mark and become a great breeder. I think you should develop them for 15 or 20 years to see what they do. Then plant a few in other climates, which we have done with the Alice Franklin.

The ones I want to do next is what they call a somatic mutation. They're not really a seed cross, they are part of the tissue that just changed. That's where all the Red Delicious (apples) have come from. You're never sure until you've had it a little while if it's stable or if it's going to go back to the original. That's a hazard we'll have to take someday.

Scott: The somatic mutation you're talking about is the Russian variety. It turned lavender-blue on us. Some of those are very striking. (The original, non-mutated Krasavitsa Moskvy is described in catalogs as "lavender-rose" ranking high in both white and pink.)

·   ·   ·

Woody: The Russians have done, in the last 50, 60 years, much of the best lilac breeding. And prior to that it was done, well, lots of places. Originally it was the French, the Lemoine family. That's why the Lilac Society's meeting is in France this year.[2]

(Woody and Scott begin driving. Just in front of the house they pause to examine a lilac grove.)

If you look over in here at least half of these varieties were Lemoines. The white one was Madame LeMoine, the one that's down by the road.

You see the bright green bush? The one just to the right of that is Victor Lemoine, named after the breeder himself.

Scott: Five rows from the shed end.

Woody: And then, this side of the green one, there are two rows. And that's President Grevy.

Scott: That's row seven and eight from the shed.

Woody: I counted them from the house originally, rather than from the shed. So when you look at the key to all of those rows...

The first lilacs were a wedding present to the folks from the hotel in Julian.[3] The negative thing we've had there is the deer have decided they like lilac. They knocked that fence to smithereens in about two weeks.

Scott: You're going to have to allow hunting or something.

·   ·   ·

Woody: Well, now that you mentioned it... Enough said.

Scott: I love the deer and I love looking at them, but there is an overpopulation, no question about it.

Woody: Way overpopulated.
(Pointing to the lilacs in front of the house.) When we were little, this was all an old apple orchard, a lot of big trees like this, and then they took those out. In 1962 they planted that bunch of lilac. We used to raise our corn and pumpkins between the lilacs. We've got some pictures of that.
We raised corn and pumpkins and gourds and stuff [downhill from there], and then we planted it with lilacs, and that has not been terribly successful.

Scott: Right. I helped plant those, and a year or two later there was a flood that killed many of them. The middle of that patch remained muddy for weeks on end.

(Driving farther, Woody pauses in front of his parent's house. A large grassy patch leads to a hill covered in both old and recently planted peonies.)

Woody: There were a few great big apple trees right in here. This otherwise was all tulips -

Scott: On the green patch, where we park cars during parties and such?

· · ·

Woody: Where the green is was all tulips, and that hill was just apples where we have peonies now. These lilacs here were a gift from the Dyars. When they sold their ranch to Cuyamaca State Park they didn't know that Grampy wanted to buy it, and they were good friends. I think the Dyars were short of money.[4] As a consolation prize in a sense they went up and got a bunch of lilacs from Hulda Klager in Washington State. These were some of the original Hulda Klager hybrids. That was put in in the '40s.

(Woody points in the opposite direction, towards the pool.)
The oldest big patch of lilac is right up there on that hill.

Scott: Between the pool and the house?

Woody: Yeah. They were some of the original ones that came from the hotel as wedding presents to the folks in the '20s—as you walk up to the pool you walk between them. This other stuff was done in the '20s.

[Driving another 100 feet or so, they pause to look toward "peach tree hill." Woody describes the closest patch of lilac, directly below his parents' house.]

This is one of the later patches that we put in. This was all pears, and previous to that it had been prunes and wheat and cherries and walnuts, all of which were marginally successful to complete failures.

Scott: Nothing lasts forever. That's one lesson of farming.

Woody: Well, you don't know until you plant something whether it's going to be successful or not. We had quite a few grape vines in that area between where the road turns there and the brush. Down this way was a narrow grape thing that we kept after we took the grapes out when I was a kid and planted peaches elsewhere, but not here. They were old seedy type grapes. You couldn't give them away now. They had good taste.

Scott: My favorite were the Concord.

Woody: The Concords are back over in front of the old shack house. I understand they have some seedless Concords now, but I don't know enough about them to know which ones would taste good.

(Woody drives along the driveway and stops about halfway to Pine Hills Road.)

One of the original roads on the ranch went right through here and came out by the peach trees. (By the culvert under current driveway, through brush and towards peach orchard.)

Scott: Um hum, okay.

Woody: Our front lake was the first dam in the Julian area, almost. There were one or two small ones around. It tells you how different things were: they took and dug a trench, which they called a keyway, from keeping the water from seeping too much across the bottom. And they hauled clay down in a pickup and filled the trench.

Scott: From the peach tree hill?

. . .

Woody: Yeah, most of it came from there. The dam was designed by the Soil Conservation Service. The first time it heavy-rained it washed out. So then Dad re-engineered it and put it together. But when it washed out you could look down and in the bottom and see the clay core where they had planted it. That was in 1938.

(Stopping where the driveway meets Pine Hills Road.)

This is Hathaway's place. Hathaways have owned it since 1929. They got it from a lady before. Stewart Hathaway came out here in 1930.

They used to call the Oak Ridge Stock Farm. Stewart was an interesting guy with a tobacco background. He actually raised tobacco there one year, a little patch. The tobacco used to hang in the barn. It obviously wasn't a success. And he had a little greenhouse. He was interested in that kind of stuff.

He called it the "Stock Farm" not because of the cattle stock but because he traded some of his tobacco stock for the ranch.

Woody's First Job

(Woody turns onto Pine Hills Road and heads toward Julian.)

This is where the road I pointed out at the other end came out. (The 'original road' went from below the ranch houses, near the front pond, up through peach tree hill, to exit near Deer Lake Park Road.) There was a cattle guard with railroad rails there (where the 'original road' met Pine Hills Road) when I was a kid. They took the rails out and they are down at the old cider house where you back in the trucks; where the building fell down (Packing House).

That tells you how many years ago that was. It also tells you how amazing it is that you remember some things from when you were just a little...

Oh shoot, I went right by the thing that I was going to show you. I have to turn around.

(Woody drives down about 1/4 mile and pulls a U-turn.)

Scott: Fieldstone Farm.

Woody: That's where I got my first job. Fieldstone Farm was owned by a family by the name of Ziesmer. Raymond Ziesmer was an attorney in Los Angeles. I took care of his lawn, his dog, two horses, numerous pigeons, numerous laying chickens, Bantam (small) chickens, his flower garden, and a vegetable garden—and got paid 50 cents a week.

At that time it was called Apple Tree Farm.

(Woody returns to Deer Lake Park Road, where he pulls a U-turn and parks with half the pickup sticking out on Pine Hills Road.)

Tolerable.

Okay, this is an interesting thing right here that I wanted to show you because almost nobody knows anything about it. But you see that bunch of rocks in kind of a circle right there? (South of 3415 Pine Hills Road on the east side of the road.) That was a charcoal pit where they made charcoal.

Scott: About 200 yards North of the Deer Lake Park Road exit.

Woody: They made charcoal here. I'm pretty sure it was used in the mines but this had fallen in before I was born. You can see there's kind of an oval with the rocks around it?

. . .

Scott: Oh yeah. Okay.

Woody: That was a pit. The way they made charcoal is that they put the wood in, set it on fire, then when it got to a certain thing they shut the oxygen off.

Scott: By pouring dirt or by—?

Woody: Here they did dirt and then they poured a little water on it. I think the reason they did it here is that there was a place where they could get some water in the wet time of year. But I think they did it mostly with dirt. Just suffocated it.

That's one of the few charcoal pits that I know of around.

Scott: Do you have any idea what they actually used charcoal for?

Woody: Yes. It was to fuel the boilers at the mines. They made steam, and they ran pipes down and had steam engines down inside the thing to pump the water out of the mines.

Scott: Oh, so on the outside there were boilers and then the pipes ran the steam, and the steam ran—

Woody: That's my understanding. But they may have also used it in some of the hammer mills to break the ore down.

. . .

Scott: Steam powered engines.

Woody: I have never known for sure, but they didn't have electricity, and they pumped water out. That would have been a logical way to do it. Or they could have generated electricity and run electricity down there using the same charcoal.

Scott: Right.

Woody: They didn't have electricity up here till around the 1920s other than your own power plants.

Scott: That makes total sense. That information really helps clarify the story.

Woody: Most people don't even know there's a charcoal pit over there.

(Looking at the Manzanita Ranch across the road.)

This is the fence that was put on the property line (between the ranch and Hoskings' property). Rick Moretti did a great job. We had him use iron brace posts on our end of it.

Now this field here, Kenneth Wellington used to raise corn in.

Scott: That's the Hoskings's field.

. . .

Woody: That used to be Jackie Elder's house here (3415 Pine Hills Road), and there were stairs that came down right there. They used to stop the bus on this corner. The stairs came down right here and he went across Pine Hills Road here to his fields. The house was built by Kenneth Wellington. He used to raise corn in that meadow. That was before I was born. Grampy told me all about that.

Van Duesen Road Development

(Driving further, Woody pauses near the entrance to Van Duesen Road.)

You can still see a row of trees that went in right through there. (Across from Van Duesen Road on Hoskings.) That was all farmed ground. When they tell you that this has never been farmed and it's all virgin country, that's not really true.

(Driving up Van Duesen Road and veering right.) Grampy and Uncle Ted bought this property from Ed Fletcher, the back part here. We owned the Timm's part,[5] this was Ziesmer's over here. They subdivided it when I was just a little kid. I was old enough so I walked along the road when they dragged it with brush; I threw the rocks off to the side before they sprayed oil on it.

Scott: It was obviously a dirt road.

Woody: Just a dirt road originally. And then they sprayed oil on it and it was an oiled road. The intent of Ted and Dad was to sell pieces 40 acres and larger. Which they did. This first 40 acres turned out to be 80 because it belonged to an attorney from Los Angeles whose name was Howard Reynolds.

Howard had a wife whose name was Silence. And if there was ever a misnomer—because she never was silent.

Scott: I've never heard of anyone named Silence.

Woody: That's why I brought it up. I thought it was kind of funny.
(Woody drove up Van Duesen, bore right.)
Grampy planted all peaches on the left side of the road.

Scott: This is where Van Duesen Road turned right at the fork.

Woody: Howard Reynolds had all this put into apples. There were dams put in on the creek over there. I think there were two on Howard's place and one on Ziesmer's place.

This house was built by Reynolds on your right. You can see the remnants of the apples. They came clear up to the edge of this field. One of the Reynolds family still owns four or five acres here. Then, approximately here was owned by Van Duesen. We sold it to him. They built this nice dam and it washed out and they never repaired it. They made it too narrow, and too small a spillway. Then there's a couple more dams up in here. Used to be a little spring up in there.

Okay, we're about up to where Webster's starts at the top of this hill. Webster's is kind of a little rectangular piece, part of what was Webster's place. We own 30 acres right in here.

(Looking at a small, empty pond bordering the road.) This is probably the worst pond we own. It leaks.

The Webster place that today is all oak trees and brush was a great pear orchard. There's hardly anything left. We'll have to tackle that someday. Tells you what happens when you don't take care of something.

Scott: We're bringing hay for Mom's horses. (Unloading a bale of hay for the horses.)

Woody: The upper end of this fence line is an interesting story in itself. When we first sold it we sold it to a fellow named Holly. And the fence was off (the property line) 15 feet or so. We had an agreement that he could just leave it. We didn't bother to move the fence. Well, Holly sold to another guy and we didn't bother to move the fence. Then the other guy got ready to sell. And he said that he owned the property (within the fence). We worked out an agreement: we let him have the 15 feet or so, and in exchange we got this little triangle here which guarantees us that we could fix the lake and have better access to the property. Which was a crappy deal in some ways but is better than no deal—which is probably what you would have had if you had tried to go to court or anything.

That's why I was such an adamant lunatic about "This fence is going to be on the [property] line!" on our home piece.

Scott: Right. So this right here is not part of the triangle.

Woody: This is part of what we don't own. A fellow by the name of Lewis owns it. He's the father of the guy who owns our packing house (formerly Manzanita Ranch store in Wynola, now called Julian Station.)

They have had a terrible time down there. They decided they were going to put a restaurant or 'coffee bar' where our snack bar was (for employees) where we had places to sit down while we were working. Then of course they had to get a health permit. To do that you have to get your water tested. Well, the water didn't pass the test. So they drilled another well.

He (Albert Lewis) had a well drilled and built a pond right next to the concrete house where Bill Cain lived. His mother, or I think it's her [Mrs. Lewis'] mother, lived in the house where Louise Andermatt used to live, the really old house. Anyhow, somehow he had a horse trough and he didn't have any back flow prevention. So the pump stopped and—this is somewhat speculative—but it siphoned all of the manure-y water from the horse trough into his well. Well then, of course, it wouldn't pass the health test.

Albert Lewis doesn't really believe in bleaching. He thought you could get away without it. And so in the long run he had to drill a second new well.

The people who rented the coffee stand... (Shaking his head in sympathy.) It was open for about two or three weeks, and it was closed for five months.

I just talked to the health inspector. It passed this week.

Scott: Well, I'm glad it passed.

Woody: They had to replace all of the underground pipes. It was a nightmare. Basically they were trying to chintz on how you got it done—and then wouldn't admit that you needed to put bleach in. He [Mr. Lewis] thought bleach would poison the water. Of course it poisons it! That's why it kills bacteria. It's not rocket science.

(Woody and Scott get in the pickup again after unloading the hay for Jane's two horses and drive further up Van Duesen Road.)

That piece (of property), from there on up Van Duesen Road was 80 acres. It belonged to Jackson. He sold to Jackson when we sold this other. Holly here, Jackson there.

Scott: We're at the four-way intersection past Websters, near the end of the road.

Woody: Richmond Jackson grew up across the street from Grampy on Fourth and Upas in San Diego. They were childhood buddies. Richmond wanted this piece, and Richmond is also the fellow who persuaded Grampy to sell him that little place where our cabin is on the home place (on Manzanita Ranch in Pine Hills). When Richmond got ready to sell the cabin, they had an agreement he'd offer it back to our family. We almost blew it because he wanted seven thousand for it and we thought that was too much. He was just ready to go to a Realtor and sell it. It would have sold in a minute! But anyhow, we managed to come up with seven thousand; Mom (Jane) and I did. It's probably one of our better investments. The house was nothing at the time. We put another $50,000 into building, fixing up the house and drilling a new well. It wasn't a gift.

How are we doing for time?

Scott: As long as you want.

Woody: Well, let's go look at the tractor work. (Two bulldozers were removing trees and brush that had died on Manzanita Ranch during the Cedar Fire of 2003.) I'll take this pickup to town this afternoon to buy fertilizer because it's supposed to rain this weekend. I want to Nabor (Obeso) to come tomorrow as well as Heriberto (Obeso) to put out fertilizer.

Scott: Are you pronouncing Heriberto's name correctly? That's pretty good. [laughs] For the first 35 years it was Herbierto.

Woody: Everybody calls him Harry. Everybody except me.

Scott: Harry's good too.

(Returning by the Fieldstone Farm and Orinoco Creek corner a semi cuts into Woody's lane.)

Woody: I don't think I want to get in front of him.

Scott: He shouldn't be cutting the corner in that big-rig.

Woody: I put reflectors on these things (fence posts on Hoskings property) because people kept driving through the fence. You'll see on our corner of Pine Hills Road I put some on too.

Scott: I remember Barney and I were at the bus stop and somebody drove straight through the intersection and flipped their car. A girl from high school. If I think hard enough I can remember who it was. (Thea Johnston and a friend.) I just kind of froze and waited for the bus as a couple people crawled out of the windows of the upside down car all covered in blood. I was like, 'Oops, I'll just stand here and wait for the bus.' [laughs]

(Woody turns back into the ranch driveway.)

Woody: That well right by the gate is our deepest well on the ranch. I believe it's 700 feet. It had very little water in it. We'd shot a well (with dynamite) in Wynola and it went from five gallons to fifty gallons a minute. So we shot this, and somewhere I have photos of the water fountain that came out of that sucker when the explosion went off. It was quite sensational.

Scott: I was there, actually.

Woody: Do you remember that?

Scott: Yeah, I do. Grammy (Alice Barnes, Woody's mom) was here. And who was the guy—?

Woody: Carter was his name; he was the well driller. He had the dynamite.[6]

Scott: He asked me if I would eat some dynamite and I was very dubious. I asked if he'd ever eaten it and he said "No." But he said he had convinced lots of people to try it.
    The explosion increased the water a little as I recall.

. . .

Woody: Not much. Hardly any. But it's been a very good well. I've been using that one to keep the pool full all summer.

Scott: So a steady five gallons a minute.

Woody: Yeah. Probably something like that. We put a pipeline from there all the way to the pool separate from all our other pipelines. The mistake I made was I only used one inch pipe. I should have used inch and a half, but I didn't. Which means that even at five gallons a minute there's some line friction.

Alice and Pedro Mireles ready to haul lilacs, April 1957. Given the length of the stems, these may have been destined for display in Marstons Department Store. The Barnes were the exclusive supplier for the downtown San Diego store.

Woody (left) and his father Franklin in 1979, Woody carrying bunches of the Alice-Franklin variety that the family developed and named.

Woody auctioning lilac plants as a fundraiser for the International Lilac Society at Descanso Gardens, 2002. Five years later, Scott and Grace (Agustin) Barnes married in the same garden.

*Picking in the rain in 2004, for number of bunches the biggest
season ever. Scott Barnes (left), Jo Geary, Jim Geary, Woody.
The picking "season" lasts three-four weeks tops—everything has
to be harvested and sold in that time frame. If a freeze or hard
east wind hits it can ruin fifty percent of the crop. Hot days
shorten the season considerably, making it impossible to pick the
delicate flowers before they wilt. Not an easy business.*

Jane used this 2007 photo to paint a watercolor portrait.

---

1. A dark purple lilac developed and propagated by Woody and his parents, Alice and Franklin Barnes.

From the "International Register and Checklist of Cultivar Names in the Genus Syringa."

'Alice Franklin', S. vulgaris

Barnes, F.L. & A.G., ca 1928; S VII

{seedling of unknown parentage}

Wister & Oppe, Arnoldia 31(3):121 [1971]

Named for Alice and Franklin Barnes, parents of Franklin Lockwood ("Woody")

Barnes, Jr.

cultivar name registered 1970; name established and accepted.

2. Victor Lemoine (1823-1911) was a well-known, French horticulturalist and plant breeder. Lilacs were his most famous accomplishments, especially the beautiful "double-flowered" breeds with flowers within flowers. This interview was done in 2012. The International Lilac Society held its yearly convention at the botanical garden of Nancy, France (Jardin Botanique du Montet à Villers-les-Nancy) in 2012.

3. The Julian Hotel. Alice Barnes (Woody's mother) grew up in The Julian Hotel from the age of 13 through high school. For a thourough discussion see *Alice Barnes—Gold Mines and Apple Pie*, pp91-101.

4. Near the present-day Cuyamaca Rancho State Park visitor center, Ralph Dyar built his house in 1923 partially from lumber salvaged from the Stonewall Mine. The house burned in the Cedar Fire of 1983; its remains can still be visited.

5. 'Timms' orchard is north of Van Duesan Road and east of Pine Hills Road.

6. Gorden P. Carter

8

COLLEGE YEARS

Scott: How did you end up at Pomona College?

Woody: Well, a variety of reasons. One of them is my Aunt Helen, Grammy Barnes' sister Helen Hunt, had gone there and had been Phi Beta Kappa.[1] Uncle Ray (Jacobs) went there for one year and then went into the army in World War I. Tot Cumming and Mary Starr had both gone there, and they were very good friends of Grammy, particularly Tot Cumming. Then the Marston family had been philanthropists there, Grampy Barnes' friends were of the Marston family from way back. I can talk more about that later.

I actually applied late; I didn't realize that February or March was late to apply to a school. And so I got accepted the day of graduation from high school, which was very exciting.

I forgot to mention that our Spanish teacher, Mrs. Patton, always took the Spanish to Padua Hills (theater), and she also had graduated from Pomona College. So she always took the class by Pomona College on the way to Padua Hills or on the way home, one or the other, in the bus. So I had a variety of people who kind-of pointed to Pomona College. I had thought about applying for Stanford but didn't do it. A couple of my cousins had gone there and been very successful.

Also, I looked at the Pomona College book and they had a pre-agricultural program. I was so dumb that I thought every college had an agricultural program at the time. So I went there thinking that I was going to major in agriculture. Well, when I got there "pre-agriculture" was actually a botany program. That turned out to be a very pleasant error on my part in that I soon was taking botany from a fellow by the name of Doctor Lyman Benson who was a well-known taxonomist. It was very interesting, and I made a lot of friends in the botany department, many of which I still have after all these years.[2]

When you first go to college you always end up with a variety of classes and I don't remember all the classes, but I can remember English. Fortunately we were assigned roommates. My request for a roommate was somebody who didn't smoke. That was the only request I had because I didn't really know anybody except Martin Dickinson, slightly, who was actually going to go there. I'd met a few people. Grammy Barnes had a pre-Pomona party for the people from San Diego County who'd been accepted, and two or three I'd run into in student government and other things, but I didn't know them well.

I ended up with Bruce Carlson as an assigned roommate, who was a wonderful person. He had won from Lockheed a four-year scholarship, room, board and tuition. Very few people ever get a four-year scholarship when you're still in high school. He was a physics major at the time.

We lived in what was called the "Vet Units." They were some old ramshackle buildings that had been built during World War II as a temporary place for military people to live while World War II was going on. A number of soldiers lived in them. They were going to tear them down. Also, they were not damageable no matter what happened, because at the middle of the year they tore them down and we moved into what was then a new building, Walker Hall.

But Bruce was a Godsend in that I was very poor in writing essays. You had to write a 500-word essay pretty near every week. That was a lot for me, coming from a school where we practically never wrote essays.

My English teacher was a fellow by the name of Fussell.[3] I went to ask him for help on how to do better, and one of the few people I ever ran into in college or anywhere who was not very helpful. He was sitting there in the front of the room at his desk, and I was sitting there in kind of a plaintive mood asking what I could do better. He said, "What do your parents do?" I said, "My parents are farmers." And he said, "Well, all farmers are dumb." That was the end of the interview. People have said, "No, it couldn't possibly have been." But it was. I sat there for a minute, and then I decided, 'Well, that was the end of the story; I'd better go on.'

Fortunately, Bruce became my savior. I would write an essay, and he would grade it. Then he would give it back to me to rewrite it. I would rewrite it, and he would grade it again. Usually by about the third time it was something he felt was acceptable to turn in. He never wrote anything, he just graded it and said what I was doing wrong. Made me write it over again.

Without Bruce's help I would have been in very deep trouble. At Christmas time I came home and I think I was getting an F in English, and a C in almost everything else. So I spent the entire Christmas vacation studying and working, and ended up getting good-enough grades.

At that time we had what was known as the "Universal Draft." Every male when he reached the age of such-and-such had to register for the draft. Then you could apply, if you were going to college, for a deferment, which meant that you could go to college without going into the military first. So there was a tremendous incentive to do well. Anyhow, every year the percentage went up but every year I managed to make it, so that was sort of the story of my entrance to Pomona.

In Pomona I took all kinds of classes, but most of my classes were botany. Many of my long-term friends were botanists, either one or two years older or younger than I was or in the same class. I could go on for days about the various field trips we took. The other major professor (besides Doctor Lyman Benson) was Doctor Ed (Edwin) Phillips. Doctor Phillips is still alive at the age of 97 and still goes to our annual botany reunion. "Botany bashes" we call them, where various botany majors over the years get together for a fun and botanizing weekend. This last year it was in the Santa Cruz Mountains in Big Basin Redwoods State Park. We've even had it a couple of times in Julian. We've gone to Death Valley and a variety of places, and I've missed some of them, unfortunately. It's always a lot of fun and you have a lot of reminisces about various things.

Field trips that we took while we were in college included Charleston Peak near Las Vegas, Ajo National Monument,[4] near the Mexican border in Arizona, the San Francisco Peaks in Arizona, Sequoia National Park and Greenville area in California, the Redwoods National and State Parks in California, and a number of others. So we got to see a great deal of the western vegetation over the years while we were in school.

Doctor Phillips was a graduate from the University of Michigan. He went to the (University of Michigan) biological station to teach ecology every summer, and one summer he invited me to go along and be his assistant. It was an interesting year, being an assistant in an entirely new floristic area. The next year, that was my junior year, and my senior year, I got invited to run the biological station bookstore because of some friends I had made back there by the name of Jim and Marilyn Wilson. Marilyn was involved with the administration of the biological station. So then after that I ended up going to graduate school at the University of Michigan and eventually got a Master's there.

I was very fortunate—doubly fortunate—while I was there in that I was assigned to a fellow by the name of Bill Benninghoff. Benninghoff was a glacial paleontologist, studying fossil columns, particularly around cold-climate areas. He'd worked for the geological survey[5] and had come to Michigan as a professor. I was his assistant, which was great. He was a wonderful man, extraordinarily brilliant. You could not find a subject that if you brought it up, he didn't know everything about.

Michigan had a very large library. I remember one incident when I mentioned a subject, and I don't remember the exact subject. "Oh," he said, "in this shelf in the library…" he described the shelf, "…is a book, and it's just exactly what you need." Which really impressed me in a library of three million volumes.

Then one night, because at Michigan, like a lot of places, the students really weren't daytime-only students. We worked nights too. I was sitting in the office, and the natural science building was kind of a triangle and our building looked into the center of the triangle. And a fellow came over, a professor I'd had in Forest Pathology, whose name was Dow Baxter, and he invited me to go to Alaska and be an assistant for him in Alaska.

Scott: He just happened to see you there?

Woody: No. I'd taken his class before. I was sitting there one night and he came over and invited me—I didn't think too much about it. But the next morning I mentioned it to Benninghoff, and he said, "He means it. Every year he takes somebody to Alaska."

So I got to go to Alaska. Doctor Baxter, a wonderful man, took me to all kinds of places in Alaska for two summers (in 1947 and 1948). I got no pay. He always apologized because —he paid all of this stuff out of his own salary, he didn't have a big grant from the government or anything—and he always said, "We can't afford to have anything but salmon and halibut." Two things which I love!

The first year I left my car at one of my botany friend's parent's house. Phyllis Dobbins, whose later name was Bravender. Her father was a vice president of Boeing. They lived out near the airport so I left my car there. And my suitcase went to Denver instead of Alaska. Well, we were traveling all the time in Alaska, there was no address for it in the suitcase, so the airline called the Bravenders and told them that my suitcase would be sitting in Denver until I got back.

So I was in Alaska for 30 days with just the clothes I had on, which was kind of an adventure in itself. And while maybe I could have bought something, I didn't. I found that you could wash things and they'd get halfway dry. Then you'd wear them until they got dry the next day. If we were lucky we were in a motel which had a steam pipe or something that would help dry them at night. We survived that way.

We started in Juno and worked around Mendenhall glacier. Dow Baxter was particularly interested in the succession of fungi on forest trees as glaciers retreated. So we would dig the roots up and he would take these samples for his research work on forest fungi. I also had worked with Dow in the summer before we went up, in addition to [working for] Benninghoff, and he was studying the effect of various creosotes on various wood samples for Consolidated Edison, because they were trying to find creosotes[6] that would last longer on their poles.

Scott: Oh, I see.

·   ·   ·

Woody: That was interesting work. I was just there one year and of course the samples were there for many years.

Anyhow, we worked around Mendenhall Glacier.[7] We took a trip on the White Pass and Yukon Railroad up from Skagway up to Lake Bennett and clear over to White Pass where we were able to look at the "barges on the marges" of Lake Lebarge.[8] Robert Service's cabin was in White Horse.

There was a forest fire burning up there the first year. The second year when we went back, the fire was still burning. It had burned under the highway in the peat and come up on the other side of the highway and was still burning a year later.

Scott: Wow.

Woody: They didn't burn with the rapidity that we have (in Southern California), but they burned quite a bit of an area. I don't know whatever happened to it; I just saw it for two years.

We also went to the Anchorage area and down around Moose Pass, which is south of Anchorage on the Cook Inlet and the Turnagain Arm. On Turnagain Arm we saw a moose and its calf get hit by an incoming tidal bore. It's a very long, shallow bay, and the tidal range is around 15 feet. The waves come in almost a foot high up this arm.[9] They hit the moose and knocked the moose calf down. We assumed it got up and got out but we never saw the end of it.

We have a picture, somewhere in my things, of a rainbow on a gold miner's cabin. We thought that was really appropriate. And we visited a number of Dow Baxter's friends. He had been going up to Alaska every summer for 19 years, and he knew hundreds of people. Anybody who was anybody in the natural resources field of any kind, whether it was geology, glaciology, forestry, were a friend of his.

Another thing we did in Anchorage was they had found an abandoned wolf pulp. They were raising it, because wolves were pretty rare even then. And I am one of the few people that was ever bit by a wolf. It was probably a two-month-old pup. But I did have a hand chomped on by a wolf.

Scott: They let you pet it?

Woody: Yeah. We were holding it.

Dow took pictures for things like the Audubon Society. One of the things he loved about me having no clothes was I always had the same shirt and pants, and he could splice them any way he wanted to. And he took the old-time film movies; I think they were 16 millimeters. His camera was his prized possession. He had a big metal trunk that he carried his things in. Wrapped all his clothes around this camera. Towards the end of summer things got a little ripe. He didn't wash any more than I did, hardly. [laughs]

We also went up to Fairbanks into Mount McKinley, saw the bears in Mount McKinley and went up to Fairbanks and went up to Circle City and went through the university.

Then another time—this was not all at once—we went out to Nome and Kitzebue on the Bering Straits, or Bering Sea. Nome was a little dumpy town. Kitzebue was pretty much an Eskimo town. There were a few other buildings. The Eskimo ladies were still chewing the blubber off, I think it was beluga whales, but I don't remember whether it was seal or beluga whale, to turn it into a kind of leather. It was very interesting.

Dow told a story about another time he was in Nome— this is not when I was there but this was one of his stories—he and one of the earlier "slaves[10]" were walking down the beach studying something. Well, night doesn't come really quickly or really dark there. In fact, in Kitzebue and that area you sometimes can get basically 24-hours of light in June. They were down there and it was getting darkish, and it was the end of summer so that there was some dark. Dow was really worried that he wouldn't find his way back to Nome. He was kind of timid, even though he did all these adventures. The assistant said, "Don't worry. We won't have any trouble." And Dow said, "Well, how do you know?" [The assistant] said, "You can tell by the smell." [laughs] And sure enough, they got to this Eskimo settlement, near Nome. You could smell it before you got there.

Scott: Because of the blubber?

Woody: Fish remains and so on.

Back to Casaview. If you went inland just a little ways there were what you call permafrost, and in the summer there would be potholes that melted (the underneath would still be frozen) which held incredible numbers of mosquitoes. That was when they first had come up with insect repellents. And so as an experiment we took and put a stripe of insect repellent down the back of my shirt or coat—I had a jacket. On the sides of the stripe you could count around 100 mosquitoes, and in the center there were none. Dow made a picture of that to show how effective the insect repellent was.

I never got a copy of it. About the only photo that he ever gave me is the one in my office where I'm overlooking a glacier.

Another thing we did was in Mendenhall Glacier area we walked up and there was an ice-cave at the base of the glacier. He had me go in there. It was a bluish light at this particular area, and he took color pictures of it. Dow wanted to make sensational photos.

We went back a week later and it had squashed flat. [laughs]

Scott: The movement of the ice.

Woody: Another place he wanted to have pictures of some-body swimming where there was ice in the water. Of course, that "someone" was me. I was nude, swimming in this ice-water. It wasn't long, I tell you what. About two seconds and you were out and trying to get warm again.

Scott: Wow.

Woody: So that's some of the Alaska adventures. Oh, one more, even more of an adventure. On the second year we went up there we decided we were going out to Kamishak Bay to take pictures. There's a place where the bears are well-known for fishing, and the salmon come up this stream and the bears sit there and catch them. You have to take a charter plane out to it. Well, we went to get this charter pilot that somehow Dow had heard about, went to his house and got in his car. We were always in rental cars or somebody else's car. And we drove towards the airport.

That should have been a little bit of a clue, because the pilot stopped at his ex-wife's house to get his camera, and it took him about 30 minutes to go into his ex-wife's house and come back out with the camera. Then we went to the airport, got in his plane, and flew out. (We took off in the water from Anchorage—it was a pontoon plane.) We were flying pretty much towards the west and I was sitting beside him and I was reading this map and I said, "You know, we're flying up the wrong valley." And he said, "No, we're not."

And we were flying up the wrong valley!

We just barely were able to clear this mountain; we had been flying in a dead-end valley. Going over this little pass, it wasn't super high, but we were coming in too low. We just made it over the top of the pass and you could see the vegetation, the rocks and stuff at the pass as you went over it.

Well, because we had done this, he had to use a lot of extra gas to get over this thing. He landed at Lake Iliamna. He was essentially out of gas. So we landed on what they call a "dead stick." No propeller running.

But anyhow, we got it up to shore, and we had sprung the pontoons a little bit.

Scott: How did you get it to shore with no propeller?

Woody: Well, I can't remember. Maybe it coasted to shore. Anyhow, we got there. We had to pull it up on shore because the pontoons were now leaking, because we hit so hard coming in.

They didn't have any aviation gas there. But they had some auto gas. So we fueled the sucker up with auto gas, bailed the pontoons out, started the motor, pushed it into the water, jumped in and flew out to Kamishak Bay.

We landed again. It's one of the areas with pretty good tides in it, probably 15 feet. We got out and we could walk across the area we had just landed in. It was all gravel and rocks—it was that shallow. And he managed to land there. And again, we pulled this thing up on a sandbar and then went to look for the bears.

. . .

Scott: [laughs] So you were still on your mission.

Woody: Oh yeah. Don't give up the mission.

But anyhow, we landed there and got out and walked up to where the bear were fishing. It was really a sensational thing, but it made you pretty nervous because the bears were everywhere. I mean the trails that went up there, there was bear poop on them. The berries were in season and the bears were, fortunately, primarily interested in salmon, not in berries. We watched that for quite a while and went back.

Well, the tide had come in and our plane had floated loose. But we'd been really lucky because there was a ranger there, and he saw the plane start to float loose and he tied it up.

By the time we got back the tide had gone back down and the plane was up on a sandbar. [laughs] So we managed to push it in, drain the pontoons, fly back to Lake Iliamna, get some more gas, and fly back to Anchorage. And then, to give you a final idea of what kind of a guy we were dealing with, we were driving back to Anchorage on a two-lane road from wherever-the-heck we landed in the water. There were a row of telephone poles along the side with a kind of a graded road. He would pass cars on the dirt on the right, around the telephone poles and swing back in.

It was obvious that we had made a serious mistake. By the time we got back Dow was ghost-white and shaking all over. I thought we were going to get killed but I wasn't going to get killed by being scared. Anyhow, we made it back and this guy passed all these crazy people on the way into Anchorage, dodging around power poles.

That was probably the most ridiculous adventure —next to dumping a tractor into the lake—that I ever went into.

· · ·

Scott: That's pretty fun.

Now when you were digging on these glaciers, I'm trying to picture it—

Woody: We did not dig on the glaciers. The glaciers had been retreating, I don't know why or how long, but if you got down say five or six hundred feet in front of where the glacier was there would be vegetation beginning to come in. If you went a little farther there were trees. There were never any "big" trees in the area. In fact, most of the trees we saw in Alaska were not big trees as you would see in country where you had redwoods. But they would be maybe six, to seven, eight inches in diameter when you got down a couple of miles from the glacier where they'd had time to grow.

We would dig the roots out and he would send them home to study the fungi on them. I don't remember the details of how they studied them, or how he preserved them long enough to take home.

Scott: It seems like these glaciers would be pretty inaccessible. Were there trails up to them?

Woody: Mendenhall Glacier, the reason it was so famous was there was a road that went right up within a half a mile of the glacier. There was a big lake right in front of it. The glacier was at the edge of the lake. It's now gone back. Even when we were there it'd gone back quite a ways. When you and Barney sent us up in 1995 the thing had retreated a mile or so. The lake wasn't even around hardly anymore.[11]

But at the time we were there (with Dow) the lake hadn't been filled in with the debris.

Scott: You guys did a lot for two one-month stints.

· · ·

Woody: Yeah. Well, it was more than a month the first time. We went up soon after school got out, and came back shortly before it resumed. I was very fortunate. I kind of had an agreement with my folks that I would work for them in the summers and they would subsidize my education. I didn't get any pay. Well, of course, there were two summers where I still got some subsidy but they got nothing, basically, because I was only in Julian for a short time.

The second summer I came back a little early for Jo's wedding to Carlyn Tuttle.[12]

Scott: Did you keep in touch with Dow Baxter after?

Woody: Oh yeah. In fact he came out and visited us once here after we were married. Then he was on his way out to visit us again and he had another friend in Arizona, and he dropped dead. He'd been in a bad auto accident in New Mexico years and years ago. And he said that all his family lived to be relatively old. He was probably sixty seven or so when we went to Alaska. Sixty five, somewhere in there. He'd been going up there 19 years. I don't remember the exact number of years, but he was a wonderful, kind, gentle man.

When he came out here (to Julian) we took fungi samples from around our big lake and down around Ramona and over around Cuyamaca for his fungi work on trees. I still have a book in here called *Pathology in Forest Practice* that he wrote. I was lucky enough to have it autographed with his picture.[13]

One of my roommates in Michigan—I had some interesting roommates—one of them was Clyde Eriksen, who is still a good friend of mine. We lived in a graduate fraternity house, which was basically nothing but a boarding room. We lived in the second floor. I can't remember the name of the fraternity. 615 Oswego is the street address.

Scott: That's what you had to tell the cab driver after your parties.

Woody: No. The parties were at the house. We didn't party much because they paid me $1,600 a year, and they took $1,000 back for tuition. So I had $600 a year to live on. I don't know what they paid Clyde, he was a little farther along. He was working on his PhD.

When we moved out of Oswego and moved down to the apartment above the Golden Apple Restaurant, right next to where we worked, we lived on a dollar a day. There were three of us: Emerson Hibbard, Clyde Eriksen, and myself. Then Clyde got married so Emerson and I moved to a different apartment. We lived on food for a dollar a day. If we were really careful at the end of the month we could either go to the Pretzel Bell[14] or the Old German[15] for their cheapest meal. Other than that we cooked.

We had an agreement, one of us cooked and two cleaned the house. We rotated. Every week it was somebody else's turn to cook. My cooking was primarily stews.

When we first got there the closest grocery store was A&P, a group called I.G.A. Grocery Store.[16] We said that stood for *I'd Gip Anybody*. [laughs] We bought a whole bunch of canned vegetables because they had a special and the vegetables were 10 cents a can, which really sounded good if you were trying to live on a dollar a day. And they were the worst vegetables you ever saw. [laughs] They were worth their 10 cents a day. Even in those days 10 cents a can was pretty cheap.

I was going to talk about some of the botany people that I

associated with at Pomona. Robert Webb and his wife Yvonne are still family friends.

Scott: Sure.

Woody: Rob was in botany with me.

Mac Jeffrey was a botany major.

James Irvine,[17] when he was originally trying to get people to come [to Orange County], offered people an orange grove, or a place to grow oranges: if they would grow oranges and stay for so many years he'd sell the land to them. Well, most of them didn't succeed. Jeffrey's grandfather did. And so Mac had grown up there, which is interesting, in that Mac grew up very close to where Jane grew up. (Jane Mathis-Barnes grew up in El Toro and Santa Ana, Orange County.) And if you go to Irvine now you will see Jeffrey road. That was named for Mac's grandfather.[18]

Lucile—Housley was her married name—was another one. She was one of the gals who was still working for the Bureau of Land Management, Department of the Interior, as a botanist when we traded out of Fort Klamath and went to Lakeview.

Scott: Oh really. That's a long time.

Woody: So we renewed our friendship. We used to visit her every time we were there. She retired at 75. She now lives in the area west of Fort Klamath in the Medford area.

Let's see. I mentioned Phyllis Bravender (Dobbins) whose parents lived in Seattle.

There was Ralph Philbrick, who was a year older.

Del (Rodney) Weins, who the day I dropped the tractor in the lake came by to visit—I was still all wet. [laughs] His wife was Carol. She also was a botanist. I think they're in Idaho now.

Barbie Breylinger, who is a botanist. She was actually at Scripps, but Scripps [students] could take botany courses at Pomona. She lives up at Flathead Lake, Montana.

Sally Ellis-Christian-Vogel. She's been married a variety of times. She lives up in the Seattle area. Sally and I always worked very hard to get the good grades in botany.

Kay Raeder-Burns was a really good friend. She was a year older. She became a teacher and ended up with leukemia. Died, and about a year later her husband Bruce Burns, who was also a good friend, died. Her dad was a professor of engineering at the University of Colorado, Boulder and I visited them there a couple of times. His parents lived at Yucca Valley, and we went out there a few times and visited them. Very nice people.

There's an interesting story. When I was at Michigan, my first year, we were short of money. (Well, every year we were short of money). I got a chance to carpool with a lady who wanted to share a ride back. Somehow I'd met this lady, Jocelyn Robe. The only contact we had was that she wanted a ride from California to Michigan and I wanted somebody to pay for half the gas. And so we did that but we stopped at Bruce and Kay's house. And they immediately decided that we were a couple. It was farthest from the truth.

Then, while we were there, Bruce and Kay were getting engaged. And Walt Bertsch, who was another botanist who grew up in Coronado, was there trying to make time with Kay, who was busy getting engaged to Bruce. I was assigned the job of keeping Walt away from Kay. [laughs]

Scott: Kay gave you that assignment?

. . .

Woody: Yeah. We were buddy friends, very good friends.

Botany classes were usually offered every-other year for your advanced classes, so you were in always with other years of students. Walt was a physics major as well as a botanist. Very bright guy. He became a professor of botany at Pomona. And he died. I didn't know what he died of. Lucile told me, "Don't you know? He was gay?" I didn't know he was gay. He was one of the first people to die of AIDS in that area. I had no idea. I was probably the dumbest kid that ever...[19]

At Pomona there were local fraternities; there were not national fraternities. I was lucky enough to get involved with one called Nappies: Nu Alpha Phi Fraternity. That was a great group of people, and many of them are still my friends after all these years.

While I was there I, you know, dated a number of people and had some serious romances, I guess. But I dated Jane.

Scott: I was going to get around to that.

Woody: I don't remember exactly how I met Jane but I did. I think we started a class on Classics of the West, or something like that, Mesoamerican Civilizations. The teacher's name was Leslie [Cousins]. This was an elementary class, theoretically, but he expected us to really understand all of the ins and outs of Mesoamerican Civilizations. We were really overwhelmed. There were probably 50 people in this class. It was very popular, the first year he'd ever taught it. A requirement-filling class. I took it for about two months, and I said, "You know, I don't have a clue. I don't know what we're doing." He would put up 50 to 60 slides in a period and expect you to know all about them. Then he'd go through and pick one or two slides out and say, "Okay, now tell us all about these slides."

So I dropped that course, one of the few courses I ever dropped. One of the wisest things I ever did.

Jane was easy to remember because she always walked in late and wore a tight sweater. So I ended up dating her a few times.

Leslie was really a tyrant. He flunked 17 seniors, none of who could graduate. All of who had to take a summer class to graduate. These were good students. I mean, this was an impossible guy to take a class from. I guess he got better because he stayed there the rest of his career.

I ended up, I think, cum laude at Pomona when I graduated.

Scott: That's pretty good. You said you started with straight Cs and an F in English.

Woody: Well, that was at Christmas. By the end of the semester I brought them all up. I got a C in English and the rest were all Bs, I think.

Scott: Because your semester ended in February?

Woody: February or something, January. I spent the entire Christmas vacation, except for maybe Christmas day and half a day before, studying. I knew I was in trouble. If you know you're in trouble and you want to get somewhere you've got to work hard. That was one of the times when I really worked hard. I'm probably guilty of goofing off many a time but not then.

.   .   .

Scott: My theory is there should be one wild card semester that you can just throw out your grades. I had a bad semester. You transition from high school where it's pretty darn easy, to college where it's... You think it's hard, it's not hard once you get to graduate school, but you think it's hard. [laughs] It's totally self-discipline. Your parents aren't there forcing you to do homework and all this stuff.

Woody: Graduate school was in one way easier than undergraduate because all of the subjects were related to what you were already doing. It made it a lot easier because you had some background. But when you're taking English, Spanish, history, religion, these are very different subjects.

Scott: When I got my MBA I studied four hours every night. But when was an undergrad, in the first year, I thought four hours for a single test was a huge amount of studying. [laughs]

Woody: Well, I'll tell you a story. One of my high school compadres who is still a good friend, Tom Tozer—his dad was the druggist in Julian—went to San Diego State and essentially flunked out. Why? Because he partied. Not that he is dumb. Tom is very bright. He became a professor of pharmacy at the University of California San Francisco and taught pharmacists all over the country.

Scott: Probably a good lesson for him to get flunked out.

.   .   .

Woody: Yeah, in a way. But it tells you that you can flunk out and be very, very bright.

We had a very good high school class, actually. Quite a bunch of good students in our high school class. And so did Martha Gwen a year ahead of me, and so did Eileen, a year ahead of her.

Martha Gwen Redding Thum, and Eileen, both went to Redlands. They were both Reddings, Robert Redding's sisters.

Anyhow, Redding was the principal up here for I think 26 years. He had a very good stabilizing effect. He probably owed his existence, although you could argue it forever, to the fact that Thelma Jacobs, who was married to Ray Jacobs, was a teacher there. She was a disciplinarian that helped him get through some scrapes that came along. Anyhow, that's neither here nor there either.[20]

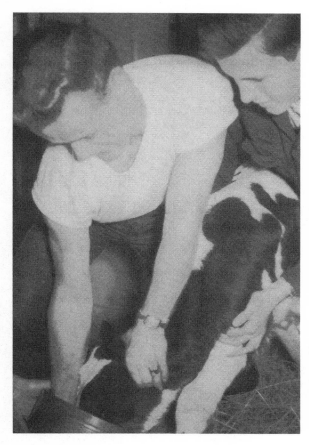

*Woody (not shown) and his friends pranked fellow dorm-mate
Beecher Dixon by bringing a calf into his room, scattering hay
and turning the whole thing into a barn. Not entirely without
compassion, they made sure to feed the calf well, 1954. The "vet
unit" dorms which were torn down soon thereafter.*

*Lyman Benson holding court with Doctor Edwin Philips
(standing on the right) with the botany students in the Mojave
Desert in their San Francisco Peaks trip (near Flagstaff,
Arizona), May 13, 1956. Woody graduated Pomona in 1957,
but the "Botany Bashes" continued unabated for decades.*

*On a botany bash overlooking Bryce Canyon, June 16, 1955.
From left Sally Ellis, Jim Bathgate (up), Ralph Philbrick
(down), Cory Almiard, Woody Barnes, Sally Remy.*

Still going strong after all these years, the botany students hold a botany bash in Julian April 9, 2009. Here they are preparing to study wild sweet peas near Lake Henshaw. Woody wearing plaid in center, Doctor Philips with baseball cap.

Woody on film duty in Alaska. Dow Baxter sold his pictures and film to the Audubon Society and others to help fund the trips.

An Inuit woman in Kitzebue on the Bering Sea, Alaska.

*Woody checks out the entrance to a cave in Mendenhall Glacier,
summer 1957 or 58.*

1. Helen Hunt graduated from Pomona College with honors in 1919.
   According to its website, Phi Beta Kappa is America's oldest academic

honor society for liberal arts and sciences, a society which "celebrates and advocates excellence in the liberal arts and sciences." It has had a chapter in Pomona College since 1913.

2. Benson, Lyman David. Recipient of the WIG award in Botany from Pomona College in 1974.

3. Edwin Sill Fussell

4. Actually Organ Pipe Cactus National Monument in Ajo, Arizona.

5. An agency of the U.S. government, the USGS provides "science about the natural hazards that threaten lives and livelihoods; the water, energy, minerals, and other natural resources we rely on; the health of our ecosystems and environment; and the impacts of climate and land-use change. As a scientific agency of the U.S. government, the USGS scientists develop new methods and tools to supply timely, relevant, and useful information about the Earth and its processes."

6. Creosotes are a category of carbonaceous chemicals formed by the distillation of various tars and by pyrolysis of plant-derived material, such as wood or fossil fuel. They are typically used as preservatives or antiseptics.

7. Mendenhall Glacier is a glacier about 13.6 miles long located in Mendenhall Valley, about 12 miles (19 km) from downtown Juneau in the southeast area of the U.S. state of Alaska. The glacier and surrounding landscape is protected as part of the 5,815-acre Mendenhall Glacier Recreation Area, a federally designated unit of the Tongass National Forest.

8. Robert W. Service was a famous poet whose subject matter was Alaska, and "The Cremation of Sam McGee" was one of his most famous poems. He spelled the lake Lebarge in the poem, presumably for its sound. Its true name is Laberge.

9. A tidal bore, often simply given as bore in context, is a tidal phenomenon in which the leading edge of the incoming tide forms a wave (or waves) of water that travels up a river or narrow bay against the direction of the river or bay's current.

10. Meaning the unpaid student assistants.

11. For Woody's 60th birthday Scott and Barney bought him and Jane a trip to Alaska that included a cruise and inland trip.

12. Mary Alice "Jo" Barnes married Carlyn Tuttle August 24th, 1958.

13. *Pathology in Forest Practice* by Dow Vawter Baxter, published by John Wiley & Sons, 1942.

14. Pretzel Bell is still in operation, 226 S Main St, Ann Arbor, MI 48104.

15. Old German is still in operation, 117 S Ashley St, Ann Arbor, MI 48104.

16. The Great Atlantic & Pacific Tea Company, better known as A&P, was an American chain of grocery stores that ceased supermarket operations in November 2015, after 156 years in business.

17. Woody is referring to James Harvey Irvine, Sr. (1867–1947) who had inherited what became known as "The Irvine Ranch" from his father, James Irvine. The "Irvine Ranch" combined 48,800 acre Rancho San Joaquin and 47,200 acre Rancho Lomas de Santiago which the senior James Irvine had purchased largely through profits selling merchandise in San Francisco during the California Gold Rush.

18. According to the Irvine Historical Society, Scottish Immigrant George Jeffrey leased an early lima bean farm on the Irvine Ranch. He noticed the favorable moisture patterns and, leasing a total of 80 acres, created a successful citrus orchard. James Irvine got the idea from George Jeffrey to plant citrus (or lease land to farmers to plant citrus) over wide swathes of the 96,000 acre ranch. George Jeffrey was prominent in the burgeoning community and, as an Orange County Supervisor, helped create its infrastructure, roads, and airport. He became known as "The Road Builder." Ortega Highway linking the coast with Lake Elsinore is named in honor of George Jeffrey's wife's family, descendants of the Spanish explorer José Francisco Ortega. His son William "Mac" Jeffrey served on the local water district and school board.

19. The Walter Bertsch Prize in Molecular Biology was established in memory of Walter, who served as Professor of Biology from 1977 to 1984.

20. Ray Redding was superintendent of Julian High School for 39 years.

9

USD AND MILITARY SERVICE

Scott: It's May 2nd, 2019. We had talked about when you taught at University of San Diego. Do you want to tell me about when you were working there?

Woody: When I first came out of the service I was looking for a place to work. I had applied to a number of places. Bob Cheesewright got me a potential job at Cate School (a boarding high school in Carpinteria), but we didn't take it because we were just freshly married, and you had to share the bathroom with students for the two of us. That didn't sound too good. Then I got a chance to work at La Jolla Country Day. That sounded very good.

Ruth Jackson, who was a prominent in Republican politics in San Diego County, as well as in the Catholic church there, helped me get a job at U.S.D. At that time the college for men and the college for women were separate. I worked at the college for men for two years. I was directly under Father Philip Murray. Above him was Father Ganahl.

Everybody told me when I went to work for a Catholic school, "Oh, they'll interfere with everything you ever do.

You'll never have any freedom to teach the truth or anything." The first day of class I was pretty nervous, of course. I had been in the service for two years, and I was a little bit rusty on things. I was teaching a beginning biology class. Father Murray came in, and I thought, "Oh my goodness. It's just what they said. They're gonna interfere."

He said, "This is Mr. Barnes. He's in charge of your class. If you don't like it, come and see me and I'll kick you out of school." That was my total supervision for two years. Total interference was zero.

Scott: Wow.

Woody: Yeah, it was very good. He came in a little later when I was in my office area, the community office area, and said, "We need somebody to teach geology." I said, "Well, I'm not a geologist, but I could probably teach the beginning class." So I ended up teaching beginning biology, evolution and genetics, and beginning geology, which was a stretch for me, but I managed to keep at least 15 minutes ahead of the kids. Not all the kids. Some of them were faster. It was a very good experience. The only thing we didn't do as much as I would like to: It was hard to organize field trips because the kids all had conflict of classes. You could go for an hour, and we could look around the mountains in San Diego County, but we couldn't take a three day trip like we used to at Pomona. Anyhow, it was a very good experience. At that time at the University of San Diego the men's school and the women's school were separate. The women's school was far better, actually. They had sent a number of nuns to Stanford to get PhDs. Their standards were higher. Later they combined the two schools, which was a very intelligent thing to do.

John Cunningham was a good friend of mine. He was

their basketball coach. I don't know quite how we ever became good friends.

But one of the kids that was a basketball player was in my class. He was doing poorly. His dad was a well known guy in San Francisco. He flew down, and I thought, "Oh boy, I'm gonna get the arm twisting."

He said, "Why is my kid doing badly?"

I was just, "He's not studying."

"Well, he will. If he gives you any trouble, give me a call." I had very good parental support.

Scott: That's great.

Woody: I think I got along very well with the kids. Several of the kids went on to law school that were in my classes. Of course, you pat yourself on the back. Actually, I didn't teach any of the classes that got them into law school, but at least one of them needed a transcript to get into Berkeley, and so I wrote down and sent to the school of Berkeley everything I had tried to teach him for the whole class. He got in. There were three of them that went up there. They were so pleased that they bought me a bottle of whiskey, which of course I don't drink, and which I think may still be in the cupboard.

It was fun to see that. Three of them became judges in San Diego.

Scott: When I was working at Manzanita Ranch Store one time, and I don't have any idea what his name was, though he probably told me, a customer came in and said, "Are you Woody Barnes' son?" "Yes." "He used to teach me at U.S.D. He was the best teacher I've ever had."

·   ·   ·

Woody: Oh, that's... [embarrassed and pleased]

I had one other fellow who wrote a letter the same way. Then Joe (Joseph A.) Sciarretta was not really a student, but I knew him down there. He was an attorney. I don't know if you heard about this scrape that Heavy (Frank) Martinez got into.

Scott: No.

Woody: I don't know all the details, but there were some trespassers on his place, and they were hunter-type trespassers. He went out and chased them off, and he had a gun with him. They called the sheriff and the sheriff arrested him. I think they didn't take him with them, they just made him sign a thing and he would appear in court. Joe Sciarretta, one of the kids that I knew, is an attorney in Ramona. He's representing Heavy. I have not heard how that came out, but Heavy was very sorry for all those things he did wrong. He was just kind of impulsive and wanted to chase people off.

Scott: Where were you and Mom living?

Woody: We were living in the same house where you grew up in across the street from Spencer Valley School in the little cement block house that Dad built. Dad built it for Bill Edic's mother-in-law. Bill Edic was the distributor of our cider for many years in San Diego. He ran Pacific Coach Packing Company Imperial brands. He was a great guy. He used to rent the big house up at the end of Wynola[1] valley where Karen lived at one time.

Bill Edic's mother-in-law rented the place across from Spencer Valley School. When she got where she couldn't do it, it turned out to be just about the right time because Jane and I were getting married and needed a place to live. So we moved into it. We were the second tenants. We were there 14 years in that house. That's why you started at a one room school with Mrs. Stanley, who was really a breath of fresh air as teachers go.

I think it was great that you guys got to actually go to a one-room school.

Scott: Oh yeah, even though I don't remember it all that well. I only stayed until halfway through second grade. Barney was there until sixth grade.

Woody: That was a unique experience that will never happen again for most of the family. You guys are getting a lot of the same kind of benefits by having your kids go to good private schools. But a public school that was a one-room school... Now it's a three-room school.

Scott: I have bragging rights. [laughs] The teacher, Mrs. (Evelyn) Stanley, was amazing. And her assistant Loralee Marcy.

Woody: I went to a three-room school for eight years. They put a fourth room on about the time we left. We had first, second, and third grade (in one room). Up to the eighth grade in those three rooms.

In our class there were two or three of us that were pretty good students and they put us in with the older students to balance the numbers out. If some teacher of lower grades had too many students, we could pretty well keep up with the students that were older. Particularly in the sixth grade or so we were in with the eighth graders.

We had some miserable teachers, some really good teachers.

Father Philip Murray was a Jesuit. He was very well-educated. He'd been educated I think in Rome, or somewhere where they have a Jesuit university. He was a gruff-appearing, soft-hearted guy.

He got sick and I went over and visited him at Mercy Hospital. He would never admit he was friendly with people but he was.

Scott: You had a long commute then, five days a week that you drove from Julian to San Diego.

Woody: Yes. And Jane was working at the Alvarado Medical Center, right by State College, at an orthopedist's office.

Scott: As a registered nurse?

Woody: Yes. McPherson, McPherson, Kimball and Smith was the name of the thing. There were two McPherson cousins, I think. One of their employees was Hubertina Thelen. She used to live down where Sears used to be near the Mercy hospital area. There was a lady that thought Hubertina was too old to work, and when they managed to force her out it took two people to replace her. Hubertina Thelen. She was probably 70 when we were there, and she was very good. We visited her several times at her house after she was unceremoniously retired. Very nice lady.

. . .

Scott: So you would commute in the same car and drop off Mom and then—

Woody: Once in a while the other way around, but 90% of the time we'd go through and drop Mom off there and I would go down to U.S.D.

Scott: Barney was saying there was some story you told about someone who was doing fairly well academically but because of attendance got failed, or got kicked out or something?

Woody: Oh. I don't remember that one right now. There was a fellow whose grandfather was from Mexico. He wasn't a Mexican but his grandfather was apparently some fairly prominent person in Mexico. He really had trouble taking tests. So I managed to find ways to give him oral tests and other things; because he wasn't dumb, it was just that he froze up when he was taking tests.

I tried to give a variety of tests. I gave some true false, multiple choice, short answers, essays, so that you covered what certain people could do well and other people couldn't do well. But this guy didn't do anything except these oral things. So we made an exception; he passed and went on through school.

Scott: Yeah. I take multiple choice tests really well, and some people don't at all.

Woody: I tried to compensate for that, recognizing that some people do well on short answers and some people do essays very well.

I tried to do a good job, and it was fun.

Scott: Why did you stop?

Woody: Well, I wanted to come back up in Julian, and Mom was tired of commuting down there. The folks were getting older and they were thinking about selling out, and we thought maybe we should come up and help them up here. Besides, without a PhD, you're always temporary.

A story I didn't tell you and probably shouldn't go into the record.

Scott: Front page.

Woody: After the first year they fired all of us new teachers. There were three or four of us in the college for men and they fired us all. I was a little bit distraught because I didn't think I'd been that bad. Another lady was equally distraught, and there was another guy, he was a jerk. But anyhow, two weeks later they called me in and said, "We'd like to give you a two-year contract." I said, "What, you just fired me?" Anyhow, I took a one-year contract instead of a two-year contract.

But really, if you're going to stay in college teaching you should get a PhD, and I knew that and I didn't want to spend three, four, five years getting a PhD. At that point in my life I'd just gotten out of the service and we were just married. I think we were only married about a month before we went to work down here, the two of us, and so I didn't want to do that. So my academic career was over.

. . .

Scott: And they fired you so you wouldn't get tenure, or something like that?

Woody: Well, that may be part of it. They fired me because they had inadvertently hired a communist, and he was propaganda-izing communism very vociferously, and I think that to avoid prejudice they fired all of us. I may be wrong, but I think that's what it was. They fired all of us but they hired me back, and so that was kind of a backward compliment. But they did offer me a two-year contract. Somewhere in my files I have a letter from Father Murray saying that they were going to have to hire two people to replace me because nobody else would be able to teach geology and biology. I wasn't very good in geology but I did it, and I could stay at least five minutes ahead of most of the students.

Scott: Mom has a picture that shows you writing a lecture for one of your classes. It looked like the house down there in Wynola but I wasn't sure.

Woody: That's where it was. We never lived anywhere else but there and here.

At that point in time we were really doing a lot down there in Wynola. The retail thing was going up (Manzanita Ranch Store) and we were still selling fruit wholesale, a lot of it, pears particularly. We were really in the pear business more than the apple business.

Scott: I should know what year you got married but I...

· · ·

Woody: '62.

Military Service

Woody: I was in the service, I think it was '59 to '61 or early '62. Anyhow, we got married shortly after I got out.

I was drafted. That's why I was in Utah for a couple years. I wanted to go overseas... so they sent me to Utah.

I had some interesting experiences in the service too. I don't know if I've run through them for you.

Scott: That would be a fun addition.

Woody: Well Dad, Grampy Barnes, was on the Del Mar Fair Board and there was an outfit that wanted to take over the racetrack. Arnholt Smith was a banker in San Diego and they wanted to take over the racetrack because it was very lucrative at that time. I don't remember all the details of how they wanted to take it over. They even went so far as to offer Mother anything she wanted if she could get Grampy to vote for them to take over.

But anyhow, at the same time something you (Scott) didn't have to deal with much, there was a draft and everybody over 18, males, had to register for the draft. Which of course I did. And you could get a deferment to go to college, which I did. All the way through school, every year you had to apply for it, and there was a deferment board.

There was a guy that turned them down. It was Dad's enemy. When Dad didn't vote for the racetrack—this guy was working for Arnholt Smith. Lou Lipton, of Lipton Savoy Café downtown.

Finally when I got to Michigan and got through school I could have gone on for a PhD but I said, "You know, eventu-

ally I've got to go in the service, I might as well get it over
with." So I just did it. I was trying to get into the Navy, I was
even taking the test up in L.A. for the Navy thing, and Lou
Lipton got me drafted. I ended up in the Army as the lowest
level private, and you could have gone to officer candidate
school but then you'd have to extend another six months or so
and maybe you'd pass it and maybe you wouldn't.

They sent me up to Fort Ord. That's up right on Monterey
Bay. I was there a couple of days while they processed you and
counted your fingers and toes and stuff. Then they sent me to
Fort Hood, Texas, which was an armored division. Sergeant
Jenkins was in charge of our group, I can still remember his
name. We went through the regular military basic training,
and one of the things that always frustrated me was that they'd
give you steel wool to take the rust off the tracks of the tanks.

Scott: [laughs] That's important.

Woody: I think they were out of places to march us that day
so they had us do that. One night we were out on night practice, and all of a sudden they stopped the night practice. It was
right near the end of my basic training, and I thought, "Good
Lord." Then they called me out by name. I figured my folks
had died or something terrible because they don't... A peon,
buck private, they don't stop things for in the service. Anyhow
they called me in and took me out of this group. I went in and
an officer said, "Sit here." So okay, I sat down.

I sat there for about four hours, and a guy came by and
said, "Why are you sitting here?" I said, "They told me to sit
here." "Oh, we just wanted to tell you you're going to Utah,
not to Europe."

I had thought I was going to be in the medical corps in

Europe and I turned out to be in the biological division at the Dugway Proving Ground in Utah. That turned out to be a very good thing too, but I didn't get to go to Europe. I wanted to go overseas. I really didn't care where I'd never had the opportunity to go overseas and I thought, "Well, you know, I'm in the service, I might as well go somewhere where I can do something for myself."

But anyhow, this turned out interesting because they assigned me to a group called Ecology and Epidemiology. It was run by a veterinarian Dale Parker who was a civilian. Dean Vest, who was a civilian, was my immediate boss. He would have loved to have me write his PhD thesis, but I didn't do it.

Basically my job was to trap mice and turn them loose—to make sure they weren't killing anything (with their experiments). They had a grid set up. I think we had ten grids. They had about a hundred traps in each one and every morning you had to be out there. In the summer you had to be there early because the heat would kill the mice, and you can't turn them loose if they're dead. You could turn them loose, but it doesn't do a lot of good. And in the winter you had to be out there early because if you didn't they'd freeze to death. So you got up around 4 AM and went out and marched up and down these trap-lines.

Scott: So they were doing some sort of experimentation with diseases?

Woody: Not in the group I was. We were in the safety group, to make sure they hadn't killed everything. A few years later they flew an airplane down a valley next to our valley and killed two or three hundred sheep. I'm pretty sure I know what they did; I think they were probably testing a nerve gas and went down the wrong valley.

Scott: Good thing you weren't trapping in that valley.

Woody: They were very careful. In a way. Careful-relaxed. You're in this place where it would be almost impossible for anybody to do anything. We lived in a housing area which you had to come through a gate, and then to go to work you had to go through another housing area. The guards there for both of them were civilian guards, but the guards where we went to work... *Lackadaisical* would be an exaggeration for how efficient they were.

We traveled in a Jeep all the time. Another guy, Ron Louden and I did a lot of that (trapping) for a year. He was with me as my senior partner, and he was from the Midwest somewhere. One day we decided these guys really weren't looking at us. We didn't have any guns or anything, so we rigged up a package and put it on my lap. It said "bomb" in big letters. We drove through the security checkpoint with a thing that said "bomb" on our lap. The guy just waved us on.

We were next to a place called T.G.Y., which was Toxic Gas Yard. That was where they stored bad stuff; we don't know what it was because I wasn't involved with it. A couple of these civilian guys were a little bit funny in the head. They had a separate guard for the T.G.Y., and they were a little bit more strict. One day a guy drove through it, and pulled out a gun and started shooting. He didn't hit either the people or the Jeep or the toxic gas, which is probably just as well. That was another incident.

I've told you my lies about badgers, haven't I? My partner Ron Louden and I went out... We had to get up early in the morning, because the heat would kill the mice the in the traps if we didn't get up early. One morning, probably about 8 AM by the time we got to this series of traps, we found a badger digging. And being young and not very bright—nothing has changed—we decided we were going to lasso it. I do not recommend this. Particularly when the only thing you had to lasso him with was our army belts.

We succeeded in lassoing him and he was not very pleased.

Scott: Wow.

Woody: A badger has claws about the length of my little finger. We pulled him out of the little hole where he was digging. It could dig so fast you can't believe it. And, we thought, well, now what do we do? We realized we'd made a mistake, so we decided the only thing we could do is drop both belts and run two different directions because he couldn't get both of us. Which is what we did.

We came back a couple hours later and got our belts. He'd shaken them off.

That's my badger story.

One of the things was that I really worked for civilians during the day. All my bosses were civilians. There were probably four or five of us at different times of year that were in the military but really worked for these civilian people from 4 AM in the morning 4 in the afternoon.

That's why I went into bartending in the afternoon. One of my friends was bartending, he said, "We need a bartender." I said, "How about me?"

It's interesting if you say, How about me? how often things work out. So I worked at a bar there for 18 months in the Officers' Club, and that was a very interesting experience because this post had visiting groups from other places like

Canada. Canadians would bring Canadian whiskey to that bar and these other things.

We had three or four customers, I think it was three, that would drink a quart of whiskey a night and still hold down a job the next day. One of them was a veterinarian that was in charge of my post. And one of them was a Mr. Mackie who was in the personnel office. And I don't remember who the third one was, but Mr. Mackie was a warrant officer. You had to have Mr. Mackie's drink there. The others weren't quite as bad, but Mr. Mackie, 4:31 P.M., you had to have his drink there.

Down they went.

He was a very nice guy and he held down a responsible job, and I don't know how he did it. It's amazing what some people can do and still function well.

The head of the post was Major Britt. He was a person with many prejudices. He didn't like anybody who wasn't a redneck, particularly a white-skinned redneck. I went in to see him. He said, "What do your parents do?" I said, "They're farmers." That was okay. He liked farmers. So I got along with Major Britt, and that was a blessing.

Major Britt was a first-class prejudiced jerk. He came in to the Officers Club occasionally and most of the people in the service were people of color, including the cooks in the Officers Club where I was bartending, and I can remember coming in one day, this cook was throwing a steak on the floor, jumping on it and spitting on it. I thought 'Man, this guy's lost it!' I walked very gingerly around, figuring he'd really gone crazy. Pretty soon the cook hands the steak to me and he said, "Give this to Major Britt." So I gave it to Major Britt. He hated Major Britt—with good reason. I had a hard time keeping a straight face knowing this thing was covered with spit and had been on the floor.

· · ·

Scott: Wow.

Woody: Going back to Mr. Mackie, the personnel officer, we became pretty good friends in spite of the fact he was a full-fledged alch-y. He...

Well, let me go back one more time. There was a colonel in charge of the thing, Colonel David Armitage, in charge of the whole post. He and his daughter there, they liked the wild horses. Really liked them. They let them run everywhere, including everybody's yards and right in the base. I mean you've heard of these herds of wild horses. He had probably 28 or 30 in there, and that's a lot.

Scott: A lot of damage to flora, I'm sure.

Woody: In desert country.

Scott: Yeah.

Woody: Anyhow, one day the veterinarian had to explain why this horse died. He had tried to treat it and it died, and he finally came up with a fraudulent answer. He said he thought the horse had been eating too many cigarette butts. [laughs] So the next day Colonel Armitage had 200 people out there on the post picking up cigarette butts so it wouldn't kill any more of his horses.

There's a lot of strange things that happen in the service that, they're humorous, they're not terribly bad, but that was one. We were out there marching around picking up cigarette butts so that the horses didn't die. I think the vet had given this one a shot for something and then he was on the hot seat.

Getting back to Mr. Mackie. I'd been in there about 18 months or so at this post and it was getting time to be moved on. There was a guy in the personnel office that did not like me. I don't remember what his name was. I do not remember why he did not like me, but he probably had a good reason. One day Mr. Mackie came in and he says, "You've got orders to get out. Tomorrow morning you get in your car and drive. Take the orders," he handed me the orders, "and drive until you run out of gas."

I didn't get out of the service but I was put in the reserves instead of being sent to Vietnam thanks to Mr. Mackie. He kept the papers away from this guy that didn't like me who would've wanted to send me to Vietnam.

Scott: So you ditched the papers somewhere?

Woody: [all innocence] Oh, I don't know where they went.

Scott: I don't understand how driving away would help... because you're still there the next day.

Woody: Well, he wanted me to get away from the post so this guy couldn't change the orders to send me overseas. I got out of the gate and I was gone.

Scott: And then you were done. And then—

· · ·

Woody: Well, I wasn't done. I was discharged from active duty. I had six years in the reserves. But I was out of that area and out of thumb of the guy who didn't like me.

Scott: Okay. I understand now.

Woody: That was an indirect result of a bartending, I think.

That was in 1959, '62, somewhere in there. Closer to '62 probably. Because I got out and then I went looking for work. It was hard to find a job. I applied at the (San Diego) Zoo and almost got a job there working for the botany department. I had a job offer at Cate's School and one at La Jolla Country Day, and then got lucky and got the one at University of San Diego. All of them were pretty good jobs, and every one of them had a connection.

It's amazing. You never ever want to burn a bridge. If there's one thing you learn in life, is that burning bridges is more than a giant mistake.

Scott: Didn't you also buy some hair clippers that you probably are still using, and start a hair cutting business?

Woody: I got those in college.

Mac Hege and I bought them and we intended just to cut each other's hair.

Scott: This is Pomona or Michigan?

·   ·   ·

Woody: Pomona. We ended up with a business cutting hair. Mac Hege was a roommate. You remember Mac Jeffrey probably?

Scott: Yes.

Woody: Mac Hege... There were four of us in what they called a suite in a dorm. The first year my roommate was Bruce Carlson. Great guy. I probably would have flunked out without Bruce grading my English.

In the second year my roommates were Martin Dickinson, who lives in Rancho Santa Fe still, and Mac Jeffrey, who just died, and Mac Hege, who just died. We had a suite. They were very good roommates. Martin became quite well-to-do. His grandfather was a doctor in San Diego. His dad was a banker and Martin became a banker. He was very successful and he married Carol Fleet.

Over the years so many things fell in place. Not by plans but just by being in the right place and not screwing up too often.

Scott: I keep thinking about the haircuts though. What did you charge for a haircut?

Woody: Well, first we just did them for each other for free, Mac Hege and I. And then people wanted them and we did a few, and we said, "You know, we're putting too much time on this." We charged fifty cents. The best investment I ever made was that clippers. We paid nine dollars for it. I cut hair there and I cut hair a little bit in Michigan, and cut hair in the service, and we are still using it. Jane cuts my hair.

. . .

Scott: It's probably saved you five grand over the years.

Woody: We figured that between Jane and I cutting each other's hair we darn near paid for our first little car, if it was all lumped together.

Colonel David Armitage's beloved wild horses grazing on base at Dugway Proving Grounds, ca 1960, Utah.

Woody on base, ca 1960.

At night at home in Wynola, Woody types a lecture for the course
he was teaching the next day at the University of San Diego.
Woody taught beginning biology, evolution and genetics as well as
beginning geology in school years 1962-63 and 63-64.

1. Spencer Valley School in Wynola, in continuous operation since 1876, was named after Wynola Valley's first settler, a hermit gold-miner named Spencer. The primary structure dates from 1904; a fire burned the original. Two rooms were added in 1987, making it a three-classroom school averaging between 30 and 35 students total between kindergarten and eighth grade.

10

CEDAR FIRE

In 2003 several massive fires burned across San Diego County simultaneously: the Otay Fire, The Paradise Fire, the Pendleton Fire, and the Cedar Fire, among others. At 273,246 acres, the Cedar Fire was the third largest in recorded state history. It was started as a signal flare by a lost hunter in the area of Cedar Falls on October 25, 2003. Driven by Santa Ana winds, it burned to within a few miles the coast before a shift in the wind drove it back eastward. More than 500 homes in the Julian area burned, though the town itself was saved by the fire crews. Fifteen people died in the blaze.

Karen Conely (Tuttle), Woody's niece, participated in the interview.

Scott: In 2003 there was major event in Julian, the Cedar Fire. Do you want to tell us how that affected you here?

. . .

Woody: The Cedar Fire was started by a guy who was lost and fired a flare in a windy situation down in the Cedar Falls area. You don't just fire a flare into the brush. But anyhow, it started it, and he survived it, which was probably a mistake. It immediately took off. The fire went west and burned clear down to Miramar across the road at Miramar Naval Air Station. Well, then the wind changed and it came back and one of the tragic things locally, I think that 13 people got killed.

Bud Lewis was a retired state firefighter. He and I were up there in Pine Hills at the Fletcher Point area looking out at the fire and the fire was coming back. Mort, his brother, had gone down to protect their property in the Boulder Creek area. And Bud said, "Mort, careful, this is a bad one."

Karen: No, they were down there hunting. It was the first day of deer season. And Mort got trapped in the way.

Woody: Heavy (Frank) Martinez went in with the water truck and saved him.

Karen: He was backing the water truck into the fire when Jerry Fry got Mort out.

Scott: The story I heard was that Heavy squirted water from the truck to douse the fire as best he could, keep the heat to a manageable level, with Jerry Fry in the spray looking for Mort.

Woody: Mort's lungs were damaged pretty badly, and he never really fully recovered from it. But Heavy Martinez got him out of there.

. . .

Scott: Those two saved his life.

Karen: Heavy and Jerry were both heroes that day. Jerry continued being one when they got back up here.

Woody: It was a wild time. The fire kept coming up closer, and we decided it was going to come here whether we liked it or not. It was down in the canyon, and the heat was such that it sounded like cannons going off when it would hit these trees. They just would explode. It was a lot of heat. So Mom (Jane) loaded up the horses and the cat and you (Scott) walked in from Julian. They wouldn't let you drive in.

Scott: Yeah, I parked at the post office and walked. First it was clear sky and then the wind shifted and it was just like snow; I could hardly breathe because I was breathing in flakes of ash. You could almost see the flames in the trees by the time I got here.

Woody: You guys took the horses and the cat and filled up lots of buckets of water. I don't remember how many buckets of water you managed to fill up, but we had buckets from the flower business, and went up to the post office and I was supposed to stay here until I couldn't take it anymore. But the fire came up here... it was very interesting. Down in the canyon it sounded like cannons going off. When it would hit these trees it'd just go boom, it was so much heat. Well, when it came up over the ridge here (the ranch is on a rise), it divided the fire two ways up these two canyons, and it actually slowed it coming to us here.

In fact we ended up with a little back-draft; you could walk right up almost to the fire and throw buckets of water on it. Unbelievable. I managed to throw buckets of water and steer the fire around our houses. When it got around the houses it was going to close the road, so I got in the car. I had the car pointed out: There's a limit to how stupid you are. Drove over and met you guys and we went down to the desert. We didn't know anything about what was happening. Several days later one of my friends calls. We were down in Imperial Valley—

Scott: At Julie Kemp's house. (Woody's niece.) We were camping on Julie's lawn.

Woody: Well, Jane and I were at Kay and Dutch's.[1]

Karen: That's who Mike and Julie Kemp bought their first place from down there in Calexico.

Woody: That's right. Anyhow, we heard that our house had survived but we couldn't come home for a while because the roads were all blocked.

Scott: I can't remember if it was seven days or ten days.

Woody: It was around seven—

. . .

Scott: Mary Lynn was the only one smart enough to bring the barbecue and some camping gear. That made our lives a lot easier. I was impressed. I thought about the valuables but I didn't think about how to survive for those seven days or whatever it was going to be.

Woody: We came back and there was still stuff burning. The amazing thing is the night before I had run the disc around some. It didn't burn any of our buildings, but it burned all those pallets right beside the shed. That can't possibly happen... but it did.

Scott: It burned a lot of aluminum pipe. Miles of fence.

Woody: We still haven't repaired some of the fence. We were lucky it didn't burn the house or the garage.

Scott: I was amazed that we had a pallet of cement blocks over by the shed. I thought, "This is great, they didn't burn and we can still use them," and I grabbed one. It crumbled like dust. The heat destroyed the integrity of it.

Woody: That's how you make cement is you heat limestone.

Scott: I guess if you heat it too much, it disintegrates, because they weren't good for anything.

· · ·

Woody: No.

Scott: They would have been great for a karate class. I could have looked very tough.

    Those are great stories.

Woody: Well, don't compare them, because every time I tell them I lie a little differently.

The Cedar Fire enveloped the farm in Pine Hills from the west.
Over the course of 10 days it devoured 2,232 houses and burned
all the orchards and open space on the Barnes family farm.
Thanks to Woody, Jane and Scott's efforts, all the buildings on
the ranch were spared.

Coming to help his parents evacuate, Scott had to park at the Post Office in Julian because the roads were closed. He walked the two miles from town to the ranch, taking this photo along the way. Firefighters managed to steer the Cedar Fire around the historic town of Julian.

Near Scissors Crossing, Jane driving with the family cat Puzzle, Woody standing, and Scott in the reflection taking the photo. They family evacuated to Calexico for 7 days, and the farm remained without electricity for the better part of a month.

Woody putting out hot spots in the aftermath of the Cedar Fire.
Massive live oak stumps continued to smolder for weeks after the
initial blaze.

Part of the ranch's original hand-dug well originally lined with
redwood planks, this trench gathered water toward the deeper well.
The fire burned the planks to the bottom and destroyed the well.

1. Kay Brockman Bishop and Leonard "Dutch" Snyder.

11

MANZANITA RANCH STORE

This covers the "Manzanita Ranch store" in Wynols, which is where they moved the retail fruit operation from Pine Hills in 1946 and the apple cider making in 1956. Please see the diagram in the Maps section.

Scott: What I think we don't have very much of is Manzanita Ranch store in Wynola.[1] A lot of people don't really understand what it was. I think the way to start is to talk about the different seasons. Because really it was a completely different business depending on the time of year.

Woody: We can talk about when we bought the property.

Scott: Sure. Start wherever you want to start.

Woody: The property was bought by the folks about 1942 and it was really just the little tin building on the corner. It was relatively primitive. It had a small store in it—it's still there, the store stall, probably 8' by 10'. The rest of it was a garage, which is what it had been used for. It also sold gasoline.

Scott: A garage, in other words, to repair cars.

Woody: Repair vehicles, yes. It also had what they call a Butler Grader in there for grading apples. Today you probably wouldn't be able to fix cars and run a Butler Grader in the same place.

We bought the property from a fellow by the name of Hawkins, he and his wife. They moved back, I believe, to Missouri. They were some sort of relative of the Marcys. I don't remember how they were related to the Marcy family, and I don't know how long they'd been there but quite a while. This was right at the beginning of World War II and of course you could not build anything because you could not get any building materials. So most of our packing was still done up at the old place in Pine Hills during that period of time.

Prior to World War II agriculture was a pretty respected profession for young people to go into. People like Henry Silvers worked for dad. Henry became an electrician and owned the gas station in Julian and did a lot of other things.

Ralph Slaughter. Chuck McCoy.

George McCain lived with the folks for a year when he was in high school.

Jackie Elder used to come over and wash bottles.

All those kids, everybody worked. But when World War II came along, all the young guys under about 40 and over 18 or 17 were in the Service. There was a shortage of labor for this, so they established the bracero program which was a legal way to bring people from Mexico up. They would work for so many months and then go back to Mexico. You had to provide them with housing and so on.

We have a picture of the first Bracero crew sitting here with Bill Loux, my granddad Bope, and Pedro (Mireles), who was one of the first people to come up.

Scott: Who was Bill Loux?

Woody: Charlie Long's sister is married to Sterling Loux. Sterling's dad Bill worked for us for years. He lived in the green house in Wynola behind the packing house. The kids were all down there, Bernadine and Sterling and Carlie. The older Billy was gone already.

Scott: Now the green house, you are talking about Andermatt's house?

Woody: Yeah. That was the original house on the Hawkins place. The Hawkins had that 40 acres, and they had the corner where the packing house was. We bought that, I think, in 42.

The place where they (the Bracero crew) lived was in Wynola. It had been a garage and packing house for the Hawkins family right when the war came along. So we converted it from a garage and a packing thing into a cooking area. We had tents around the outside on platforms where these guys lived. We built the restrooms there at that time. That was before we built the packing house in Wynola. The war was over by the time we built the packing house.

The garage (as housing) was just a temporary thing before

we built the cement block house in back where Bill Cain[2] lived for a while and had the funny restrooms.[3]

Scott: That would be an interesting photo of that gas station with tents around it.

Woody: When we bought it, it had a little Butler grader in there (for sizing-sorting fruit). I got a terrible shock from it. Everybody said, "You're not getting a shock." I was barefoot, of course, so I got a shock.

Scott: I'm not sure what a Butler grader is.

Woody: Well it has holes like this and you put the apples in, each one of the holes gets bigger. Grading fruit.

Scott: I see.

Woody: The little ones would drop. I think it had about four sizes, maybe only three. The holes were lined with rubber and it would take and dump it into the next one. If it didn't go through it dumped it into the next one. They were in a sequence.

Right after the war, Dad was able to get building materials.

Dad had traveled all over with his Farm Security Administration job in the 30s and early 40s and he had seen a building up in Pasadena made out of cement blocks,[4] but they stacked them straight rather than every other one staggered like most buildings. So he looked up the architect and found out why. The architect said, "Well, there's no strength in the bricks. It's all in the reinforcing steel." And so dad had the building engineered by somebody, and I think it was the same architect, and Jo has pieces of the original plan. So around 1946 we were able to get enough materials to build it.

All the cement blocks were built in the parking lot, by us. I was 11 at the time, but I even tamped some of the cement into the forms. We still have one of the forms in the old cider house that we used to make those blocks. Then they assembled them. The original building was just a rectangular building. They put in an F.M.C. (Food Machinery Corporation) grader and sizer.

Jo had a copy of the plans and the engineering. The County (San Diego County) one time accused us of having... Some one of our friendly neighbors accused us of having an unreinforced concrete building. They wanted us to tear it down. I knew it had steel because I was there when they built it. I had some pictures of the steel sticking out. But the County sent two guys with a metal detector to detect the metal in the things. The inspector didn't know how to run the metal detectors. I had to show them how to do that and to show him the place where the metal actually showed through. So that building was passed by the County as having reinforcing steel, which I know it did.

There was no bathroom. There was no refrigeration, originally. We had a refrigerator over at Hawkins, that little green house where Louise (Andermatt) used to live. There was a refrigerator there—one of the first in the mountains. A lot of the insulation at that time was sawdust from the sawmills between two (walls of) one-by-fours or one-by-sixes. The wonderful thing about that was it was a happy home for termites once they started on it.

The other thing was that the gas they used at that time

[for refrigeration] was sulfur dioxide. I don't know if you remember Virgil Walker?

Scott: I don't.

Woody: Virgil Walker worked for us after World War II when he got out of the service. I went over there one day and he was working on the compressor, and the sulfur broke loose, and he said, "Run!" So I said, "Okay." I figured he knew. So we ran away.

It was very toxic stuff. Then they went to freon which was completely harmless to people but people thought was harmful for the environment.

That was the only refrigerator we had for a while. Then the two (walk-in) refrigerator rooms under the apartment were put in about 1949. They were World War II surplus from Camp Elliott down in San Diego. They managed to haul them to Ramona legally and then these guys managed somehow to get them up the road. There were two buildings. They built more blocks (to tie them together with the main building). Didn't know what to do with the roof, so they put an apartment on it.

Scott: Nice little place, actually.

Woody: Yeah. Then the next thing they did was to put a loading/unloading dock for our fruit right outside the easterly end closest to the garage. Kind of an L-shaped thing that you could drive a truck in and unload it. It was designed originally to be unloaded by hand. Not long after that we got our first forklift. Fortunately they designed everything level enough so that you could drive a forklift over it. It was an old Towmotor, one-ton Towmotor. We unloaded stuff for years with it.

We loaded the trucks by hand, put the boxes on directly. We were still shipping most of the fruit we grew. We sold a little bit there at that front porch thing, which we call a store, which was half as long as it is now. (In the front of the Manzanita Ranch store building in Wynola.) They didn't have the space where the gift shop is now. They had no refrigeration (originally) so we were only open for a few months there in the fall. Gradually it expanded and we got refrigeration and so on.

Dad had always been going to put refrigeration on the west end (the opposite end of the building from the Camp Elliott refrigerators). Originally they used ammonia refrigerators up north. He'd been up there and seen a lot of those big refrigerators. They used to dig a hole and put the refrigerator equipment under the building. So he had the hole dug while he was preparing the building. We never built that—for years. Then we filled it in and had a loading dock. Then we bought that first refrigerator building which is now their beer garden (after getting the two walk-ins we had from Camp Elliott). That was a pre-fab. A very good refrigerator.

Scott: Pete (Pedro Mireles) would always hit the door frame by leaving the forklift a little too high. [laughs]

Woody: They built the packing house with showers so there was a place for the pickers (bracero crew) to take a bath. But anyhow, things were primitive in those days, comparatively.

Then we built the place behind Louise's on Orchard Lane with multiple baths and multiple stoves and put the tents around the outside of that building. Bill Cain's second house.

In '46 we were still making the cider up in Pine Hills. And

as you know that building is a little bit dilapidated. So they extended the building in Wynola out about 50 feet. They already had the loading dock, but they went from the loading dock all the way down almost to the end of the other building, and built a tin building to make a room for making cider (in 1956). Where they made cider for many, many, many years.

You made cider there.

Scott: There are photos somewhere.

Woody: So there is proof that you were there.

A few years later refrigeration space was becoming a problem because we were selling everything retail. We were holding it (holding the fruit in storage). There was an outfit in Los Angeles that was selling a prefab building. We bought that and brought it down. Milton Angel built the dirt underneath where the big refrigerator was. Bud Davis—Stan Davis was just about to retire at that time—but Bud Davis did the cement work on that. And Henry Silvers, that was one of his last projects. He said, (speaking very slowly) "I don't know, boss, I've never used 440." But he was very, very smart. He just sounded dumb. He had gone to Berkley and flunked out because his eyes were so bad he couldn't read.

440 is the electricity voltage. There is 110, 220, and 440. It requires a little bit more insulation and so on.

The posts for the refrigerator were put into 50-gallon barrels put into the dirt and poured solid. We thought we were going to have a clear (ceiling) span but the engineer—I think Dick Zerbe did the engineering—said it wouldn't hold up without those posts so we put them in.

Anyhow, that was about the end of the building. We had, in the mean time, paved the parking lot out to the west and all the way around the building with spray oils. That was a big improvement. It kept the dirt and dust way down. We puttered along with that for quite a few years.

That was when we were still shipping pears to the canneries.

There were lots of long-time friends in on this, talking about Henry Silvers and so on. Fred Farmer had the property right next to us. We managed to buy a sliver of that to make the parking lot a little bigger. We should have bought the whole thing but we didn't have much money.

I don't know if I ever finished telling you about Bob Duggan. Every morning when he'd come in (into Manzanita Ranch store in Wynola). We had breakfast together. I don't know how many years. Originally with Floyd Lewis and Bill Cain, but eventually they passed away and it was just Bob and myself. Somebody else once in a while. We'd sit there in front of that old Franklin Stove and I'd say, "How are you, Bob?" And he'd say, "I'm mighty fine. My nose is a-running; my feet's a-smelling." That was every morning's greeting. (Woody's voice breaks up.) I still love that greeting.

Scott: I remember when Bill Cain would come in a lot, and sit in front of the fire and sometimes we'd warm hot coco on the edges of the stove there. Those were good days.

Woody: Dad and Mom were amazingly good workers. They just worked like crazy all their lives.

Scott: They were very happy about it.

Woody: Oh yeah. They enjoyed it. At least I think they did.

·   ·   ·

Scott: That's great stuff. Do you have anywhere any old photos or anything we can use as a prop next time?

Woody: There were very few photos because we had an old box camera and film was fairly expensive. You forget the difference in economics. I can remember how glad Dad was at Christmas one year when he gave Mother, I can't remember if it was three one hundred dollar bills, or two one hundred dollar bills. They were going to take a trip that year. That was enough money to take a trip on. They had been skimping by for a long time. I think that was the trip we didn't go with them on; they got somebody to babysit.

They were incredible workers. And, like I say, they started with very little. Grandpa Barnes bought the property here (the ranch in Pine Hills). I think what he did was Uncle Hark (Hartwick) got the property on Fourth and Upas. Instead of getting half of it we gave it all to him and Dad had already gotten this piece—to avoid someone claiming they had a half interest in this piece. Grampy Barnes bought all of those other pieces of land around the county. He bought 240 acres in Wynola (at the end of Orchard Lane). He bought this and that. With Len Webster, a longtime friend, he bought two or three hundred acres in the Del Mar area and raised lima beans and barley. Bruno Denk, from a famous family down there, managed it for a year or two for us. But Grampy and Len had an agreement: If it ever got to a thousand an acre they would sell it.

They did, which was good. People laugh and say, 'Why did you do it?'

Well, there were two things. One was the agreement. Two, Len needed the money.

Dad got Len a job with the Farm Security Administration, the group he worked for. They moved down to Ibis Street in the Hillcrest area. Len and Edna were a wonderful couple. They had two boys, Jack and David.

It was good because they got their five hundred an acre, and we had our five hundred an acre.

The lady and her husband who bought it, it was 20 years before they made more money on it. That tells you how slow things were back at the time of the war.

You can't believe that you could be raising lima beans and barley on dry land in Del Mar. It's like El Toro (i.e. the Moulton Ranch in Orange County—Jane's family ranch); that's what the Moultons were doing in El Toro. They did it longer. It was an interesting time. But there wasn't any water. They hadn't brought Colorado River water into those areas either.

Gold Spotted Oak Borer

Woody: I sent a copy of our rainfall records up to these guys that are studying these trees [live oak trees infested with gold spotted oak borer beetles]. All I've done this winter, other than bookkeeping, is work on trying to save oak trees (on Manzanita Ranch in Pine Hills).

If you go over beyond Julian Elementary School where the road turns and goes north towards Volcan, towards Banner Canyon, the trees are dying by the dozens. Some of ours look pathetic and have beetles all over them, but compared to theirs ours look good. If you go up to Julian on the right side of Julian Grade there are lots of dead oaks. This is one of those things that you didn't anticipate coming, obviously. Nobody could have. It may change the looks of this ranch.

Scott: I'd like to walk and look at one that you know has it.

·   ·   ·

Woody: You really hardly can tell except when they're leafing. You see the exit hole in the bark which means that the beetles have already been there quite a bit. Unlike pine beetles, it usually doesn't kill [the oak trees] in one year. It usually takes three or four years to kill them. But it costs between 25 and 50 bucks, depending on the size of the tree, to treat them for one year. And we don't know if it works. I've spent about $2,000 trying to save the trees around the house. If it doesn't work, I've thrown away $2,000. But you have to do it next year too, so it's $2,000 more.

(A delivery man arrives with a package. Scott signs for it.)

Scott: Is this art supplies for Mom?

Woody: No, it's Xtandi (prostate cancer medicine) for Woody.

Scott: Ah. Where would you like it?

Woody: Just set it on the table. I'll open it.

I'll tell you another interesting thing. I was on a clinical trial for 36 months on this Xtandi stuff. And it helped... Kept the cancer pretty stagnant, didn't eliminate it but it didn't grow. It shrank it at first.

Well, the experiment was over. So then, you take a little bottle like the one that's in there, it's a pretty expensive co-pay. (During the trial, the medicine was free.) I said, "Okay, we'll do it."

They have at U.C.S.D. an ombudsman who helps the negotiating with companies for the price on your medicines.

Well, first they wanted $13,000 a month. That's very steep. While we were still down at U.C.S.D. they reduced it to, I think it was $4,300. By the time I picked up my prescription, they had reduced it to $1,000 a month, maybe $1,300.

The ombudsman kept working on it.

He said, "Send me your first two pages of your income tax." I said, "Well, they're high." He said, "Doesn't bother us. Send it anyhow." So I did.

I got a phone call from him, "You're going to hear from an outfit. I've got a year's supply coming for you free."

How's that for a reduction?

Scott: That's a crazy... I mean, what a crazy system! That should not exist. I'm glad you got the discount, but there should not be such possible variation. It's unbelievable.

Woody: That pretty well got us up to the years you remember. While my memory is still halfway good I'd better quit.

The Barnes family sold the Manzanita Ranch store in Wynola... twice. After the first sale in April of 1995 the buyer declared bankruptcy and after a lengthy struggle the family recovered it[5]. Woody and Jo then transformed the store by adding antiques and consignment sales, changing the focus from locally grown produce and cider to gifts, and returning it to profitability. Later they sold it to Alejandro Orfila, the former Argentinian ambassador to the U.S., who turned it into an Orfila Winery tasting room. Today called "Julian Station," the store is owned by Albert Lewis who specializes in making hard apple cider. Julian Station has several tenants including a beer garden and taco bar.

The first Bracero crew at Manzanita Ranch. Pedro Mireles is second to left, back row (no hat). Bill Loux is squatting in the front row, fifth from left. 1943 or 44.

Franklin L. Barnes (right) holding the architectural plans with Bill Cain on June 13, 1946 as Manzanita Ranch store is built. The cement blocks were formed in the parking lot in front of the building. Woody at age 11 helped tamp the cement into the forms.

When they ran out of good, used lumber for the roof, they had to switch to using green, uncured Julian lumber. To this day from the inside one can see larger gaps between the boards where the Julian lumber shrank more than the well-cured imported lumber. Photo from June 13, 1946.

A rare heavy snow Manzanita Ranch store in Wynola, 1969, elevation 3,645 feet. Come rain or snow, Woody kept the store open 364 days a year.

Woody bottling cider in the Wynola Ranch store, 1959.

Woody and his mother Alice holding up large, sorted pears, 1971.
The washing-sorting machine would drop the sorted pears in the
round bin to the photo's left.

The cider press in the background was used first on the ranch in
Pine Hills, and then moved to Wynola in 1956. This photo,
from the fall of 1972, shows three generations of operators:
Woody (left), Franklin, Scott, and Barney.

*A busy fall weekend at Manzanita Ranch, Woody in yellow
giving apple samples ca 1977. During the busiest Apple Days
weekend in the 1970s the cars would be parked on Highway 78
for up to a mile out of Julian and Manzanita Ranch would
employ 15 or more store personnel.*

Woody on the propane powered forklift. Every day weather permitting he would haul a dozen or so bins outside to attract customers and put them away at closing.

Because of a fire in the Town Hall, the annual spring Flower Show was moved to the fruit packing and storage area of Manzanita Ranch. Coincidentally, Julie Tuttle's planned outdoor wedding was also moved there from the ranch due to an impending snow storm.

Woody walking his niece Julie Tuttle down the aisle of jams and jellies for her wedding to Michael Kemp at the Manzanita Ranch store, May 7, 1988. Julie's father Carlyn had passed away two years before. Behind Woody and Julie stands the iconic lunch counter.

Angela Conley and Scott Barnes rock out to the live band De-Railed at Julie's wedding. Band members Wayne and Ross Moretti, Roy Sulser, Mark Thompson, Duane Garrant, Adam Cauzza.

1. Manzanita Ranch is currently called Julian Station and is owned by Albert Lewis and Lydia Frausto.
2. Willard Cain, a carpenter famous for saying "Measure twice and cut once," and "Never hang a door after two in the afternoon."
3. You had to go outside and around the back of the house to get to the restrooms. Scott helped pour a slab so you wouldn't have to walk on dirt.
4. Likely this was the Bullocks building, built in 1944. Address 401 S. Lake Avenue, Pasadena, CA.
5. The Buer Family Trust, represented by Tanya J. Robinson, held Manzanita Ranch and accompanying 40 acres from April 1995 until February, 1997.

12

WOODY AND JO REPRISE

This interview with both Woody and Jo occurred on September 20, 2019 after both Woody and Jo had a chance to read the draft of the entire book. Besides a few corrections, they both brought up topics that hadn't been covered sufficiently.

The Toboggan Slide

Scott: I think Jo wanted to talk about some new things?

Jo: I was only making suggestions of things that I thought were important to Woody's youth. The two things that I thought of were the Jeep, and the toboggan slide.

Scott: That's fine.

Woody: When we were kids we used the toboggan slide fairly often. When you guys came along (i.e. when Scott and Barney were young), I cleared the same exact track that we used for the toboggan slide. We were only able to use it about once because we just didn't get enough snow. We used to get more snow. We used to even have friends come up and spend the weekend so we could play in the snow and go down the toboggan slide.

We wore Grampy out many times.

Jo: Because he'd have to pull the toboggan back up. The slide goes right down [from the top of the hill] to the canyon well.

Woody: You wouldn't get snow on that thing for 15 minutes nowadays. Oh, you would, but not much. Not enough to slide on. I think we used it one day when you were kids.

Scott: I can remember three or four at least, but it was not often.

Woody: No. And we didn't invite people up from San Diego to slide.

Jo: It would be melted by the time they got here.

Scott: Is the toboggan the wooden one that is in the garage?

Woody: That's the second one. The first one wore out completely.

They actually put a rope tow for skiers over at Laguna when we were in high school. It was there for a year or two. I don't know exactly where it was because we never had the luxury of going to Laguna.

Jo: '49 was a great year [for snow].

Woody: I can remember one time this toboggan was going really good. We went out—there was a little lake—sliding out on the lake. We sat up for a second and just thinking...

Jo: ...the ice broke and we sank in about six inches, just enough to get really wet.

Woody: You don't have any idea how cold you can get walking up from down there, with...

Jo: ...ice in your pants.
    We used to make snowshoes with the cleats that you would put on the pear box ends to make them a little taller so you could stack them and it wouldn't bruise the fruit. We'd take two of those, one for each foot, and nail bottle caps on the bottom to make snowshoes. Then we would walk on the ice with them.

Woody: To tell you how much cooler it was, the pool was about half or two-thirds full, we hadn't completely drained it for the winter like we sometimes do. We had gotten a cold spell. We went out on the ice, and Jo went through the ice. That was a close call, because it is pretty cold when you go through ice and get all wet.

Jo: It's hard to get out.

Woody: It was hard to get out, even though you knew right where you were.

We used to go out on that little pond below the well when it froze over. (The same place the toboggan broke through the ice.) We even piled up the snow there, thinking we would make it last through the year, but it didn't.

Jo: Another thing that we never mentioned is the year (it had to be before 1944, because it was before the pool), Dad nailed some two by 12s together, two of them like paddle boards. At noon every day in the summer he'd take us down to the lake so we could go swimming on these paddle boards. You know, splinters...

It didn't make any difference.

Woody: That's right.

Jo: Later when we used to go fishing we had the boat down there. When we were older we didn't have to have chaperons. The dog would go with us, and if we didn't let him in the boat, the Springer Spaniel would swim all the time we were out there. Well, that kind of interferes with fishing.

.   .   .

Scott: Do you remember the dog's name?

Jo: Butch. Before that, when I was really little, they had a collie named Wag.

Woody: Wag One and Wag Two.

Jo: Before that they had Ramsey McDonald who was a Scottish Terrier or something, the little black thing.

Woody: The boat was called the Red Wood, because Red Brown who worked for the electric company salvaged one from Lake Henshaw that was too bad for them to use. He and I, mostly he, but the two of us rebuilt the thing. We used it at our lake for several years. That was the one the dog used to swim around, the Red Wood.

Jo: Butch was a fun dog, but he was a chicken thief.

Woody: We were still raising chickens.

Jo: When we butchered the chickens, they always chopped the heads off. Sometimes we had races with the headless chickens —see whose headless chicken would go the furthest before they dropped. I mean, who needed a toy store?

Then they'd bring them over, because you had to boil water to pour on them to be able to pull the feathers off. So mother would boil water and we'd pluck the feathers off down in the garage. More than once that dog would slip in there and grab one of those plucked chickens and off he'd go.

Woody: He also would break the netting on the coop and grab a live one. He didn't kill them. He'd carry them around live, and then bury them in the leaves. Of course, they didn't last too long.

Jo: He did that with kittens too. We had lots of cats. He was so jealous that if he could get to the kittens, he would take them, carry them just like the mother cat did, push the leaves aside and cover them up.

Scott: And bury them alive? That's terrible.

Jo: Oh, the mama cat would dig them out and take them back to her "hiding place"—which was usually in one of the hollow branches on an oak tree or else on a patio cushion.

Woody: I had a horse adventure too, once or twice, but Jo had a more exciting one. Mine was when the horse would get down and roll.

Scott: While you were on its back?

· · ·

Woody: Yeah. He'd get tired of having you on his back, lie down and roll. But Jo had one when they were over at the Timm place; they had the horses over there, and Mrs...

Jo: McClain.

Woody: Jo was riding out and the horse was kind of spooky, and Mrs. McClain came running out of the house yelling at her.

Jo: With a broom.

Woody: ...and scared the horse. The horse spooked and ran, dropped Jo on her head on the pavement on Pine Hills Road.

Jo: If you ever wonder why there's a bump right there (on the road, not my head).

Woody: May explain a few other things. She was pretty much out for two weeks in her bed. The dog was the only thing that seemed to console her. Butch would come running in and jump up on her bed, and it seemed to be very therapeutic.

Scott: Maybe he brought her some chickens or something that nourished her.

. . .

Jo: I wasn't supposed to be jiggled around. I had a concussion and a fractured skull. So they were always being very careful, tiptoeing around, talking quietly. And that dog would leap from the bedroom door to the bed. But he was worth it. He was a great dog.

The Yellow Jeep

Woody: The Jeep was an interesting story. After World War II, the government had lots of vehicles left. In fact, they took Jeeps off of those islands and dumped them in the ocean to get rid of them. But this one...

Scott: You got the yellow Jeep right after World War II, then?

Jo: It was camouflaged color when we got it, and we had to paint it. That was part of the agreement when you bought one.

Woody: I don't think so, but it was anyhow.

Jo: It was.

Woody: It was caterpillar yellow. The same paint they put on yellow caterpillar tractors. Virgil Walker did the painting, and we bought it... well Lowell Zornes was a veteran, so he could get one. If you were a veteran you could buy these used vehicles. And then Lowell didn't need it, so we bought it. Lowell Zornes was Pansy Signi's second husband, really a nice guy.

We used that Jeep for years and years. We first put on a pruning tower. There was an air compressor in the middle of the Jeep, and a tower that we could go around and prune trees with, using compressed air (to squeeze the pruning shears closed) instead of muscles. It was very good. We used it for a number of years.

Jo: The tower took the place of hand pruning with the ladders.

Scott: It must have been a little bit dangerous, that pruner that snipped—

Woody: Oh yeah. The pruners, at least one or two of them, are still down in the old cider house. The air compressor is over in the tractor shed.

Jo: I think Scott meant from riding in the tower with the snippers in the bumpy Jeep.

Scott: I assumed you stopped it to prune.

Woody: Yeah, you did. It was a platform with a railing around it. It hung for years in the shed. We finally got rid of it.

Then Jo and I used to use the Jeep all summer to spread squirrel poison, which was strychnine bait at that time. Of course, I let her handle the strychnine so it wouldn't hurt me any. I was generous. But I got to drive.

We used hundreds of pounds of that stuff and it was very effective. We never had a incident, but today you can't even buy strychnine. So, that's a historic note.

Jo: Then later we had a blower on it to blow dry spray on stuff.

Woody: We had a duster which you could put on the back and use it for dusting the pears with copper dust for fire blight. They still use copper dust; it's still approved to use.

Jo: Well, don't put that in the oral history or they'll outlaw it.

Scott: Now Jo, you told me a story about Dad (Woody) taking the Jeep somewhere in quite a precarious spot, is that right?

Jo: The one that I remember, and I don't know whether Tommy Tozer was with you or Winston or somebody, but you went up and around the Peckham place, and got on a rather precarious spot and walked home.

Woody: Yup. Grandpa (Franklin Barnes) used to take care of the Peckham ranch. That was another one of the orchards we didn't own but we took care of. They had a reservoir-swimming pool combination up on Cedar Creek, way up in the canyon. Every year, Grampy went up and cleaned it out. There was a little trail that went to it.

Well, I drove the Jeep down the trail and pretty soon it got so narrow that the wheels fell off the trail. I don't remember who was with me; I thought it was you (Jo). But anyhow, we walked back from the Peckham ranch—which is several miles, and Grampy went up and looked at it, jacked it up a little bit and drove it out. Once again, rescued.

Another time with the Jeep we were gathering pine cones. Jo and I gathered a lot of pine cones in this Jeep because we could sell them at the store for a dime. We were driving up toward Julian Grade from where Hutchinsons lived there in that Timm place, and we got going so steep that the gasoline was low, and it wouldn't suck into the engine, and it stopped on that hill. So we walked home and Grampy came over, backed it down, got it where it was level enough, started it up and drove home.

I think those are two of our bigger adventures with the Jeep.

Jo: Right, and gathering the bottles.

Woody: Oh yeah. Jo and I would drive down to Wynola and at that time people would throw out beer and pop bottles, and they had a deposit on them.

Jo: Three cents for the little ones and a nickel for the quart ones.

Woody: Most weeks we could gather enough between here and Wynola to pay for the gas so we could keep driving.

. . .

Scott: That's a lot of trash thrown out of windows.

Woody: Well, they didn't use to be as pristine, and there were lots of people who—

Jo: Drank.

Woody: Most of them were beer bottles, sure, but we got pop bottles too.

Scott: Okay.

Pink Truck

Woody: The Cheesewright family had a little cattle truck when they were in the cattle business up here. Grampy (Woody's dad) sold part of the Webster place on Deer Lake Park Road to the Cheesewrights.

That is how we hauled our cattle around from one place to another because we used to have them here on the home ranch, and rented this Strick place (next to the Big Lake). And then we had the Drury place up on the corner of Frisius Drive and Deer Lake Park Road. We sometimes hauled them up there. But we always hauled them to the Julian Grade or to the part of Wynola that wasn't an orchard.

We would have some of the most bizarre corrals when we first started. But we finally bought a good corral with a good loading chute from an outfit in the mid-West. Portions of the good corral are still in use, or still available over at the Webster place where mom used to keep her horse during part of the year. So anyhow, we got our money out of that old corral. And then we donated the pink truck along with the green water tanker that we used to fill the sprayer with, and the Jeep, to the Motor Transport Museum in Campo.

Jo: Didn't you donate the green Chevy pickup too that had the curved windows on the side of the cab?

Woody: I remember the other three clearly, but I'm not so clear about that one.

Scott: That was a cool pickup. I was never ambitious about working on cars, but if I was, I would have restored that.

Jo: You (Woody) graduated in '53, and that was a new truck when you were a freshman, so that must have been like a '49.

Scott: The thing I remember best about the pink truck was taking the lambs to the Del Mar fair to show them in 4-H and FFA. I was telling my kids that there were no seat belt rules, so you would let me stay in the back with all the manure blowing around. It was great fun to jump up and grab the overhead bars and just swing as the truck went around the corners toward Ramona.

Jo: There was no seat belts so you couldn't get in the cab. But you could swing with the s_ _ _.

Scott: It was better if it was swept out.

· · ·

Woody: That was Mom's driving, too. (Jane drives considerably faster than Woody.)

Scott: Mom was driving. I even did it with Eric Mortenson. We both went back there. Swung and ate cold Dinty Moore stew out of a can.

Packing House in Wynola

Woody: We ought to talk a little more about the packing house in Wynola. We moved there in 1946. It was built in '46. This was really beginning of the heyday of fruit production in Julian.

We always raised many, many more pears than apples. Originally we sent a lot of them to San Diego, Andrew's brokerage company. I think those names are still in the file. That was Helmus Andrews, whose wife was Billy and daughter was Patsy. And who's nephew was Meatball.

Jo: I think his name was really Harold Butley. Meatball was what they called him. He was about as big around as you are, Scott. Even skinnier.

Woody: As fat as my finger.

Jo: Just like a pencil.

Scott: But they called him Meatball? That's hilarious.

. . .

Jo: They lived across the street from the Andrews.

Woody: Andrews primarily sold potatoes wholesale, that kind of stuff. Later he sold their business to Tom Segawa. Tom was really a good guy. He was one of the people from the Japanese internment during World War II. Which was a serious mistake —but the country did it.

Dad (Franklin Barnes) had a lot of Japanese friends. When they first interned them, we tried to help by salvaging some of their building materials and stuff, as the government took over their properties. I can remember going to Capistrano and taking down some of the building. Some of that stuff is what we built part of the sheds with around here.

Jo: And the tree house.

Woody: Now the tree house, I think the lumber came from barns the folks took down. I don't remember exactly. It was used 1x12 redwood and other type of lumber. A lot of pine wood.

They still had lumber mills in Julian at that time. There were two of them at least. During World War II they cut a lot of lumber at Volcan Mountain, and off of North Peak in Cuyamaca. Birdsells had the mill out toward Cuyamaca, and Ralph Slaughter had the one up on Volcan, which a lot of people think is an area that was never harvested or anything.

Jo: A.G. Foster had one at the top of America Grade, right where Starks used to live. On the flat above Newman Road where the little house is.

Woody: That's an era that's long gone. In fact, I think that Foster moved his sawmill down to where Betty (Ritchie) Porter lived in Wynola.

Jo: Well, he married Betty's mother.

Woody: I used to haul the sawdust from down there when I was in high school up to my jump pit for high school jumping. I wasn't a very good high school jumper, but I did jump.

When we got the packing house going the fruit business was really at the peak. There was good demand for fruit, and we were shipping our fruit via Porters down to Andrew's in San Diego, and then he distributed it around San Diego, up as far as Long Beach, and occasionally to L.A.

Jo: A lot of our stuff was sold in the Safeway stores at that time.

Woody: Yeah. When Safeway became a big chain that was the end of our ability to sell them pears. They didn't want to deal with anybody that couldn't supply all of California with the same pears the same weekend—so that their ads looked good.

Then we went to canneries. The first cannery we used was Kern's in Los Angeles. Porters used to haul the fruit up there. They hated to go up there but they did. A few years later we also sent them to Productos Kern's in Mexicali. And then Kern's quit dealing with us, and we sent them all to Productos Kern's.

Porters really hated to go down there because you had to leave your truck and let somebody from Mexico drive it over the boarder and back. You hoped they came back. They always did so for us. An outfit called Max Limegrubber hauled the fruit from then on down.

And Max's had a driver with just one arm, and he was a character. He liked to hurry. Just below Highway 78 and Yaqui Pass Road there are some dips in the road. He once hit the dips so hard that it broke the trailer in half and dumped 20 tons of pears on the road in the state park. That created quite a bit of a confusion. Fortunately, Productos Kern's owned them when they left our place. They sat there for a while and rotted, and disappeared, but... that's another story.

We used to sell a lot more pears. One year we sold 54 semi-loads of pears to Productos Kern's. They had a buyer named Dan Bray. He was a very good buyer. He looked out for the long term; he wanted to build business relationships. We even went to one of the Productos Kern's family weddings.

He got killed in an airplane crash, and Archie Chavez took over. He was a nephew or something of the owners. Things went downhill from there. The final thing was one year, we had 250 tons of pears in the building waiting to go to Productos Kern's, and they quit hauling them. So we had to haul the pears out and dump them. That was pretty much the end of the pear business. It was a big business for us. It was a significant loss.

Scott: You said they used it for nectar.

Woody: They make pear nectar out of it. Both canneries did.

·   ·   ·

Jo: By Kern's—nectar in the little soda pop size.

Woody: It was very popular with the Latin people, and I don't know where they all distributed, but I know the L.A. cannery distributed to L.A., and Productos Kern's probably distributed in Mexicali.

Scott: I had always thought they were used for canned or jarred pears.

Woody: No. It was nectar.

Jo: Juice.

Woody: You got it dead ripe, squished it, put a little sugar and water in it, and sold it.

The pear business died very suddenly. With that we were down to very few pears that we could sell. From then on we were very much dependent on the retail store. We had been gradually building it up, and it went up rather rapidly because at that time Julian was beginning to be known for its apples and so on.

My mother—Grammy Barnes—always made pies. We used to figure she made close to one a day, year round. Well, everybody wanted pies, so we started hunting for pies.

We were the first people in Julian to make pies commercially. I may get my sequence of pies mixed up, but Kriegers made pies for us at the Girl Scout Camp[1] and down in the basement of the Town Hall. And then we started getting them elsewhere.

. . .

Scott: Was Mr. Krieger using Grammy's recipe?

Woody: Yes. Mother oversaw the first batches. We weren't making thousands of them. If we made a hundred a week—in the fall we'd make 150. But in the off season we didn't (make pies) because we were pretty much out of good apples. We were buying some apples for cider and processing—I'm sure some of those ended up in the pies. We far outgrew the amount of local grown apples back in the 40s. We had to buy cider apples even back then.

Later Jo found an outfit in Michigan that would fly in frozen pies that were really quite good. Among other places was Smart & Final, and Martino's, a bakery in L.A. Martino's used to delivery them. And then Jo was getting them from some place in Michigan, brought out frozen. Do you remember those? We were selling a lot of pies. That was before anybody else was selling pies in Julian.

We gradually went out of the pie business when everybody else went into it. But Martino's continued to sell them pretty much up to our end. They used to bring them down from L.A. I still have some tins in the cupboard from Martino's.

The fall was the busy time and the most fun time, although we always had good times there in Wynola. Business was rapidly getting better. We would hire as many as 13 kids and adults on weekends to handle the business at the store.

Jo: Eighteen, frequently.

Woody: Ralph and Bev (Beverly) Kulk had the gift shop. (They rented a space for a gift shop in the front of the building.) And then Rick and Colin ran the antiques upstairs. Kulks came after Rick and Colin had left.

Woody: Rick and Colin would sell a truckload of furniture every week. Unbelievable. They took a truck to L.A. and came back with a load of antiques every week and sold them. They were a great group. Colin still lives in Julian.

We were still selling our flowers wholesale... and still do as a matter of fact. We sold a lot there at the store, but we would sell quite a bunch of them wholesale. We would take flowers down to them in San Diego. We took truckloads (or station wagon-loads) to Marston's department store for their displays, hauling them dry, usually. We would sell lilacs, hyacinths, daffodils, lily of the valley, and peonies.

All of us made many runs (to San Diego, around 60 miles each way), but Jo got more than her share, and so did Grammy Barns. They'd get up at five in the morning and deliver those things, come back up and get ready for the next day.

Jo: When I was working at Cuyamaca (Rancho State Park), I would load up the old blue van. Do you remember the old blue van?

Scott: I loved that van because you were sitting right in the front window, and it was very tall.

Jo: I hope it never talks, but anyway... I would take flowers to the wholesale market at Carlsbad and then go down and deliver them to one florist in La Jolla, and one up on Washington, Joys, and then go down to the wholesale flower market off of Market Street, San Diego and then get to Cuyamaca to work by seven in the morning.

The wholesale places were always open. The other places I just left them on the doorstep.

Scott: Oh really?

Woody: A lot of times at Adelaide's (flower shop in La Jolla) you'd just pile them on the doorstep and drive off.

Scott: Amazing.

Jo: But fortunately they come and get them now.

Woody: That's really true. Big difference. We still sell them to Adelaide's and to Lily's.

Apples became more important, and like I say, we had apples running out our ears. But we also went into preserves and nuts and other kinds of things. Canned fruit, olives, and we hunted around for various people to do the packing for us.

George Perris , for example, who lived up on Red Hill in Tustin, used to do the fruit for a long time. The Utt Juice Company used to do a lot of the preserves (i.e. jams, marmalades and jellies). And then Stone Cellar did a lot of the preserves. E. Waldo Ward did a lot of the preserved fruits, relishes and stuff. They were all wonderful people to deal with.

The nuts we used to get from Torn & Glasser. I can't think of Ben's last name, but Ben was the guy that dealt with us most of the time at Torn & Glasser, and he was a character. Torn & Glasser was down in the wholesale market on 8th street, in L.A. and a lot of times I would work at the store until it closed at six or seven, drive up to L.A. so I could be there at 4:00 or 4:30 AM when they opened, and pick up various kinds of fruits too. We used to go some of the fruit booths.

Jo: And the dried fruit.

Scott: Did you sleep in your car? Or did you—

Woody: There was a motel I found that was cheap enough to sleep in, and it was much better than a car. I would be there at four or five in the morning, get that stuff and bring it home. And then all week the ladies that worked for us would pack it in little bags and have it ready for the weekend. That was only during the fall when we were that busy that we had to do that kind of hours.

It was suicidal, but there was one thing about it. If you drive up to L.A. late at night, and you leave early in the morning, you're not fighting all the traffic, you're just fighting a little of it. But I wouldn't do it now.

Freddy Slaughter and his family did it for a while (for the Julian Cider Mill) and he now has it shipped. Finally we had all our stuff shipped to us. It was much more satisfactory. But you had to establish a good relationship with people before you could do that.

We used to get olives from Corning. There were seven olive companies when we first started going up to Corning. (This was long before we had a cattle ranch in Corning.) They gradually got down to two. One of them made a mixed vegetable pickle relish that was quite good.

· · ·

Jo: Gardinera.

Woody: Gardinera, yeah. It was quite good. When they quit, we never did find anybody who did it as good as that. Now there's one olive company in Corning, and there's only about two in the state.

Jo: But there's a few vineyards.

Woody: Yes.

Jo: Many took out orchards and put in vineyards.

Woody: They were planting olives by the ton up there, but now they are mostly for oil.

Jo: When we were selling here at the ranch in Pine Hills, before Wynola, everyone bought quantities. They'd come up (from the city) and get two or three boxes of fruit, because they canned and preserved, and things like that. Even when we first opened Wynola people would buy by the box.

But as society progressed, quote unquote, they just bought a bag, or they'd drive 60 miles and buy four apples, and they'd think they'd gone out to the country and bought apples. I mean, we sold quantities and quantities of fruit, but it changed from boxes to bags. That's when we converted everything to bins, so we didn't pack and sell them. They'd bag their own and bring them to the scale.

. . .

Woody: When we first started packing down there at the store in Wynola, we'd sell people five to 10 boxes. First the larger boxes, then the half-bushel boxes, which are much more practical. We'd have pallets of those half-bushels sitting all over, and they'd disappear like crazy. Then suddenly the light turned on and we realized we were going to sell everything in teeny bags, just as Jo said.

Just pick the apples in a bin and bring them in.

We raised a lot of apples for a combination of cider and selling retail. I remember one year hauling 30 or 31 bins of Jonathans out of the Golden Delicious orchard. One weekend when they were done picking I went up with a forklift, loaded them on a truck, and hauled them down to the store. Nobody picks 30 bins of Jonathans anymore. But we did.

Scott: Especially out of the Golden Delicious orchard. Did I hear that wrong?

Woody: We called it the 'Golden Delicious orchard,' but it had Jonathans and Red Delicious in it also.

Scott: Just checking.

Woody: Grampy had put a mile plus of pipe down to the pear orchard for irrigation from the spring that was up on the hill (at the end of Orchard Lane in Wynola, near Volcan Mountain). They built a dam up there. It was a great system. On the west side of the creek was all pears. Most of the east side was apples. Not all of them. We had 100 crabapple trees. One year when we were making preserves and stuff, the juice people, Mr. Shellhouse wanted a load of crabapples. We took 20 tons to Mr. Shellhouse. [laughs] He accepted them and paid for them.

Scott: [laughs] He never wanted them again.

Woody: He made jelly out of them. George Perris was still doing all the preserves when that happened. They were all Hyslop crabapples.

The fall got busier and more fun in a way as the years went by. We sometimes had as many as 100 cars parked in our parking lot during the fall.

Jo: One of the big attractions to get people to stop during the spring, right across the street from the store were rows of hyacinths and peonies and lilacs and lots of flowers.

Woody: One year when those lilacs were absolutely in their prime, in one day I picked over 250 bunches of lilacs myself, and carried them across the street to the store. You just leaned in, snip, snip, snip, grab five bunches (12-14 stems per bunch), walk over to the store, put them in water. There's nothing like that growing anymore, because they were at the peak of their production.

We saved our newspapers all year to wrap lilacs in.

Jo: Tot Cummings saved all her newspapers and brought them up also.

· · ·

Woody: We wrapped them in wet newspaper to take home. Messed up everybody's cars... and everybody was happy doing it.

We also cut lilacs all around the community, including Ray Jacob's, Tot Cumming's, and Stanley Davis's in Mesa Grande... and various others.

Scott: Oh, it was great. The other fun times of the year were the pumpkins. Bins and bins of pumpkins.

Woody: We raised pumpkins up here in Pine Hills for a while. When they planted these lilacs, we raised pumpkins between them. That was in '62 or so. Then as the lilacs got bigger, there wasn't room. And we raised field corn, sweet corn. We used to eat most of that. Indian corn, gourds, pumpkins, what else? I don't know. That was most of what we raised.

We soon learned that it was a lot cheaper to buy pumpkins than to grow them. The bins that you saw came from Van Groningen's, and they're still in the pumpkin business up in the valley. We'd buy a semi-load of pumpkins from Van Groningen, and even a few white ones.

Jo: Ghost pumpkins. I have a picture of my three girls sitting out here in the pumpkin field, when the lilacs were little bitty bushes, and the pumpkins were all ripe and orange.

Scott: Christmas trees were a long tradition also.

·   ·   ·

Woody: We raised Christmas trees but we first started getting them many years ago from Volcan Mountain. Oh boy, I can't think of his name who owned it.

Jo: Ed Rutherford. He had bought it from Hans and Mary Starr.

Woody: I actually worked for him. He owned the trees and it was a separate business during Christmas, and eventually he got tired of doing it. And Lee Hunt, who used to be a neighbor here—

Jo: Lived in the Madden's house on Pine Hills Road and worked for the Soil Conservation service.

Woody: His wife was Carmen. Linda Lee and Wendy were his girls.

Jo: Before they moved to Oregon they had David.

Woody: In Oregon, Lee had a property with Christmas trees. He'd bring us a load. And we got a lot of trees off the San Isabel Indian Reservation, and a few off of the Los Coyotes Reservation.

Jo: Don't forget, you grew quite a few for a while, too, across the street from the store, behind the lilacs.

· · ·

Scott: Some were you-pick.

Woody: Christmas was always a fun time because everybody was in a good mood. During the fall, which was our busiest time of year, we'd have 13 or 14 people working on weekends at the store. Most of the people paid cash. The girls all had aprons, or not all of them, but some of them had aprons and scales out front. They made change out of their aprons. It was a different era. You wouldn't do that in today's world, but we did.

Jo: The kids couldn't do it that way anymore, because if they don't push a button on a cash register they don't know how to make change.

Woody: We had to do some educating, but they were wonderful kids, most of them. We really enjoyed it, and we still see a lot of them that worked here in Julian and other places. In fact, I was in Julian yesterday or the day before, and a lady said, "Hi. You gave me my first job." She had two little kids about this high, and she looked well middle-aged.

It was a very interesting period, one that probably could never be duplicated. We did a lot of business. Had a lot of fun. We were beginning to get run down and you didn't make much money, in spite of the number of things you did.

In fact, if you go way back, when I was in the Service, Grammy and Grampy almost sold the entire place—the ranch here and all the other properties, for $180,000. And then I said I wanted to come home, so they kept it... probably to their regret.

Then we reached a similar place. Grammy wanted to sell out and we were getting kind of tired. We looked around and we found a lady who was far smarter than we were, but not particularly honest, Mrs. Robinson. We sold to her, and she never paid anything, declared bankruptcy twice. I know you can't do that, but she did. We got it back and ran it for a few more years, and then sold to Mr. Orfila for all cash, which was just the store property, and that was a very much of a blessing.

Jo: When we did get it back [from Mrs. Robinson], Woody and Jane had already ventured into the cattle business, and so I agreed that I'd come back and help with the store operation if I could put in antiques. So I retired from State Parks a couple years earlier than I really intended to. But it worked out fine.

A lot of the antiques were things we purchased for resale. Others were consignment items. Consignment items were mostly from local people who had things they wanted sell.

Woody: Jo was the super antique manager of the store. It was beyond us.

I don't think I mentioned Edith Vedova, but Edith worked for us for probably 35 years. Absolutely wonderful person. She liked people; people liked her. We went to school with her sons and daughters. Jim Vedova still lives up here.

Jo: And Vicky and Barbara and Susie.

Woody: Her husband Cleto used to haul our cattle when we shipped them up to Chino to sell them for butchering or slaughtering, or to Escondido to Talone's to be butchered. He had a better truck than we did. We had a little tiny truck that was only fit for running around Julian. But Cleto knew how to deal with the Chino people and the Talone people.

Grampy was beginning to get Alzheimer's at that time. It was pretty easy for people to take advantage of him, such as Pedro (Mireles) did. I think he was the most egregious digger advantage of him. It was fairly easy, because Grampy was very congenial but he didn't know what he was doing.

Jo: There was a time when I was doing the payroll, and I always did the payroll on Friday nights because the employees wanted their checks on Saturday, but I used to sit down at the counter on Friday nights down there, and we had as many as 79 people on the payroll during the peak of the picking season, including the packing people and the store people. Fortunately, that was only for four and a half to six weeks. That was particularly during the time when some of the pickers were being trucked up from Fallbrook Citrus.

Woody: We lived across the street from the Spencer Valley school, where you guys (Scott and Barney) were in school when you were little, and then when we moved up here, I really never had a day when I didn't want to go to work. I always had a good day. A lot of interesting people, a lot of interesting customers, and a lot of customers that came back year after year. You gradually got to know quite a bit about them. Of course, some of us were talkative.

Woody and Jane continue to live on Manzanita Ranch in Pine Hills, and Jo and her husband Jim reside part time in Woody and Jo's parent's house a few hundred feet away. Woody still manages the farm, and there isn't a day he doesn't want to go to work.

. . .

~by Scott T. Barnes, December 27, 2019.

Taken in 1971, Woody was appointed to the California State Board of Forestry by Governor Ronald Reagan in October, 1971. From left, board members Whit Carter, Morse H. Salisbury, John T. "Kelly" McGinn, Woody Barnes, Waller Reed, Lamar Johnston.

For his 80th birthday, Jo Geary offered Woody a Scrapbook of Magical Memories, *from which came a number of the photos used here. From left rear: Karen (Tuttle) Conley; Sherlice Theroux; Julie (Tuttle) Kemp; Jo. Front: Jane Barnes; Woody; Mary Lynn (Tuttle) Cravey.*

Jo and Woody in the old Jeep circa 1947.

*Jo and Woody in the same old Jeep just before donating it to the
Motor Transport Museum in Campo.*

*December 2000 Woody and Jane brought the four-wheeler to
Julian from Corning when they sold their cattle herd.*

*Riding in the buggy, Woody was Grand Marshal of the Julian
Fourth of July Parade in 2007.*

---

1. In Camp Winacka, 4720 Boulder Creek Road.

13
FAMILY PHOTOS

Held July 28, 1962 at the Episcopal Church of the Messiah, Jane and Woody's wedding was presided by Reverand Wesley A. Havermale, dean of the Long Beach Convocation. Carlyn R. Tuttle was best man and Lewis M. Mathis and Glenn E. Mathis Jr. were ushers.

The wedding was on the Moulton Ranch in Orange County.
From left Glenn Mathis, Charlotte Mathis, Franklin Barnes,
Jane (Mathis), Woody, Alice Barnes.

Tony Guerrero's strolling four piece Mexican orchestra provided the music. A newspaper article said Woody "donned a Dior blue Italian silk suit with black accessories." Certainly the one and only time he was so dressed!

Jane and Woody moving into the cement block house across the street from Spencer Valley School and Manzanita Ranch. As I like to tell people, the little 1,200 square foot house had no central heating or air, no insulation, and no color television.

Woody reading to Scott (left) and Barney in the Wynola house.
Jane turned this photo into the 1970 family Christmas card.

Inevitably sad goodbyes. Grandchildren Kaylynn (left) and
Elizabeth (Ellie) love visiting Manzanita Ranch. Taken in
2016.

*Like her grandmother, plein-aire oil painter Nellie Gail Moulton,
Jane has become an accomplished watercolor artist. On
Christmas, 2017 she presented Ellie with her portrait at the house
in Julian.*

The Barnes family has many Christmas traditions, one of them being the "search through the dumpster" when someone inevitably throws away a gift in their haste to clear the wrapping paper from the floor. December 25, 2009.

SCOTT T. BARNES

Jo and Jim Geary, in front of a live oak in Julian, Dec 2, 2012.

Woody and Jane Barnes in front of a dogwood tree in Julian,
Dec 2, 2012.

The family in Gilbert, Arizona. From left Diane Barnes, Barney Barnes, Chelsea Taylor, Caden Taylor (front), Lance Taylor, Adalyn Taylor (in Lance's arms), Grace Barnes, Kaylynn Barnes (front), Elizabeth Barnes (front), Gladys Knight, Emmalee Barnes (rear), Scott Barnes, Jane, Weslee Barnes (rear), Woody.

Jane's side of the family has begun bi-yearly family reunions. The 2015 reunion was held in the Grand Californian Hotel, Disneyland. From left: Diane Barnes, Barney Barnes, Adalyn Taylor (front), Minnie, Weslee Barnes, Jane, Woody, Elizabeth Barnes (front), Kaylynn Barnes (front), Scott Barnes, Grace Barnes, Caden Taylor, Mickey.

BIBLIOGRAPHY

Available Online

Alessio family. "John Alessio, 87, Businessman and California Political Force," by Kenneth N. Gilpin. The New York Times. April 5, 1998.

Angel, Milton. 240 Years of Ranching: Historical Research, Field Surveys, Oral Interviews, Significance Criteria, and Management Recommendations for Ranching Districts and Sites in the San Diego *Region: Attachment I, San Diego County Ranching Interviews*, "Interview with Milton Angel," by Heather Thomson. July 30, 2001.

Beck, Darrell. "The Angels of Mesa Grande." Ramona Home Journal. June 18, 2015

BO-SE (selenium, vitamin E). Drugs.com website.

Bracero program. Wikipedi website.

Cattle prices. "Historical Cattle Prices." Ag Decision Maker. Iowa State University.

Cletrac Tractor. "Cleveland Tractor Company: Ohio Family Starts and Ends with Cletrac," by Bill Vossler, Farm Collector Newsletter, July, 2010.

Cumming, Lucy Sawday "Tot." "On Memory's Back Trail

the Land and Cattle Empire of George Sawday." Ramona Home Journal website. p5667.

Drug Store. 2134 Main Street, Julian. Miner's Diner website.

Dyar family. Hidden San Diego website.

Edic, William "Bill" family, Pacific Coast Packing Company. "Local man turns 102," by Adrienne A. Aguirre, The San Diego Union-Tribute, April 16, 2005.

Electricity in Julian. "Julian Historic District Design Guidelines," by the Architectural Review Board of the Julian Historic District.

International Lilac Society. International Lilac Society website.

Graber Olive House. Graber Olives website.

Halgrens in Ontario. Haltrans website.

Hoskings Ranch. "Julian residents object to Linden Blue's backcountry development plans," by Dorian Hargrove, June 22, 2016. San Diego Reader.

"Luxury development approved for Julian," by J. Harry Jones, The San Diego Union-Tribune. March 3, 2016.

Holcomb, Charlotte. "Highway 94 Club," by D. Craum, 2014.

Hostage Crisis. "1979 Oil Crisis." Wikipedia website.

Housley, Lucile. "Implementation of 2002 Survey and Manage Annual Species Review." Bureau of Land Management. March 14, 2003.

Hubbell, James T. website.

Irvine, James Harvey, Sr. Wikipedia website.

Jeffrey family. "The Jeffrey Family in Irvine," by the Irvine Historical Society. March 28, 2017.

Julian Hardware and Mercantile, 2111A Main Street from 1975-2013. "Farewell, Friends," by Ann Reilly Cole, Julian Journal. Aug 15, 2013.

Klager, Hulda hybrids. Hulda Klager Lilac Gardens website.

Knight Hollow Nursery website.

Lilac breeds and breeders. "International Register and Checklist of Cultivar Names in the Genus Syringa," by Freek Vrutman, July 2016.

Lemoine, Victor. France info: 3 Grand Est website: "La plus importante collection de Lilas Lemoine au monde," by Thierry Pernin, May 13, 2015.

Manzanita Ranch. "The History of Manzanita Ranch," by Tracy Rolling. The Julian Journal. April 1, 2009.

Marston Department Store. "Honoring a local legend," by Katherine Hon. San Diego Uptown News. September 8, 2017.

Marston family. Wikipedia website.

McCoy family. Legacy.com website.

Moulton-Niguel Water District. "Moulton-Niguel Votes District, Sets Board," The Tustin News, October 27, 1960.

Nappies: Nu Alpha Phi Fraternity website.

Nicholson, Roger. "Ranchers grudgingly accept Klamath water-sharing pact," Capital Press, by Tim Hearden, March 14, 2014.

Oberlin School. Julian Union School District website.

Olivenhain. Denk Family. "Remembering Harley Denk," by Ruth Marvin Webster, Hartford Courant, September 30, 2008.

"Otay and the Castros," by Ceasar Castro. South Bay Historical Society Bulletin, July, 2016, Issue 13.

Padua Hills Theater. Wikipedia website.

Palmer cider press. YouTube website.

Phillips, Edwin, Wig Award winner Pomona College. Pomona College website.

Ramona Mainstage Theater. The San Diego Reader website.

"Ramona Mainstage. The Original Ramona Theater," by Darrell Beck. *The Guide to Ramona, California.*

Ramona, Turkey Capital of the World. "Ramona Then,

Ramona Now, part one," by Sharon Doubiago, July 14, 1994. The San Diego Reader.

Rancho Guejito. Valley Center Historical Society website.

"Rancho Guejito — Southern California's land that time forgot," by Mike Anton, The Seattle Times, June 13, 2007.

Rancho Santa Ysabel. "Santa Ysabel Crossroads of History," by Darrell Beck, The Julian Journal, Aug 14, 2014.

Redding family. "Eileen Tellam Looks Back On A Lifetime In Education," by Ann Reilly Cole, Julian Journal, June 15, 2017.

Redding, Martha Gwen (Thum). "Parade A Special Event For Julian Old Familes," by Bobbi Zane, Julian Journal, August 1, 2007.

Rice's brickyard/Rose Canyon. "Rose Caoyon Brick." Originally Pacific Beach, December 30, 2017.

San Diego Central Line. "Sprinter Follows Historic Route Built More Than Century Ago," by Paul Sisson, The San Diego Union-Tribune, November 25, 2007.

San Diego Imperial Cattlemens Association membership roster 2010.

San Vincente Dam. "The Ghosts of San Vicente Reservoir," by Darrell Beck, Ramona Home Journal, September 1, 2013.

"Rain Adds Billions of Gallons to San Diego Water Reservoirs," Coronado Eagle and Journal, Volume XXXI, 4 February 1943.

(Feb 4, 1943 "not yet completed" but capturing water...) "San Diego Project," by Robert Autobee, Bureau of Reclamation.

"On Memory's Back Trail: Foster Station, Atkinson Toll Road and Mussey Grade," by Darrell Beck, Ramona Home Journal, March 23, 2017.

Spencer Valley School. "Spencer Valley School Celebrating Over 130 Years," by Bobbi Zane, Julian Journal, February 6, 2008.

Thorpe, Edmund Carson and Rose Hartwick. *Women in World History, A Biographical Encyclopedia.* Published by Gale Research, Inc, 2002.

Thorpe, Lucian Carson. *A History of California and an Extended History of its Southern Coast Counties* by James Miller Guinn. Historical Record Company, Los Angeles, CA 1907.

"Individuals Who Died on Hilton Head, South Carolina, During the Civil War As Listed in Known Burial Orders and the Roll of Honor Buried in the Government Cemetery on Hilton Head Island," by Heritage Library, Hilton Head Island, South Carolina, p60.

Tulare Farm and Equipment Show. I.e. World Ag Expo. Wikipedia website.

Turkey Inn. "On Memory's Back Trail: Tales From The Turkey Inn," by Darrell Beck, Ramona Home Journal, July 1, 2013.

Tule plants. "California Bulrush," by U.S. Department of Agriculture.

Utt Juice Company. Tustin History.com website and Wiki-pedia website.

E. Waldo Ward. E. Waldo Ward & Son website.

Warner's Ranch. Vista Irrigation District website.

Webster, Len and Edna. "Julian Pioneer Cemetery records," compiled and contributed by Steve Paul Johnson, December 19, 1999.

Witch Creek School. Historic Julian website.

Zerbe, Dick (Richard). Julian Historic District Design Guidelines by the Architectural Review Board, September 27, 1989.

In Print

Barnes, Scott T. *Alice Barnes — Gold Mines and Apple Pie.* New Myths Publishing. ISBN 978-1-939354-04-4. 1999.

Beck, Darrell. *On Memory's Back Trail: The History of Ramona and the Backcountry of San Diego County.* Backcountry Press. ISBN 978-0615125145. 2004.

Jasper, James. *Trail-breakers and History-makers of Julian and Roundabout.* 1928.

Julian Union High yearbooks. 1950-1953

Lewis, David. *Last Known Address, The History of the Julian Cemetery.* Headstone Publishing. 2008.

McGrew, Clarence Alan. *City of San Diego and San Diego County: The Birthplace of California, Volume 2.* American Historical Society. 1922.

Metate. Pomona College Yearbook 1957.

Miller, James Guinn. *A History of California and an Extended History of its Southern Coast Counties.* Historical Record Company. 1907.

Webster, John. *Originally Pacific Beach: Looking Back at the Heritage of a Unique Community.* 2013.

INDEX

ABOUT NEW MYTHS PUBLISHING

Publishing the finest in fantasy, science fiction, and nonfiction.
See our entire collection at NewMythsPublishing.com.

Made in the USA
Columbia, SC
06 August 2021